For Jim . . . for his love and support . . . forever.

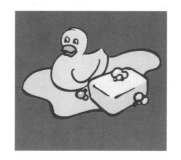

mes
ar-Olds
THIRD EDITION

...CHOLS

by

...ears

AMERICAN LIBRARY ASSOCIATION
Chicago   2007

Composition by the dotted i in Bookman and Tekton using QuarkXPress 5.0 for a Macintosh platform

Printed on 50-pound white offset, a pH-neutral stock, and bound in 10-point coated cover stock by Data Reproductions

The paper used in this publication meets the minimum requirements of American National Standard for Information Sciences—Permanence of Paper for Printed Library Materials, ANSI Z39.48-1992. ∞

Library of Congress Cataloging-in-Publication Data

Nichols, Judy.
    Storytimes for two-year-olds / Judy Nichols ; illustrated by
Lori D. Sears. — 3rd ed.
        p.   cm.
    Includes bibliographical references (p.) and indexes.
    ISBN 0-8389-0925-6 (978-0-8389-0925-6 : alk. paper)
    1. Storytelling—United States.   2. Children's libraries—Activity
programs—United States.   I. Sears, Lori D.   II. Title.
Z718.3.N5   2007
027.62'51—dc22   2006023915

ISBN-10: 0-8389-0925-6
ISBN-13: 978-0-8389-0925-6

Printed in the United States of America

11   10   09   08   07   5   4   3   2   1

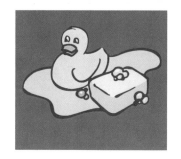

Storytimes
for Two-Year-Olds
THIRD EDITION

JUDY NICHOLS

Illustrated by
Lori D. Sears

AMERICAN LIBRARY ASSOCIATION
Chicago   2007

While extensive effort has gone into ensuring the reliability of information appearing in this book, the publisher makes no warranty, express or implied, on the accuracy or reliability of the information, and does not assume and hereby disclaims any liability to any person for any loss or damage caused by errors or omissions in this publication.

Composition by the dotted i in Bookman and Tekton
using QuarkXPress 5.0 for a Macintosh platform

Printed on 50-pound white offset, a pH-neutral stock, and bound in
10-point coated cover stock by Data Reproductions

The paper used in this publication meets the minimum requirements of
American National Standard for Information Sciences—Permanence of
Paper for Printed Library Materials, ANSI Z39.48-1992. ∞

Library of Congress Cataloging-in-Publication Data

Nichols, Judy.
    Storytimes for two-year-olds / Judy Nichols ; illustrated by
Lori D. Sears. — 3rd ed.
        p.   cm.
    Includes bibliographical references (p.) and indexes.
    ISBN 0-8389-0925-6 (978-0-8389-0925-6 : alk. paper)
    1. Storytelling—United States.   2. Children's libraries—Activity
programs—United States.   I. Sears, Lori D.   II. Title.
Z718.3.N5   2007
027.62′51—dc22   2006023915

ISBN-10: 0-8389-0925-6
ISBN-13: 978-0-8389-0925-6

Printed in the United States of America

11   10   09   08   07   5   4   3   2   1

Contents

Preface

In 1981 I faced my first toddler storytime armed with a few journal articles, three months' research into the characteristics of toddlers, and ten years' experience with preschool storytimes. During preparation, I felt confident, thinking, "How different from preschool storytime can it be?" Then I faced the room full of wiggling, distracted tots whose parents were frantically trying to get them to sit still for that first program. I realized I was in uncharted waters, and I was scared stiff!

Two-year-olds (the core of the toddler group that ranges from eighteen to thirty-six months of age) had well-known reputations. They were labeled the *terrible twos.* Is there a more challenging or more confusing time of life for children and parents? (Perhaps only teenagers have as many mood swings and strong preferences.) Toddlers stand at the crossroads between babies and preschoolers. They enjoy watching, following, and copying others. They eagerly share their discoveries and show off what they learn, but they do not like to share toys or to participate in group activities. They understand more than they can communicate with their simple sentences, yet their vocabularies expand every day. Toddlers like to repeat tasks and activities as they develop listening skills, self-control, and the ability to follow directions. Progress is there; you just have to look for it.

When I first proposed a toddler storytime, coworkers and parents reacted alike: "Great idea! But it'll never work here." Toddlers were seen as unpredictable, undisciplined, and too young to participate in any group activity. Parents voiced reluctance about bringing toddlers into the library, fearing they might be disruptive or destructive. Unfortunately, some staff members agreed.

At that time, our branch library was in a middle-class neighborhood where the number of toddlers had increased noticeably. Parents were seeking "meaningful" activities for their tots, but few preschools accepted children under three years old. Book publishers were just beginning to realize this demographic target. Our library had some materials for toddlers and we were adding more, but these items were not circulating well. Parents had difficulty finding books appropriate for their young children, prompting comments about the library "not having anything for this age." Thus, our toddler storytime was born.

After advertising with a poster in the library and talking to parents with toddlers as we encountered them, we developed a once-a-week program to run for six weeks. We decided to take registrations and limit the number to ten children accompanied by their parents, because the room we would use was very small. On the first day, we had five children in the program, but after the first program, three more parents called to enroll their toddlers. After the second week, we were full with a waiting list, and by the end of that six-week session, we had two pages of names waiting for a second session to begin. Storytime parents told others, and word quickly spread through the neighborhood and across town.

At the end of the first session, we started another six-week session, offering three storytimes at different times of the day and week. All three programs filled the first day of registration, and a waiting list formed. Limited by staff, we stayed at three programs a week.

It soon was apparent how important the toddler storytime had become to families. They drove across town to attend. Fathers took time off work to bring their tots when mothers could not. Grandparents brought grandchildren, and neighbors, babysitters, and family friends attended with little ones when parents could not. Vacation plans, appointments, and out-of-town visitors were coordinated around the storytime calendar.

Statistical results were immediate and gratifying. Circulation of picture books and parenting materials increased. We noticed more families coming to the library together and an increase in circulation in all categories. Program attendance was great, and participants called to let us know when they would be absent. Requests and comments showed that most patrons were interested in this program. Older patrons were enamored by the "cute-appeal" of toddlers in the library. Toddler storytimes sparked more interest in our library than any other activity.

We experienced some unexpected benefits as well. Within a year our first toddler graduates began entering preschool storytimes for three- to five-year-olds. We discovered that they were much calmer, more eager to attend, and more willing to participate than other beginners. They knew what to expect and what would be expected of them in a library program. Shy and frightened three-year-olds clinging to parents became an oddity. Preschool storytimes were less stressful and more focused for both the storyteller and the children.

Another unexpected thing was the fierce loyalty that is a characteristic of toddlers. Parents told of taking elaborate detours when the library was closed, because their toddlers would demand to go inside as soon as they saw our building. Visiting relatives, friends, and family were brought to the library by proud tots as part of a city sightseeing tour. It was the kind of community support every librarian dreams of.

As our program progressed, we discovered that toddler storytime had become as important to parents as it was to their children. Some parents had never participated in structured learning experiences with their children. They were amazed at how much their toddlers knew and the level of skills they displayed. Following the role model of a storytime leader, parents remarked that they were now playing more with their children at home. They also enjoyed discovering parenting materials, media, and other resources available at the library. Some first-time parents saw storytime as a support group, finding support from others as they shared ideas and problems. Playgroups formed around toddler storytimes.

And they kept coming! Preschool storytime enrollment increased. Families visited the library regularly even during programming hiatuses. Habits learned early in life can be powerful, and parents will return to places where experiences with their children are positive.

All programs evolve. Through trial and error, routines and storytime structure that worked time after time settled into a pattern. A handout for parents was added to the program. It included titles of books, words to the fingerplays and songs, and follow-up suggestions. Guidelines were developed to share with other librarians interested in toddler programs.

At national and regional conferences, children's librarians gathered and talked about their programs. Those of us doing toddler storytimes discovered that we had all gone through the same research, the same trial-and-error process. We each reinvented the wheel. There were a couple of articles in journals, but there was no one source to turn to for ideas and information. Other librarians interested in toddler programs didn't know where to begin.

With these factors in mind, *Storytimes for Two-Year-Olds* was first published in 1987 and expanded in 1998. This work was designed to introduce the special considerations and materials needed for toddler storytimes along with routines and structures that have proven successful. This book offers planning considerations, a program structure, and fifty topical themes with examples of appropriate books, storytime props, fingerplays, songs, and activities to be used in programs. Follow-up ideas and crafts for parents and toddlers are included with each theme. Notes to librarians are provided, giving practical tips and descriptions of how certain materials were used in storytimes.

——— What Have We Learned? ———

In the years since this work was first published, toddler storytimes have grown in popularity and spread through libraries everywhere. Long-standing toddler programs continue to be offered and are popular. Programming for toddlers in libraries has been proven to be not only doable but enjoyable as well.

Children's librarians have battled the *shhh* stereotype for years, an image that does not reconcile itself well with the presence of young children in libraries. Toddler programs encourage more families to bring children of all ages to visit libraries, a trend seen in changing collections that include more board and cloth books, toys and puzzles, and picture book materials featuring simple illustrations and stories appropriate for the youngest listeners. Publishers have responded to increased demand for baby and toddler materials, sometimes favoring format over appropriate content. Large bookstore chains have even started toddler storytimes to bring in customers.

We learned that the adults who accompanied toddlers to programs were not always their parents. Grandparents, babysitters, friends, and even nannies brought children to the library because parents worked. We found that evening programs were more successful at attracting working parents, who sometimes attended together or alternated to spend time with older or younger children. With that in mind, the word *parent* is used in this edition to signify any accompanying adult.

Although this work was aimed at librarians wanting to create or enhance storytimes for toddlers, we learned it was useful to many non-librarians. Parents, teachers, counselors, early childhood educators, and others working with young or developmentally delayed children have expressed their interest in the resources and activities included here.

When this book was first published, Head Start programs, preschools, and day-care centers did not include toddlers in their programs. Children had to be three years old and potty trained before they could be enrolled. Now early childhood educators and caregivers accept not only toddlers but infants as well.

Research into the developing brains of babies and toddlers has revealed that children learn much earlier than was once thought and that early learning actually enhances the complexity of their brains. We now know that babies and toddlers need to be enriched with language (rhymes, songs, and stories), movement, and visual stimulation, all integral parts of a toddler storytime. This *need* cannot be overemphasized. Babies and toddlers absorb knowledge, much like sponges soaking up water. Librarians and early childhood educators now know that very young children can, and must, be targeted for special programming. Many libraries now offer lap-sit programs for even younger children (babies three to fifteen months old).

A partner to infant brain research has been a shift in our understanding of how children learn. *Emergent literacy* recognizes that children learn about reading and writing long before they are conventionally taught to read or write. Research has shown that young children need to experience the sound of letters, see how letters form words, discover that words have meaning, observe others in literacy activities, and have the opportunity to explore print on their own. The most frightening part of emergent literacy research is the realization that children who start school without these skills rarely catch up.

How literacy is shared with children is as important as the act itself. Children learn most from books when they are actively involved. *Dialogic reading* makes children participants in the process (reading pictures, answering open-ended questions, predicting outcomes, and retelling the story). Toddler storytimes promote dialogic reading between parent and child by modeling these behaviors during the program and guiding parents during the quiet reading time.

In the second edition of this book, the number of themes was increased to fifty to reflect many libraries' year-round commitment to toddler storytimes. Action rhymes were updated and songs added for each theme, and parent follow-up ideas were expanded. Every effort was made to reflect the increased awareness and understanding of the multicultural world in which we live. Whenever possible books, rhymes, and crafts were selected to represent differing cultural perspectives. Consideration was given to varying abilities, with sign language words, materials appropriate for children with visual impairments, and titles featuring characters with disabilities.

The connection between families and libraries has received much attention in recent years and has been reflected in more family programming and changes in materials collections. Storytimes for targeted age groups, such as toddlers, have come under criticism, since they do not include older and younger siblings. Toddler storytimes were developed for one child and one adult to attend together, because of the emotional and developmental needs of children this age. Programming for families should be an essential part of library services; however, the special needs of toddlers continue to make programs designed and presented for them alone a wise option. Toddler learning is fast-paced and multidimensional. Their special needs are best met in small groups where they have the undivided attention of adults. This encourages them and prepares them for participation in family programming.

What Has Changed in This Edition?

In this edition, all the thematic booklists have been updated to reflect newer titles, but some older titles have been retained on each list. These are still found in libraries and continue to be appropriate for toddler storytimes. Because library programs must be conducted using titles available in library collections—large and small—it is not appropriate to list only new titles. The criteria for selecting appropriate books for toddlers appear in the chapter "Program Elements," in the section "Books."

The fifty themes remain the same. Space for notes has been retained in each theme, to encourage librarians to bring their own preferences and talents to programming. The professional bibliography has been updated and expanded to reflect new resources available to aid children's librarians in programming for very young children.

A Few Words of Thanks

No program is solely one person's creation. I am most grateful to all the children's librarians who have shared their ideas and materials with me at workshops and through correspondence. My heartfelt appreciation goes to all the administrators who understood the need for and gave support to toddler programs. As librarians are encouraged and supported by many, writers are the same. To the generous souls who made the first edition possible (Becky Arnold, Linda Bogush, Mary Lou Dwyer, Theresa Overwaul, Patrick Hogan, and the late Nancy Renfro) and those who aided and abetted the second edition (Debbie Lewis, Gwen Harris, Terri Bird, Jane Dean, Jean Hatfield, Pat Rogers, Nina Hand, Lisa Hattrup, Fran Stallings, Hiroko Fujita, and Joan Grygel), I thank you from the bottom of my heart. And without Amy Woolf, Patrick Hogan, and Laura Pelehach, this third edition would not have happened. But most of all, I thank my loving and supportive husband, Jim.

Acknowledgments

"Someone Is Creeping," "I Shut the Door," "Pound Goes the Hammer," and "Make a Valentine," reprinted from *Let's Do Fingerplays* by Marion F. Grayson. Copyright 1962 by Robert B. Luce, Inc.

"Eskimo Clothes Pin Birds" adapted from *Look At Me: Creative Activities for Babies and Toddlers,* by Carolyn Haas. Copyright 1987 by Carolyn Buhai Haas. Published by Chicago Review Press, Inc., 814 North Franklin Street, Chicago, IL 60610. Permission granted by the author.

"Busy Windshield Wipers" from *Preschool Story Hour* by Vardine Moore. Copyright 1972 by Scarecrow Press, Inc. Permission granted by the publisher.

"Rainbow," "Turn-Around Faces," "I Know An Old Lady Sack Puppet," and "Caterpillar/Butterfly Sock Puppet," adapted from *Puppetry in Early Childhood Education* by Tamara Hunt and Nancy Renfro. Copyright 1982 by Nancy Renfro Studios.

"Bears Everywhere," "Doughnut," "I Dig, Dig, Dig," "Houses," "Monkey See, Monkey Do," "Where are the Baby Mice?," "Sometimes I Am Tall," "Boom! Bang!," "Wind Tricks," and "Five Winds," reprinted from *Ring a Ring o' Roses: Stories, Games, and Fingerplays for Preschool Children.* Copyright 1981, Flint, Michigan, Public Library.

"Finger Circle Puppets," "Ping-Pong Family," and "Zipping Bag Book," adapted from *Toddler Theme-A-Saurus,* by Jean Warren and Judy Shimono. Copyright 1991 by School Specialty Publishing, used by permission.

1
Planning Considerations

Many considerations go into planning any kind of program, and the same holds true for toddler storytimes. Understanding of the characteristics of this age group, careful audience preparation, the physical location, time of day, and program format are vital concerns.

The most pressing consideration with toddler programs is the length of toddlers' attention spans. Toddlers are easily distracted—the slightest noise or motion may rob you of their attention. Don't panic! This same distractibility makes their attention easy to recover. Being able to focus and maintain attention is a learned behavior. Toddlers develop this skill by focusing their attention (on objects, images, words, and actions) for increasingly longer periods. It is a gradual process, and they get better at it each time they do it.

Although toddler storytimes are developed around this primary consideration, the following concerns are also important:

1. Toddlers have not yet mastered the motor skills necessary for small hand movements—common to most fingerplays.
2. They have limited group experience and social skills, and they are shy and do not readily share with others.
3. They have abundant energy that needs to be channeled—often—into physical activities, such as marching, jumping, and the like.

4. Toddlers react strongly to changes in their routines and environments.
5. They are at the crossroads between dependence and independence, needing a familiar adult nearby for security yet demanding to do things for themselves.
6. They find it difficult to grasp abstract concepts and sketchy illustrations.
7. They like to touch things and learn from physical contact with objects.

This fascinating mixture of insecurity, independence, and limited skills requires careful planning and preparation. Toddler storytimes use more visual aids, repetition, and physical activity than preschool storytimes. Parents are active participants and role models, helping their children to stay focused, cooperate, and feel secure. A variety of programming materials are used to capture toddlers' interest, encourage cooperation, and help them participate in activities and routines.

Participant Preparation

Parents cannot be observers in toddler storytimes. From the beginning involve them and enlist their support in preparing their tots for programs. Many parents may have little experience with storytimes and may not understand what the program entails.

Registration helps make a toddler program successful. Limit the size of the group to ten to twelve children with their parents, depending on the size of the story space. Large groups over-stimulate toddlers. Registering in advance makes parents take the program and their participation in it more seriously, especially when it is popular and there is a waiting list. Gather the following information: child's name and nickname, parent's name, the name of the adult who will accompany the child (if not the parent), address, phone number, and child's birth date. Begin registration four to six weeks prior to the first program. Offer an orientation session the week before the storytime starts to introduce parents and children to the story space, the storyteller, and each other, and to answer questions. This is also a good time to make sure everyone has a library card.

When parents register, give them an orientation letter (see figure 1) or brochure describing the toddler storytime and explaining how cooperation between parent, child, and storyteller makes this a quality experience for all. Putting this information in writing helps parents and children know what to expect and what is expected of them. It also reinforces parents' roles as participants and eliminates the "Nobody told me that!" lament that is common to all children's programming.

You will reinforce this information verbally at the beginning of each session. This helps everyone stay focused on what is happening and why. For example, as children line up to enter the story space, tell them what to expect: "We will march into the story room together. See the rug spots on the floor. You pick one to sit on with Mom (or Dad). You can sit together on the same rug spot." This is information from the registration letter.

Always talk to the child! This keeps the child the main focus at all times. Parents listen to instructions people give to their children and will follow those directions. If you give directions to the parents, the toddlers no longer think the program is for them—and they will act accordingly. Talking directly to the child puts both parent and toddler at ease and encourages them to listen.

Physical Location

The Library

Libraries offer programs to bring people into their facilities, to familiarize them with library services and resources, and to encourage them to check out materials. Toddler storytimes work in all types of libraries—from large, well-staffed libraries with ample budgets and separate programming rooms, to tiny libraries housed in a couple of rooms and relying on donations for materials and volunteers for staff.

Before offering any programming, examine the materials collection that targets the programming audience. For toddler storytimes, a well-defined picture book collection with titles appropriate for infants and toddlers is essential, with a collection of board books on low shelves or in baskets. Adult collections should include a parenting section with books on child development, tips for raising toddlers, and activities to do with them. Magazine collections should include at least one parenting title. Identify a space near the children's area where a temporary exhibit of parenting books can be displayed during toddler storytimes. You can also use this display as an introduction to other areas of your collection of interest to parents (craft books, cookbooks, songs, games, or media).

Examine the library's hours of operation to find the best time for a toddler program. Common times are mornings and early evenings. Afternoon programs vary by location, but many are not as successful because most toddlers need afternoon naps. Evening programs encourage working parents to participate. Pairing an evening toddler storytime back-to-back with a preschool or family program works well, often bringing both parents and their children to the library at the same time. For very small libraries, toddler storytime can be scheduled 30 minutes before the library opens to keep distractions to a minimum.

Encourage parents to arrive early so that children have time to get settled before the program begins. If possible provide a place other than the *story space* (where the program is held) for parents and toddlers to gather before the

FIGURE 1   Sample Registration Letter

Storytimes for Two-Year-Olds

(name) _____ is scheduled for storytime on

(day) _____ at (time) _____ AM/PM for 20–30 minutes. Programs begin

(date) _____ and continue for six consecutive weeks.

For many children this will be their first group experience. Your cooperation and assistance in the following ways will make it more successful for your child.

1. Visit the library with your child and talk about the storytime before the first program. Explain that there will be stories, fingerplays, puppets, songs, and games, and that you will enjoy them together. If you would like to see the story room, we will be happy to make arrangements.
2. Bring only the toddler who is enrolled in the program. Older or younger children should not be part of this activity. If child care is a problem, ask the librarian for suggestions that have worked for others in the past.
3. Attendance is important! Activities of one week are often dependent upon those shared the week before. Please call (phone #) _____ if you cannot attend.
4. Once the program has begun, no one will be admitted to the story space. Two-year-olds are easily distracted, and latecomers become the focus of attention. Please plan to arrive early. Parking notes: _____.
5. Name tags will be provided for your child and yourself. They will help everyone get to know each other and feel at ease. Please talk about wearing name tags with your child and practice pinning something to your child's shirt so he or she will feel more comfortable with this process.
6. We will hold each storytime in the story room and will enter together when it is time to begin. There will be rug spots on the floor for seating. Let your child choose the place you will sit together, with your child on your lap or in front of you. Dress comfortably to sit on the floor. If you have physical restrictions that prohibit sitting on the floor, please call the library so other arrangements can be made.
7. If your child becomes restless or uncooperative, please step outside for a few moments. This helps everyone else to concentrate and your child to focus on your wishes. When your child is ready, you may quietly rejoin the group.
8. This is a time for adults and children to fully participate in planned activities together. If you want to chat with a friend, please do so before or after the program.
9. Toddlers enjoy watching others rather than participating themselves, especially in situations new to them. Please do not insist that your child join in any activity. If you participate and have fun, your child will soon join you.
10. A storytime handout will be provided each week, listing books, fingerplays, songs, and rhymes used in the program along with a craft idea and follow-up activities for you to do at home.
11. Plan to check out books for your child to take the storytime experience home with you. Some books will be in the story room for you and your child to choose. The librarian can show you where to find others. To apply for a library card, ask at the checkout desk.

Our goal is for everyone to have a good time. With your help, we can develop and nurture your child's love of books and the library. Library staff will be happy to assist you before or after storytime with the selection of books or other library services.

program begins. This gives them the opportunity to choose books, greet friends, chat, and play. Provide a basket with simple puzzles or toys to keep little hands busy while they wait. Be certain there are enough materials for each child to have one. Toddlers do not share.

Story Space

The best place for a toddler storytime is a small room with a door, free from distractions like ringing telephones or noisy book drops. If a small story space is not available, create a cozy area in a larger room by arranging chairs, book carts, or tables around it. For libraries without separate meeting rooms, the story space should be as far as possible from the door and telephone.

A compact, well-defined story space is preferred. Toddlers need clear boundaries in their worlds and find it easier to stay focused in small spaces. The story space should be small, just slightly larger than the seating space needed for the group, with designated places for children and parents to sit—even in carpeted rooms. Arranging *rug spots* (carpet samples) or small flat cushions in a semicircle facing the storyteller ensures that everyone can see and hear. This keeps the storyteller close enough to hold toddlers' attention. Figure 2 shows a suggested arrangement of the story space.

Always make a ceremony of entering the story space together with the parents and toddlers. It sends a clear signal to everyone that the program has started. If the library only has one room and children are waiting in the story space, create an activity to remove all of them from that area so you can all enter it together. Part of your opening routine could be to line them up on one side of the room, then march in a circle as you sing a welcome song or chant a nursery rhyme. Lead them back to the story space and direct them to find their seats in the story circle. If you do not follow this procedure and allow them to gather early in the story space, parents chat more with each other during the program and toddlers get restless. They find it difficult to settle down once they have been playing and running in the area unless you help them enter it as part of a ritual.

Display books around the perimeter of the story circle, behind the rug spots. Leave enough room for children and parents to get up and down without knocking the books over. They should be close enough that even shy toddlers can reach one. Books on display create a festive environment for the program and provide parents with choices of other appropriate titles for their children. Books can stand on low shelves, on small tables, or even on the floor behind your audience. Books can define the story space, especially in a larger room, but they are more than decoration. Toddler storytimes should include an opportunity for children to select a book to share with their parents. Do not worry if a restless child retrieves a book during the program; it is not a problem unless it distracts others.

Format

A toddler storytime *session* consists of once-a-week programs lasting six to eight weeks. Libraries often present several sessions a year to accommodate demand (two in the fall, two in winter/spring, and one in the summer). Programs within each session can be offered at several times each week (mornings, afternoons, and evenings). Once preparation is done for a toddler storytime, it makes sense to present it again when there is a demand. Some libraries take short breaks between sessions to register participants for the next one and to prepare for it.

Group size should be limited to ten to twelve toddlers with their parents (see the "Story Space" section earlier in this chapter), and the size of the story space may be the determining factor. Schedule storytime programs to last about 20 minutes, each filled with fast-paced action and stimuli broken into short (2- to 4-minute) segments. Storytimes at the beginning of a session are often shorter than those at the end, because toddlers learn to focus and participate more every week.

Toddlers seem more cooperative and alert in the morning, and storytimes offered between 9:00 and 11:00 a.m. have proven successful. Afternoon programs (for toddlers who do not

FIGURE 2   Suggested Story Space Arrangement

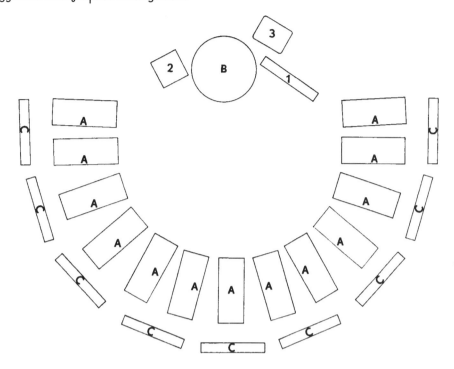

A. Rug spots (carpet samples) are placed in a semicircle close enough to the storyteller so that all parents and children can see and hear. Each parent and child shares one rug spot.

B. The storyteller sits on a low stool or on the floor with the following within arm's reach: (1) flannelboard on a low easel, (2) a low table or stool for display, and (3) storytime materials (books, puppets, flannelboard figures, handouts, etc.) in the order they will be used and kept out of view behind the flannelboard until needed.

C. Books are displayed around the perimeter of the story space on low shelves, tables, book carts, or the floor. They are to be used in quiet time activities, and they can help define the story space in a larger room.

take naps) work best between 1:30 and 3:00 p.m. Evening programs between 5:00 and 6:30 p.m. are popular with working parents. When selecting a time and a day of the week, contact other agencies and organizations to avoid conflicts and to let them know your program exists.

One of the most important considerations when programming for toddlers is to choose a time with a minimum of distractions. Move as far away from the front door and checkout desk as possible. Take the telephone off the hook if it can be heard in the story space. Avoid programs on the morning the trash truck picks up. Take every precaution against being interrupted. Every interruption becomes a distraction to toddlers, who must then refocus their attention.

Be consistent with your program. Start on time. A vicious cycle develops when programs start late. Waiting for latecomers penalizes those who arrived on time, rewards latecomers, and ultimately encourages everyone to arrive later next time. Take your program seriously and start when it is scheduled to begin. If special circumstances occur (bad weather, street construction, or parking nightmares), ask the on-time group if they mind waiting a few minutes. If a parent calls when running late, consider it a special circumstance when it is an isolated incident.

Be firm about program rules. If you decide that latecomers will not be admitted to the story space once the program has begun (and this is *strongly* recommended), make that clear from the beginning—no exceptions. It is unfair to those who have arrived on time to have the storytime interrupted by latecomers. Toddler storytime is structured so that the opening routine prepares toddlers to focus their attention and participate. Late arrivals miss that structure and distract others, often negating the opening preparation. This forces you to deal with an out-of-sync child or start again at the beginning to reorient everyone.

This rule may seem harsh, especially for parents caught on the outside with a disappointed toddler. Tardy parents are often harried and embarrassed. When possible, another staff member should interact with them, explaining the problems caused by entering the story space once the program has begun. It is important to listen to their complaints and concerns and invite them to wait until the program finishes (it only lasts 20 minutes) so their children can get handouts and talk with a storytime puppet—a favorite activity. The puzzles and toys used with children before the program will come in handy now. The staff member should console the parent with new books or magazines or offer assistance in selecting books. This special attention often calms parents and helps time pass more quickly. Most parents are cooperative, but some are not.

If a tardy parent leaves before the program ends, mail that week's handout to the *child* with a note to the parent saying, "We missed you both." Mention how much you appreciate their cooperation and how eager you are to see them next time. Enforcing a rule about latecomers benefits everyone in the long run. I've known people to arrive 15 minutes late for a program that only lasted 20 minutes! Be firm—for yourself, for others in the group, and for the children who become restless and disruptive when they miss out on storytime routines. Rarely will a latecomer miss a second program when this rule is enforced.

Program Themes

Plan each toddler storytime around a specific theme. This makes selection of materials easier and helps focus toddlers' attention. Themes can be specific (Birthdays, Dogs, or Picnics) or general (Spring, Family, or Weather). Themes should center on objects and events familiar to toddlers: family, animals, daily routines, play activities, and holidays. Support each theme with all program elements: books, fingerplays, songs, flannelboards, action rhymes, and puppets.

The themes listed later in this book are intended as guidelines. Each is based on a successful program and is intended to help you get started. When you become comfortable, personalize these by adding your own favorite stories, flannelboards, action rhymes, and fingerplays. Develop new themes by mixing stories, fingerplays, and songs from different programs. Songs and fingerplays are indexed to help you locate them. Toddler storytimes work best when you enjoy the theme and the materials. Don't be afraid to repeat a rhyme or story, even within the same program. Toddlers love repetition, and it's easy to change a story from a book to a fingerplay or a flannelboard. You can even create some broad new themes, such as "My Favorite Things," "The Color Blue," or "Thursday Stories."

Program Handouts

It is important to give a handout to parents each week listing the books, fingerplays, and rhymes used in the storytime. Program handouts can include

- titles and authors of stories (those shared in the storytime and a few more)
- words and actions for fingerplays or songs used in the program
- follow-up ideas or a craft project for parents and children to do at home

- a brief mention of a library service, other programs, or a parenting resource (book, magazine, video, or CD) available at your library

The size of handouts can vary, from full- or half-page to bookmarks. Make them festive and colorful.

The benefits of program handouts offset any time and cost of producing them.

1. Once produced, handouts can be used again and again, because themes are repeated from one year to the next.
2. Handouts are a printed reminder of the program, encouraging parents and toddlers to talk about storytime and repeat the fingerplays and rhymes at home. Including a follow-up or craft idea keeps the library at their fingertips for weeks to come.
3. Handouts help parents select *appropriate* books for their toddlers during future visits. Long after storytime sessions have ended, parents continue to use handouts to find books for their children and to make recommendations to others.
4. Handouts provide a record of storytime programs. Keep the handout master with thematic program materials and add notes to recall what worked and what needs to be revised.
5. Handouts become a guideline for new or substitute programmers, helping them understand the basic components and plan for toddler storytimes.

The impetus for writing this book (now in its third edition) came from a collection of toddler storytime handouts shared with other children's librarians at a national conference.

Program Record-Keeping and Materials Storage

Keep a written record of the materials and activities used in each program, the order in which they were presented, and how they were received. This helps you maintain a quality program and prepare for future ones.

Gather all materials to be used in each toddler storytime session so they are on hand when needed. One suggestion is to keep books, puppets, handouts, flannelboard figures, and the like in magazine storage boxes (one for each theme) along with notes from previous storytimes. When you are ready to do that program the next time, everything you need is at hand. In an emergency, a substitute programmer can step in knowing where to find everything needed and what was planned for the program.

Keep statistical records (enrollment, waiting list numbers, day and time of programs, attendance, etc.) as you do for all library programming. Statistical and population-service information can be collected for children's programs where they register in advance, helping protect these services from cutbacks during budget crunches. Statistics help determine which days and times work best in your community, as well as indicate where additional programs are needed.

Periodically conduct program surveys. Ask participants what elements of the programs they like best (and least). Invite comments and suggestions. This can lead to additional library services and programs as well as strengthen your base of support in your community . . . and those comments provide ammunition when competing for budget dollars.

Surveys and statistical data let you evaluate services and programming in terms of community needs and expectations. Surveys can be taken before offering a toddler program to determine the level of interest in the community or at the end of a storytime series to evaluate how the program is meeting your patrons' needs. Design questions based on what you want to know. The following are examples of survey questions:

What day of the week is better for your child and you to come to storytime?

Do you prefer morning, afternoon, or early evening programs?

What time works best?

What part of the storytime do you enjoy the most?

What part of the storytime does your child like best?

Always leave a space for comments and suggestions.

——————— Troubleshooting ———————

The most difficult part of working with toddlers can sometimes be interacting with their parents. Common problems are addressed below. Some challenging situations show up during registration, while others surface week to week through the session. Most conflicts can easily be resolved by talking with the parent.

When talking to parents about problems, *always* ask them to step aside out of earshot of others. This lessens embarrassment and encourages their cooperation. Without laying blame, simply state, "I need your help," then explain the problem. Never blame the child . . . or the parent. Think of problems as difficulties that need resolution and parents as your partners in solving them. It is best to speak with parents immediately following the program where the problem occurred. Face-to-face contact is best, but a phone call will suffice if parents leave before you can catch them. It is vital to address the problem before the next program.

The situations presented here are examples, and the recommended solutions are guidelines. You will know your parents and children better than anyone making blanket statements in a book. There are exceptions to every rule. Don't be afraid to try something different. Follow your instincts when faced with situations that do not conform to those discussed here, but stand your ground to protect the quality of your program.

Not Yet Two Years Old

The first problem that often surfaces is the parent who wants to enroll a child who is younger than your guidelines permit. We've all heard, "But *my* child is so mature for her age." In fairness, some twenty-month-olds are ready to participate in toddler storytimes, and a few three-year-olds do not have the emotional and social maturity, making them too young. With that said, chronological age is still the best criterion.

When your program is filled to capacity and there is a waiting list, it is easy to stick to your guns, only accepting two- to three-year-olds. When there is room in the storytime, it is more difficult. Parents can be persistent. Explain that the program was designed for two-year-olds to attend for one year, so they can graduate to preschool storytime by the time they turn three. This helps parents accept an age limitation. Starting too young means the child must repeat some programs next year. (Actually, toddlers could care less. They love repetition, but precocious parents usually do not.) As a last resort, give the child a trial period, inviting her or him to visit a toddler storytime on a trial basis. This should demonstrate whether the toddler is ready to attend.

One Child, One Lap

Another problem that arises during registration involves parents who want to enroll twins, triplets, or friends' children with only one adult accompanying them. Toddler storytimes work best when one child and one adult interact together: listening, talking, playing, and reading together. As one library puts it: "One lap, one child." When one adult must divide his or her attention among multiple children, it just does not work as well. One of the children often feels left out and acts accordingly.

One successful solution for this problem is for the parent to ask another adult (grandparent, neighbor, or friend) to come along as a second "lap." This allows all children to participate and spreads the joy of the program. Another option would be to enroll the children in an evening session so that both parents (or other adults) could attend together. There have even been cases where one twin was enrolled in storytime and the other in a different activity (preschool, recreation program, church program, etc.). At the end of the session, they switched places for the next one. I am aware of cases where multiple toddlers have attended with one adult, and it worked out fine. In other situations, it has been disastrous. This should be a positive experience for all children and parents. One lap, one child is still the best way to ensure that.

Siblings

Because toddler storytimes were designed for one child and one adult, it is best when older or younger siblings do not attend. Older children want to help, often stepping in to do things for toddlers instead of letting them do it for themselves. The presence of younger siblings can cause distractions, and they often demand attention for themselves. When toddlers and parents interact solely together without the presence of other children, they build strong bonds where toddlers can demonstrate what they are learning to their fully attentive parents. Occasionally, emergencies necessitate that a sibling be brought along to storytime, but this should not be a regular occurrence. Parents should understand this requirement of the program when they enroll. Child care is always a problem, but there are ways to make it work.

One solution is to have the parent bring along a friend, neighbor, or relative to spend time in the library with the older/younger sibling while the parents and toddlers are in storytime. This becomes an opportunity for children to know the other adults in their life. Other options include forming babysitting co-ops with other parents so that one parent and toddler attend one session, then they trade with others for the next session. Many churches and child-care centers offer Mom's Day Out programs. Some may be willing to work with the library to provide child care during toddler storytimes in exchange for an occasional storytime of their own. Options exist for child care for siblings, and under no circumstances should children be left unattended in the library.

Talkative Parents

One of the most common problems of toddler storytimes (or any program where adults attend) occurs when parents talk to each other during the program. They may be old friends who have not seen each other for a long time, or parents who have just met and discovered they have something in common. Chatting distracts others, defeats the intent of child and adult sharing experiences, and drives program presenters to distraction. The real problem is that these toddlers do not have their parents' undivided attention, and their behaviors will begin to reflect that fact.

The best way to stop this behavior is to prevent it from happening. From the beginning, make clear to parents that they and their children are expected to *participate together* in storytime activities. Include this statement in all introductory materials and orientation sessions. If chatting happens during the program, intervene through the children without stopping what you are doing. In the middle of a story, add some action that ties into the story and requires the adults and children to interact: "Janie hugs her puppy. Let's all give our parents a hug." Or "This is the top of the tree. Show Mom the top of your head." This interrupts parents' conversations and gently draws them back into the program. If the talking happens during quiet time when parents are supposed to be looking at a book with their children, use a book as bait: "Michael, give this book to your mom and show her the monkeys in it."

For persistent problems, talk to the parents after the program—together or separately—following the troubleshooting guidelines discussed earlier. Start by asking for their help. Tell them that you can see how much they enjoy each other, but you would appreciate it if they could visit together before or after the program. As a last resort, prevent them from sitting close to each other by guiding their children to different sides of the room as they enter the story space: "Mary, there is a red rug spot for you over here. Look, Michael! Your favorite green rug spot is over there." Sneaky, but effective. Parents don't mean to be disruptive and don't realize they are causing a distraction. They must understand that it is important for them to actively participate with their children. Be firm.

Child Discipline

Disciplining toddlers is a tricky situation, but it is the parents' responsibility. Parents have different boundaries and levels of patience. It helps them if you identify acceptable behavior during the orientation: being wiggly, wandering around the room, wanting to hold books or toys, and watching but not participating in activities. This helps parents recognize situations that need their intervention: crying, tantrums, hitting, struggling, or bothering others. During orientation, offer suggestions for actions parents can take if their child becomes disruptive or distressed: talking quietly with the child, moving from the circle to a corner for a chat, or even stepping outside the room until the child is ready to return.

If a situation occurs, stay focused on the other children and continue the program. This makes clear to the parent of the unhappy child that you are not going to discipline the child. If the parent does not attempt to improve the situation, quietly suggest an option: "Perhaps you want to step outside with her for a few moments until she is ready to return."

Not Ready for Storytime

Toddlers mature at a widely varying rate. Sometimes children who are chronologically two years old are not ready for group activities. It quickly becomes evident and can be disruptive to others: unable to focus attention, squirming, squealing, running around the story space, jumping on others, or knocking over program materials. Most parents quickly realize this as a problem and voluntarily withdraw their children until a later session. Occasionally, a parent is totally engrossed in storytime activities and seems oblivious to the child's behavior. If the child's behavior threatens others, quietly suggest to the parent that they both step outside a while to let the child calm down. If they return and the child is still out of control, talk with this parent after the storytime. Explain that you have noticed that the child doesn't seem to be enjoying the program. Reinforce to the parent that toddlers' interests often change dramatically within a few weeks, and suggest that they enroll in the next session.

Parents Who Force Participation

Toddlers enjoy watching others. They will participate when they are ready and when they feel comfortable. Some parents become anxious when their children are not participating (especially if they are in a group where most of the other children are). They may push their children to do fingerplays, participate in activities, sing songs, or have contact with a storytime puppet. This can elicit strong resistance from the toddlers and can lead to a meltdown. When you see parents pushing their toddlers, quietly discourage them by saying, "It's okay if she doesn't want to. If you do it, she eventually will, too." If the pushing becomes an ongoing problem, talk with the parents after the program to reassure them that their children are normal. Remind them that toddlers love to watch others and they will join in when they are ready. Reinforce how important it is for them as parents to participate, becoming role models for their children.

2
Program Elements

The toddler storytime begins when children enter the library and ends when they leave. In the 45–60 minutes intervening, a series of well-planned elements come together to form an enjoyable program that promotes trust and learning for children, supports and informs parents, and puts another feather in the library's programming cap. Beginning with the simple acts of greeting the child and pinning a name tag on a shirt . . . continuing through opening routines to the actual storytelling program and quiet time activity . . . and ending with closing routines and final good-bye hugs given to a puppet, toddler storytimes can become the favorite children's program offered in your library.

When asking for cooperation or giving instructions in this program, it is important that you speak to the children and not to the adults. Talking to the children directly, making eye contact, and smiling at them as you do lets them know that this is *their* program. It makes them feel special and the center of attention, and toddlers like that. Tell children what you want them to do, and parents will listen and help their children comply. Do not rush them. Toddlers need time to hear and assimilate what you are saying. Repeat your request if necessary. When you begin giving directions to the parents, you are telling the children that they are no longer important, and their behavior will mirror that.

Toddler storytimes must be fast-paced and highly structured to hold the short attention spans and developing listening skills of young tots. Do not expect a lot of response from toddlers at first. The program should flow smoothly from one element into the next without delays. The following program elements have proven effective and combine easily to create a well-balanced toddler storytime.

When interacting with toddlers, physically get down on their level whenever possible. Greet them sitting in a small chair, and conduct the program from a low stool or sitting on the floor. Toddlers can be very shy, and they feel threatened by adults who are standing or walking toward them. It is important for them to see your face so they can begin to know and trust you. Consider the world from their point of view: everything looks enormous, and most of what they see is taken up with people's bottoms, knees, and feet. They hear disembodied voices coming from above them, and they rarely are eye to eye with people who are talking to them. Can you remember the last time you talked with someone much taller than you, how uncomfortable it was, and how hard you found it to concentrate on what they were saying? Stay low. Sit still. Let them come to you.

Don't let toddlers be pushed into situations or participation in activities. They learn much about their worlds by observing, and they need to feel very comfortable before participating. You must be their advocate. Whether the children are receiving name tags, participating in activities, or getting their fingers "tasted" by a puppet, well-meaning parents compare their children with others in the group and will sometimes push toddlers into situations where the children feel uncomfortable. Your awareness of the child's response and a constant reassurance, "It's okay if you don't want to have your finger tasted today," help both parents and children relax and enjoy the experience.

Avoid "yes or no" questions when interacting with toddlers before and during programs. Rather, offer them choices. Don't ask, "Do you want me to pin your name tag on?" which can legitimately be answered, "No!" Instead ask, "Where do you want your name tag pinned?" or offer alternatives, "Shall we pin your name tag on your collar today or on your pocket?"

Name Tags

Ask participants to arrive 10–15 minutes early so they have ample time for children to settle down, get their name tags, and feel comfortable. Everyone in the program should wear a name tag: the storyteller to set an example, the parents to remind them of their participation, and the children to give the storyteller a handle (each child's name) with which to conduct the program. The first close contact between child and storyteller is the name tag encounter.

As parent and child enter the library, ask "Are you here for the toddler storytime?" After they have removed their jackets, invite them to come to you to get their name tags. Ask for the child's name, speaking to the child and looking at the parent only for confirmation or for an answer if the child is shy. Giving children name tags is an excellent way to greet them, and it provides a one-to-one bonding experience for child and storyteller. Be patient. Resist the urge to go to the child who is reluctant or slow. Letting the child come to you reduces stress for the child and promotes trust.

To encourage children to approach you, point to the name tag you are wearing and tell them you have one for them just like it. If some children are still reluctant, involve them in another way by asking them to "help" by coming to get their parents' name tags: "Here is Daddy's name tag. You can give it to him." (This is another good

reason for parents to wear name tags.) Children will approach, take the name tag from you, and give it to their parent. Then the tots watch carefully to see what the parent does with it. Toddlers love to help. Don't rush this process—trust takes time. They will want to assist you each week in handing out parents' name tags.

Attach the name tag to a child's clothing with a small safety pin, or thread the name tag with loops of yarn that slide over the child's head. Resist well-meaning parents when they attempt to take name tags from you directly—it is important for you to interact with the child as much as possible. Once a child is close to you, show the name tag and ask where he or she would like you to pin it. For very shy children, let them watch you pin name tags on others. As a last resort, let the parents pin the name tags, saying how much you will enjoy doing that next time.

Name tags should be colorful and durable, laminated if possible to prevent them from being pulled apart or chewed into pulp. A simple clown name tag made from basic shapes lends itself very well to this program and creates several opportunities during the storytime to draw attention to it. Print the child's name in large letters on *both* sides of the name tag. This way it can be read if it flips over during the program. Parents' name tags do not have to be elaborate: a square or circle is sufficient. Printing the child's name in small letters on the back of the parent's name tag helps get the tags paired together again at the end of the program.

Before the Program

Toddlers need time to "shift gears" before the program begins. They are very sensitive to changes: from being cooped up in a car seat to the freedom of moving on their own, from being bundled in layers of clothing to less restrictive attire, or from outside temperatures to inside ones. After they have received their name tags, encourage them to browse for books or play until it is time for the program to begin. Provide appropriate puzzles or toys with which they can play while they are waiting. Have enough toys or puzzles because toddlers do not readily share. Toddlers expel a lot of restless energy before entering the story space, and parents can use this time to chat with friends and select books, making their active participation in the program easier.

Start the program on time, and enter the story space together as a group. Letting parents and children straggle into the space where your program will be held robs toddlers of the structure they need in storytime. The clearer the boundaries and the stronger the signals, the more secure toddlers feel and the better their cooperation will be. If parents and children must wait in the same space you use for storytime, make it part of your opening routine to call them out of that space, reentering it as a group.

Within the story space you should have arranged seating markers to indicate where you want parents and children to sit. Rug spots (carpet samples) are perfectly sized and economical for this purpose. Children choose where they will sit with their parents.

———— Opening Routine ————

Opening and closing routines are the "security blankets" for toddlers during storytimes. Young children feel comfortable and safe knowing exactly how programs will begin and end. Parents benefit from observing how structure and repetition can be used to calm and focus the attention of toddlers. Opening routines have four basic parts.

1. Come with me! entering the story space and getting settled
2. Look at me! refocusing toddler's attention on you
3. Do with me! a participation activity done with you
4. Watch me do! directing children's attention elsewhere yet still under your control

This progression moves toddlers from concrete concepts to abstract thinking, step-by-step.

Come with Me!

Use a sound maker (bell, tambourine, favorite song, etc.) to signal that it is time for storytime to begin and that you are ready to enter the story space together. Have the children gather their parents and line up for storytime. Reassure children who are involved in a puzzle or toy that they can return to it after storytime is over. By making children responsible for getting their parents lined up, you continue to reinforce that this is their program. Create a ritual for entering the story space, marching to recorded music, singing a song, or chanting a nursery rhyme together. As children enter the story space, they choose where to sit that day. If you have children who only want to sit on one color of rug spot, make sure there are a couple of rugs in that color to avoid conflicts. Use this opportunity to separate "talkative" parents by encouraging their children to sit on opposite sides of the room.

Look at Me!

As children and their parents are getting settled, there is some confusion and you must redirect their attention back to you to continue the program. Although a sharp, loud sound would accomplish this purpose, it can also excite or frighten young children. The method recommended is to provide stimulation that children can actually feel against their skin as you move among them. The puff of air from a folded fan, the tickle of a feather, or dangling ribbons and placing a pretend "something" in their hands all provide physical sensations that can be delivered in a gentle, nonthreatening manner and from a slight distance. Children's attention will become riveted on you, and their curiosities will be piqued. Continue talking throughout this process, calling each child by name and explaining that this is bringing *listening dust* to make them better listeners.

Do with Me!

Immediately follow the attention-getter with a participation activity that can be done while everyone is seated: a welcoming song with everyone vigorously waving, a fingerplay, or a hand-clapping rhyme. Whatever the activity, it should be the same every week. Keep movements large, and don't go too fast. This keeps toddlers' attention focused on you and releases restless energy. Making eye contact with parents lets them know you expect them to do the activity with you. Children will follow their parents' leads. A favorite opening fingerplay is "Open Them! Shut Them!" (see figure 3). The "Hello!" song found in the theme pages for Friends also works well.

Watch Me Do!

Follow the participation activity immediately by redirecting their attention to a flannelboard activity. Flannelboards combine tangible elements, which can be moved and touched, with abstract concepts such as counting, colors, and story structure. This process is necessary for children to listen and understand the stories that will follow. This will be the first introduction to the "watch and listen" storytime model for toddlers.

FIGURE 3   An Opening Fingerplay

Open Them! Shut Them!

Open them! *(hands held in front, fingers extended)*
Shut them! *(close fingers tightly)*
Give a little clap. *(clap hands)*
Open them! Shut them! *(repeat)*
Put them in your lap. *(lay hands in lap)*
Creep them, creep them *(wiggle fingers slowly up the front of the body)*
Up to your chin. *(stop hands at chin)*
Open your mouth, *(open mouth wide, keeping fingers on chin)*
But don't put them in! *(fling hands outward and upward)*
Open them! Shut them! *(repeat first actions)*
Give a little clap.
Open them! Shut them!
Put them in your lap.

It is here they will first practice their listening skills and their abilities to concentrate.

Keep it simple. One easy flannelboard is a shape puzzle that has seven basic shapes (two circles, a rectangle, a triangle, two stars, and a crescent). When the puzzle pieces are rearranged, they form a clown that matches children's name tags. Name each piece as it is moved on the flannelboard, and explain how its relationship to other pieces has changed. For example, "I put the triangle above the circle. The rectangle goes between the triangle and the circle." Then direct children's attention to the matching name tags, having children point out one of the shapes to their parents. While they are thus engaged, remove flannelboard pieces and put them away. When their attention returns to you, be ready to begin the first story. (Clown name tags and the shape puzzle patterns can be found in appendix A.)

Story Program: Story, Activity, Story

The body of each storytime, sandwiched between opening and closing routines, is the story program—the part that changes from week to week. Including two or three short stories that are alternated with activities to get children up and moving, the story program must flow smoothly and quickly to hold toddlers' attention. The following chapter includes fifty thematic story programs that have been assembled, complete with suggested books, songs, and fingerplays, for programmers to use.

Stories can be presented and repeated through a variety of formats: books, fingerplays, flannelboard presentations, creative dramatics, music, puppets, and realia. Alternate stories (any aspect of the program where children are sitting and listening) with activities that allow children to move and release pent-up energy. This story-action-story pattern should continue in quick succession throughout the program. It will allow toddlers to gradually improve their listening skills and lengthen their attention spans without overtaxing their need for physical activity.

Books

The selection of books to use in toddler storytimes has gotten easier, and books are more plentiful. There are many fine books for this age group, and the criteria for choosing the best to use in storytimes follow:

1. Illustrations should be simple and clearly defined against the backgrounds, making them easy to see from a distance. Objects and characters with bold outlines are best. If illustrations are questionable for toddlers, adapt the story to another format: fingerplay, flannelboard presentation, creative dramatics, or puppets.
2. Characters should be kept to a minimum: no more than three or four.
3. Stories should be repetitive, either in the actions of the characters or with repeating refrains or dialogue.
4. The story should move quickly from beginning to end in a linear fashion. For longer stories, drop some of the characters to shorten the story for use with the group.
5. The plot (if there is one) should be very simple with no subplots. Books without plots (concept books or those identifying familiar objects or animals) can also be used.

Repetition is essential for toddlers to help them understand what is happening (compre-

hension), to recall events and characters (using memory and imagination), to anticipate action in the story (reading readiness), and to hear words used to tell the story (expanding vocabulary). Children greet a familiar story as an old friend and are eager to share it again and again. This means the same story can be used more than once during the program. Varying the format (first as a book, then through a flannelboard presentation or creative dramatics) makes the repetition less tedious for parents and the storyteller. Toddlers enjoy the same story presented in a new package.

Fingerplays

Fingerplays and action rhymes are essential to toddler storytimes. Interspersed between stories, they help channel restless energy, allowing toddlers to concentrate better on the stories that follow. The combination of movement, rhythm and rhyme, and following directions are welcome additions to any storytime.

Standard fingerplays must be adapted for use with toddlers. Their fine-motor skills are not yet developed enough for them to succeed with the small finger movements most fingerplays employ. Recall the last time you saw a toddler struggle to display two fingers when asked his age, and you better understand the problem. Convert favorite fingerplays into large motor activities, with broad movements using arms, legs, and the entire body to replace smaller finger motions. These bigger motions also help toddlers release more restless energy.

Whenever possible, incorporate sign language (American Sign Language or Signed English) into action rhymes. Many signed words are appropriate for use with toddlers, and teaching them a motion to use with a spoken word is more meaningful when the motion has added meaning. They are learning another language.

Flannelboard Presentations

Flannelboards come in many sizes, small enough to hold in one hand or large enough to be placed on an easel. They can be purchased commercially or made from cardboard covered with felt or a carpet sample glued to a piece of wood. Flannelboard figures can be simple shapes or elaborate characters, made from paper, felt, or fabric. Flannelboard stories offer great freedom and variety to a storytime program.

1. Flannelboard stories help hold the attention of toddlers, providing movement and action not only within the action of the story but in the telling of it as well. Toddlers like to watch the storyteller put figures on the flannelboard, move them around, and take them off again. They also like to help with this process.

2. Pictures in books are abstract concepts. Toddlers do not always recognize and respond to a two-dimensional illustration as being representative of a "real" object. Although flannelboard figures look two-dimensional, they can be held and moved, thus forming a bridge for toddlers between the concrete and abstract.

3. Flannelboard figures allow the use of stories that are too long or have illustrations inappropriate for use with toddlers in group situations. When converting a book to a flannelboard format, always display the book so that parents will know they can take that story home to share one-to-one with their children. Illustrations that do not work in group situations are usually appropriate for use individually with children.

4. Flannelboards allow the expansion of fingerplays, songs, and rhymes into visual formats, enhancing storytime themes, reinforcing language, and providing additional material for toddler programs.

5. Flannelboard activities allow the use of elements unavailable in appropriate book form. For example, use a flannelboard traffic light during programs about colors and cars.

6. The flannelboard presentation expands a story or rhyme into a different format, giving toddlers the repetition they crave while keeping the material fresh for the storyteller and parents.

Easy flannelboard figures can be made from pictures cut from magazines or discarded books. Gluing pictures to felt or to strips of sandpaper will hold them in place on a flannelboard. The pictures in coloring books are simple enough to make good flannelboard patterns, cutting them out of felt and decorating them with wiggly eyes or trim. Examine some of the excellent books on creating flannelboard figures listed in the professional bibliography, and

make some of them part of your children's programming collection.

Store flannelboard figures in large clasp envelopes, and keep them in a file box or file drawer with the contents noted on the outside. Rather than making duplicate figures, note on the outside of the envelope which figures are "borrowed" from another set.

After using felt figures in a storytime program, remove them from the flannelboard and put them out of view of the children. "Out of sight, out of mind" is an excellent adage when working with toddlers.

Creative Dramatics

Creative play comes naturally to toddlers who love to play and pretend, but it needs to be encouraged in their parents. Acting out events in a story or pretending to be one of the characters allows children the opportunity to stretch, get the "wiggles out," and concentrate better when they return to their rug spots. Keep it simple. Encourage parents and children to hop like bunnies, fly like butterflies, or chug around the room as train cars. Creative dramatics can quickly be added to a program if children still seem restless after a planned action rhyme, reinforcing the theme in children's minds.

Creative drama can also be used as an integral part of telling the story. When using *The Carrot Seed* by Ruth Krauss in a garden-theme program, toddlers can actively mimic the action in the story as they hear it, planting the seed, watering it, pulling the weeds, and finally harvesting the giant carrot from the garden. They stay focused on the story and involved in it from beginning to end.

Acting out certain elements of a story carries it beyond the moment of telling. By helping toddlers recall what they have seen and heard, you are leading them through the steps of using their memories, filing and retrieving information, as well as letting them reexamine, practice, and play with the vocabulary they heard. Parents are encouraged to participate in creative play with their children while the storyteller is modeling the process for them.

Music

Toddlers like to listen to music, dance and march to it, and sing. Music can be used upon entering or leaving the story space as children line up and march with their parents. It can accompany storytelling, fingerplays, stretching activities, and creative play.

Music can be made by the storyteller, by the entire group, or by using recorded tapes or compact discs. Include as many different opportunities as possible to share music in your storytime program. Give children the opportunity to play purchased or handmade musical or rhythm instruments.

If you play an instrument, share that talent in at least one storytime program. Children need to be exposed to music in all its varieties and sources. Also include singing a cappella so parents realize that music made without instruments or recording devices has value as well. *Everybody* can sing . . . some of us just don't carry tunes as well as others. Children do not care if you sing on key, and parents will be encouraged by your enthusiasm to sing out loud also, regardless of what they think of their own singing voices.

Action songs with movements and songs with lots of repetition work great with toddlers. Words (instructions) should be sung clearly and slowly. Keep actions simple enough for toddlers to follow along, or demonstrate the actions before introducing the song. Songs with choruses and refrains, such as *Old MacDonald Had a Farm*, are popular and a great deal of fun for everyone.

Realia

Realia are any objects used to enhance or illustrate a program theme. Many objects work well in toddler storytimes: A toy rake and watering can are perfect additions to the gardens program, allowing children to take turns tending a pretend garden. A basket of artificial fruit makes the colors in *Mr. Rabbit and the Lovely Present* more real. Toddlers also enjoy musical instruments, holiday items, and costume pieces.

Because toddlers are still in the tactile phase of learning, give them ample opportunities to explore objects by touching and holding them. Keep two considerations in mind when using realia in toddler programs. The first is safety. Choose objects that do not have sharp points or edges, small pieces that can fall off or be removed by tiny prying fingers, or toxic surfaces that might find their way into a small child's mouth. The second consideration is planning enough time in your program for children to touch and handle the objects.

Because they are fascinated by new and unfamiliar objects, toddlers are sometimes reluctant to release them or to move on to the next part of the program. Keep the object in your control. When you let them hold it, ask that it be returned to you. You then pass it to the next child. Young children will relinquish an object to an adult, but they will not always do so to another child. Put the object out of sight before moving on to the next part of the program.

Puppets

Puppets are one of the most popular elements in toddler storytimes for many reasons. Puppets provide a nonthreatening introduction to a new environment, to new routines, and to a new group situation. They allow close, physical contact between the storyteller and the child, which builds trust and friendship. Puppets provide another tactile element to a program that stimulates senses, as each child can touch or be touched by them.

Puppets are usually smaller than toddlers, who are accustomed to being smaller than everyone else. This gives children a feeling of importance, power, and self-confidence. Talking and listening to puppets give children the opportunity to practice their language and listening skills. Because they are so popular, the use of puppets helps children recall the storytime program and its elements better after they get home.

Several different kinds of puppets are used in toddler storytimes: story puppets, storytime mascots, and fingertasters. Story puppets are those used in sharing a story in the program,

such as a glove puppet used with *Caps for Sale* by Esphyr Slobodkina or stick puppets used with *Freight Train* by Donald Crews. Storytime mascots are familiar figures present in all storytime programs, and they perform specific duties, such as introducing stories or participating in the opening routine. Fingertasters are sock puppets that "taste" children's fingers, again stimulating another of their senses and bringing them into close contact with the storyteller.

Storytime mascots and fingertasters are not toys. They are powerful programming tools that should be used only by the storyteller. Allowing children to play with them (other than interacting with them while they are controlled by the storyteller) robs the puppets of their effectiveness and confuses children as to the roles the puppets play in the program. If children are interested, make sure there are some washable, kid-sized puppets in with the puzzles and toys that they play with before and after the program.

Giving puppets specific jobs to do during storytime helps define their purpose and personalities.

1. A host puppet says "hello" and "good-bye" or leads participants into the story space and through opening or closing routines.
2. An assistant puppet introduces the storytime theme, brings books for the storyteller to share, gives directions for what comes next, and leads songs, creative play, or fingerplays.
3. A role-model puppet displays either preferred behavior (following directions and using listening skills) or undesirable behavior (putting clothes on wrong or playing unsafely). Children enjoy correcting the puppet's behavior.
4. A puppet can participate in telling the story, becoming a character in it or narrating it.

The most popular puppets in most children's programs are fingertasters. Made from socks (the pattern is in the Mealtimes program and appendix A), the only necessary features are button eyes . . . and *no teeth!* A fingertaster can be hidden in a pocket or a small box and emerge toward the end of the program to "taste" fingers and say good-bye to children. To say young children *love* getting their fingers "tasted" is an understatement. They become ecstatic! The puppet "licks" or gently "sucks" on children's fingers, then tells them what "flavor" they are that day . . . and it changes every day! For toddlers, the experience of having their fingers "licked" is more appealing because of the vicarious stimulation of their senses of taste. But they don't really care what they taste like. They will come back again and again to have their fingers, elbows, noses, and toes "tasted."

It is very important to have a puppet say good-bye to children as they leave. Toddlers need time to interact with the storyteller and each other. Often children are still processing the storytime program and what they heard and saw. They need time to "shift gears" again, preparing to leave the premises. As they interact with a puppet at the end of the program, parents can gather their belongings or engage in a friendly chat with a neighbor. A puppet can provide a gentle prodding, saying "Good-bye! Good-bye!" when parents are ready to go and children are still reluctant to leave.

Inexpensive puppets can be purchased or easily made from old toys, material scraps, or throwaway items. When purchasing a puppet, look at its face and particularly the eyes. Are they visible? Is the puppet inviting to look at, so that children will be drawn to it? Big puppets are enjoyable for older children, but they may overpower toddlers who prefer smaller characters. Puppets should be sturdily constructed with no small pieces that might become dislodged and be swallowed. They should be made from washable materials (felt cannot be washed). Avoid puppets with teeth, or remove the teeth, as they are threatening to young children.

When making puppets, keep the eyes close to the mouth to make the puppet more vulnerable. Do not add teeth.

Puppets are gentle creatures that often act shier of the children than the children are of the puppets. Puppets should never be used to roughhouse, make loud noises, or hit each other. When children strike at a puppet, immediately pull the puppet away saying, "Oh, please do not hit him. He does not like being hit." Then present the puppet back to the child saying, "But he does like to be petted and hugged." Children will respond with appropriate behavior.

Do not let parents force toddlers into contact with the puppet. Move the puppet away from the child if you sense resistance or fear.

Quiet Time

A quiet time may seem out of place in a highly structured program for active toddlers. However, it fits in well as a transition between the last story and the closing routines, and it serves several purposes.

1. Quiet time is an opportunity for parents and children to interact one-to-one, reinforcing what they've been doing throughout the program and encouraging them to re-create it at home. A few moments of sharing language works well, such as reciting nursery rhymes or playing a color-, parts of the body-, or clothing-identification game. Letting children choose a book from those displayed in the story space and share it with the parent guarantees success, since the books on display are all appropriate for the age group.

2. A few quiet moments allow children and parents to process the storytime experience before they face the flurry of activity associated with leaving the library. They will retain more of the program and will talk about it more at home when they have this opportunity.

3. Quiet time is a good change of pace for toddlers. Storytime was filled with fast-paced, highly structured, and very active elements. This relatively unstructured time lets them begin to return to their own schedules, pacing, and agendas.

4. Quiet time allows the storyteller a few moments to gather program materials together, to ready handouts and giveaway items for distribution, and to prepare for the closing routine.

Be aware that some parents may use this time to chat with each other rather than interact with their children. Give instructions to their children to get the parents involved again: "Bobby, ask Dad to sing the 'Twinkle, Twinkle' song with you." Make it clear to parents that quiet time is an integral part of the storytime program, and be firm about it.

This quiet activity will be short, and children will react to it based upon their own levels of maturity. Usually during the first program of the session, you give directions for the quiet activity, and within 30–60 seconds you will notice some children already growing restless from inactivity. It is very rewarding to see these same children's tolerance and willingness to spend quiet time with parents extending every week. By the last program in the session, you may have to interrupt them to close the program. Use the appearance of restless behavior in two or more children as your cue to start the closing routine.

Closing Routine

As with the opening routine, the closing routine should be the same every week. Begin by removing name tags and trading them for program handouts. The fingertasting puppet then appears, tastes fingers, and says good-bye as children leave the story space.

Name Tag Removal

As you notice children getting restless during the quiet time, ask them to have their parents remove both name tags, and have the children bring them to you. Start with the restless children. This is a low-key activity that allows others to finish their quiet time activity and to remove their name tags. Exchange each set of name tags for a program handout.

The only changes to routines in the final program of a session is that the children can take their name tags home with them. Instead of asking for the name tags to be removed, tell children they will be able to wear them home, then distribute the handouts. Be prepared for some children

to "insist" that you take the name tags back. Toddlers like their routines to be consistent! If this happens, simply hand the name tags back to the parent when the child is not looking. Tell the children that you will still be at the library when they come to visit, even when there is no storytime. Invite parents and children to attend any future programs being offered for families.

Returning Listening Dust

When all name tags have been returned, refocus attention on you by asking that the children return the listening dust you gave them in the opening routine. Tell them to brush all that dust off their clothes and their hair and to give it back to you. Cup your hands to receive the "dust" from them, and then pour it into the pocket or box (or wherever) in which the finger-tasting puppet is hiding.

Fingertaster

Carefully remove the fingertaster from its hiding place and place it on your hand. For the first session, the puppet should act very shy and frightened of the children. Let them coax it to interact with them. Explain that the fingertaster has no teeth (open its mouth so they can see) but that it loves to lick fingers (demonstrate on yourself). Ask the nearest parent if he or she would like to have a finger tasted. Move the puppet very slowly toward the parent for a "taste." Make the flavor something fun that will cause the parents to laugh and make the children want to participate. Then sit still and ask who wants their fingers tasted. Let children come to you, taking as much time as they want. Call on those who have not come forward, but if they decline it is okay.

Saying Good-Bye

When all children who want their fingers "tasted" have come forward, tell them it is time to say good-bye for the day. Tell them that the fingertaster would like to give them a hug and say farewell before they leave the story space.

This allows parents time to gather belongings together. Singing a good-bye song or chanting a rhyme, have everyone line up at the door and exit the story space together.

This final activity is the least structured part of the program. Some children need more time to talk with the puppet or have their fingers caressed repeatedly. Letting parents and children leave the story space as they are ready is an acceptable alternative, while you remain seated and let the puppet chat with children or say good-bye. If children are reluctant to leave, the puppet gets involved, waving farewell, calling out "Bye Bye!" and "See you next week!" or even directing the child's attention to something outside the story space. The parent will be grateful for your assistance, and you won't have a crying child leaving your building.

Follow-Up

Check to see if anyone arrived late and might be waiting in the children's area to receive the week's handout. Let tardy children interact with the fingertaster, and show parents the books used in the program and displayed in the story space. This helps them feel that they didn't miss out on everything.

After gathering together and storing all story-time materials, record attendance and absences for your statistics. Make notes in your story file or in this book about which stories and activities worked well (and which didn't). This saves you a lot of time and recrimination when you repeat the program theme.

Match parents' and children's name tags together so they are ready for the next program. If you mail handouts to absent children, do so immediately. Children love to get mail, and parents will soon see the value of having a list of appropriate materials and activities for their children. It also encourages them to come the following week. If postage is a problem, clip the handout to the name tags of the absent children so they can be distributed the next week when name tags are handed out. If children are absent for the final program, mail their name tags and handouts to them with a note that you hope to see them soon in the library.

3
Program Themes

Gathered together in this chapter are fifty thematic programs for toddler storytimes. Each theme includes sixteen titles appropriate for toddlers for use in the storytime program or to be recommended to parents and caregivers. Next are fingerplays/action rhymes, including at least one song. These are followed by suggestions of activities to enrich the theme and a craft for parents and toddlers to pursue together at home. Any of these components can be shared with parents in program handouts for each theme.

To reflect the multicultural world in which we live and work, books, rhymes, and crafts representing different cultural heritages were included for each theme wherever possible. Editions of recommended titles in languages other than English are noted in the bibliography of titles used in the programs, as are differing formats such as pop-up and big-format books. Special consideration was also given to varying abilities within themes, including a sign language word for each theme, books with textures and movable parts for children with visual impairments, and books in which characters with disabilities are prominent.

The titles were selected with the intent of broadening the way themes could be used. For example, in the spring theme you will find titles for a program on spring, on Easter and Passover holidays, and on eggs. This format will give you flexibility and additional ideas to make the storytimes individual and keep them fresh.

Although some titles would be appropriate with several themes, they have been included in only one place. Feel free to trade titles between themes as appropriate. An effort was made to include the work of as many authors as possible, again to broaden choices. The "in print" status was checked on all titles. A few "out of print" titles were knowingly included if they were titles common to most children's collections.

Because the selection of stories and activities is a very personal issue, dictating which materials should be used is a disservice to storytellers and audiences alike. Therefore, in this edition program notes are less structured and include *suggestions* of how certain titles or elements can be used instead of a sequential, step-by-step outline for each program.

Program notes include a sign language word, with directions for introducing it into storytimes, as well as giveaway ideas and instructions for each theme. However, giveaways should be used sparingly so they do not become the primary focus of storytimes for toddlers or parents.

Space has been provided in each theme for you to make your own program notes. Record which stories worked best for you and which did not. Make note of new titles appropriate for use with the theme or of old favorites that were not included in this edition. Jot down the unplanned things that happened during the program that you want to repeat the next time, and write ideas shared with you by others. Feel free to leave out verses of rhymes and songs that do not work in your situation and to create new verses of your own. Add pages and create your own themes, using favorite books and activities or subjects of interest to toddlers in your community. A wealth of information and ideas passes by us every day. When you find something interesting, make a note of it. Who knows where it will lead? That is how the first edition of this book began.

——— Autumn (Halloween) ———

Books

Apple Farmer Annie
MONICA WELLINGTON

Autumn Is for Apples
MICHELLE KNUDSEN

Corduroy's Halloween
B. G. HENNESSY

A Dark, Dark Tale
RUTH BROWN

Fall
   (Spanish: *El otoño*)
MARÍA RIUS

Humbug Witch
LORNA BALIAN

It's Pumpkin Time!
   (Spanish: *¡Tiempo de
   calabazas!*)
ZOE HALL

Maisy's Halloween
LUCY COUSINS

Max's Halloween
ROSEMARY WELLS

On Halloween Night
FERIDA WOLFF AND DOLORES
KOZIELSKI

One Fall Day
MOLLY BANG

Pumpkin Day, Pumpkin Night
ANNE ROCKWELL

Red Leaf, Yellow Leaf
LOIS EHLERT

Spot's Halloween
ERIC HILL

*What Will You Be for
Halloween?*
MARK TODD

Word Bird's Halloween Words
JANE BELK MONCURE

Rhythms, Rhymes, and Fingerplays

Autumn Leaves

Leaves are falling from the trees *(flutter fingers down)*
Yellow, brown, and red.
Falling, falling from above.
One landed on my head! *(hands on head)*

Jack-O'-Lantern   (tune: "I'm a Little Teapot")

I'm a jack-o'-lantern, *(arms form large circle)*
Big and fat.
I have two eyes, a nose, and a hat. *(point to eyes
    and nose, put hands on head)*
Children come at Halloween *(make beckoning motion)*
From miles and miles.
Put in a candle and *(mimic the action)*
Watch me smile. *(fingers to corners of mouth, smile big)*

Two Little Ghosts

A very old witch was stirring a pot, *(make stirring motion)*
Ooo-oooo! Ooo-oooo!
Two little ghosts said, "What has she got?" *(shrug shoulders)*
Tippytoe, tippytoe, tippytoe . . . *("walk" fingers up arm
    or tiptoe in circle)*
Boo! *(clap hands sharply)*

Parents' Follow-Up Ideas

Take an autumn walk and talk about the changes in the seasons.
Collect leaves that have fallen from trees and sort them by size or
color. Help your child notice changes in temperature that require different clothing or changes in play habits.

Together visit a pumpkin patch or a supermarket to choose a pumpkin, the traditional autumn vegetable. Even if you do not want a traditional jack-o'-lantern, cut a design in the pumpkin and introduce your
child to a vegetable lantern. Your toddler can help scoop out the seeds
and push the cut-out pieces out of the pumpkin shell. Put a votive candle inside and light it. Then turn out the lights to enjoy your pumpkin
lantern. Do not leave children alone with a burning candle.

Keep a "dress-up box" filled with old clothes, hats, scarves, shoes,
and handbags for children to use while pretending.

Paper bag costumes are fun and economical. Two books to help
you with ideas and construction of them are Goldie T. Chernoff, *Easy
Costumes You Don't Have to Sew,* and Nancy Renfro, *Bags Are Big! A
Paper Bag Craft Book.*

Craft

Wild Thing Sack Puppet

You will need: small paper sack (lunch-sized or smaller)

glue

scraps of material, paper, yarn, felt

crayons or magic markers

pipe cleaners, trim, buttons

Using the bottom flap of the paper bag as the face of your puppet, draw or glue on it features that appear on the upper half of the face: eyes, brows, nose, cheeks, and mustache. Under the flap of the bag, draw the mouth so that it is visible only when the flap is raised. Add tongue, lips, and chin. Use teeth sparingly.

Decorate the rest of the bag with your scraps and odds and ends, using glue. Let the glue dry thoroughly.

To operate, place the sack over your hand and move the flap (mouth) up and down as the puppet "talks."

Program Notes

Sign Language

HALLOWEEN   Cover your face with both hands and slowly move your hands apart as though taking off a mask.

Note: Do *not* use this program as the first one in a series. Toddlers need time to develop trust for the storyteller and others in the group before asking them to participate where others are wearing costumes.

The week prior to presenting this program, invite children to attend in costume. If the storyteller is in a costume, do not wear a mask or full stage makeup. Spend time having each child stand and admire costumes, including children who are not in costume ("Jerry is dressed as a happy boy"). Some children may be shy of others in unusual clothes. The storytime puppet wearing a costume (no mask) will reassure them. Have children remove all masks or cumbersome costume pieces before beginning the opening routine.

When using the rhyme "Two Little Ghosts," start by saying "Boo!" together to avoid startling anyone. Next practice the sequence, "Tippytoe, tippytoe, tippytoe . . . Boo!" a couple of times so they will know when the Boo! shows up in the rhyme.

Make a flannelboard jack-o'-lantern for the "Jack-O'-Lantern" rhyme, using familiar shapes: a large orange circle, a green rectangle (hat), three yellow triangles (eyes and nose), and a large crescent (mouth). Let the children help put the face on the jack-o'-lantern.

Giveaway "ghosts" can be made by covering lollipops with facial tissues and securing them with tape.

Fingertaster "tastes" autumn foods, such as apples, corn, pumpkin pie, nuts, etc.

Children exit the story space in a Halloween parade or as fluttering autumn leaves.

———————————————————— Notes ————

Babies

Books

Buenos Dias Baby!
LIBBY ELLIS

Come Back, Hannah!
MARISABINA RUSSO

Don't Wake the Baby!
WENDY CHEYETTE LEWISON

Good Night, Baby
CHERYL WILLIS HUDSON

Hello Baby!
LIZZY ROCKWELL

I Heard Said the Bird
POLLY BERRIEN BERENDS

The New Baby
   (Spanish: *El nuevo bebé*)
MERCER MAYER

Over the Moon: An Adoption Tale
KAREN KATZ

Peter's Chair
   (Spanish: *La silla de Pedro*)
EZRA JACK KEATS

Spot's Baby Sister
ERIC HILL

We Have a Baby
CATHRYN FALWELL

What Does Baby Say?
KAREN KATZ

What Shall We Do with the Boo-Hoo Baby?
CRESSIDA COWELL

Where's My Baby?
H. A. REY

Whose Baby Am I?
JOHN BUTLER

You Are My Perfect Baby
JOYCE CAROL THOMAS

Rhythms, Rhymes, and Fingerplays

The Baby

Shhh! *(finger to lips)*
Baby is sleeping *(hands to cheek, palms together)*
Don't wake her up! *(waggle finger and shake head)*
Shhh! Baby is sleeping *(repeat motions each time)*
Don't wake her up!
Shhh! Baby is sleeping
Don't wake her up!
We don't want to make Baby cry. *(crying motion: fists to cheeks, rotating back and forth)*

Walk on tippytoes *(touch fingers lightly to knees)*
Don't make a sound. *(finger to lips)*
   [repeat both lines twice more]
We don't want to make Baby cry. *(crying motion: fists to cheeks, rotating back and forth)*

The baby's AWAKE! *(eyes wide open, make "surprise"*
      motion with hand near shoulders, palms out)
She's crying, boo-hoo *(fists to cheeks, rotate back*
      and forth) [repeat both lines twice]
Baby, sweet baby, don't cry! *(gently pat cheeks*
      and shake head)

We'll tickle the baby *(wiggle fingers under chin)*
Under her chin . . . [repeat both lines twice]
Baby, sweet baby, don't cry! *(make "crying" motion)*

Baby's stopped crying! *(stop "crying" motion)*
She's starting to smile *(make BIG smile)*
      [repeat both lines twice]
I LOVE my baby. *(make hugging motion)*
Bye, bye! *(wave)*

Hush Little Baby   (song)

Hush, little baby! Don't say a word.
Mama's gonna catch you a mockingbird.
And if that mockingbird won't sing,
Mama's gonna buy you a kite and string.
And if that kite and string won't fly,
Mama's gonna bake you an apple pie.
And if that apple pie is sour,
Mama's gonna grow you a yellow flower.
And if that yellow flower has bugs,
Mama's gonna give you kisses and hugs.
Hush, little baby! Hush.

Parents' Follow-Up Ideas

Tell your toddlers stories of when they were little babies and how they changed as they grew. Use photographs or videos but also tell stories without pictures. Talk about how excited you were when they came into your family, how you needed to do almost everything for them, and how happy you were with each of their "firsts" (coo, smile, word, and step). Snuggle your toddlers close as you talk about how they are changing. Emphasize that you love them the same through all stages of their lives.

Toddlers should have soft toys to cuddle and play with regardless of their gender. They are never too young to learn to show tender, loving care for toys, pets, or other children.

Animal babies are called by many different names. Expand your toddler's vocabulary by sharing these names in a game. Use a picture book or coloring book for animal pictures and say, "Here's a dog! Baby dogs are called puppies. What are they called? Puppies!"

cat—kitten	bird—chick	cow—calf
horse—colt	duck—duckling	bear/lion—cub
goat—kid	sheep—lamb	rabbit—bunny

Craft

Bubble Cup

You will need: small plastic/paper cup (5-oz. size)

old washcloth or piece of terry cloth

rubber band

plastic straw

hole punch

liquid soap

spray bottle with water in it

Punch a hole in the side of the cup one inch from the top. The straw should fit snugly in this hole. From the washcloth cut a circle larger than the mouth of the cup and secure it over the top of the cup with the rubber band. Spray water on the cloth to moisten it and smear a little liquid soap over it with your finger.

Have your child blow into the straw and bubbles will erupt from the top! Since there is only air inside the cup, the child will not get soap or water in the mouth if he or she sucks on the straw instead of blowing. If the bubbles stop, check to see if the straw is bent, cutting off the air supply. Also, check the cloth to determine if more water or soap is needed.

Cups can be labeled with the child's name and decorated with markers, fabric scraps, or pictures. The cloth can be removed and washed or replaced as needed.

Program Notes

Sign Language

BABY   Form a cradle with your arms, as if holding a baby, and gently swing arms side to side.

Introduce the theme with a storytime puppet or doll dressed as a baby. Let each child who responds with a baby-type behavior (cooing, fussing, no talking) hug the puppet or rock a doll in a shoe box cradle. As this is happening, talk about what "big boys" and "big girls" the toddlers are and how different they are from babies who can do very little for themselves.

Peter's Chair is a good story for a flannelboard.

Giveaways are big boy/big girl medallions made from posterboard circles glued to ribbon loops.

Fingertaster "tastes" soft foods, such as mashed bananas, oatmeal, mashed potatoes, etc.

Children exit the story space taking their "babies" for a walk.

─────────── Notes ───────────

—— Bath Time ——

Books

Baby's Bathtime
   (Spanish: *¡Al agua patos!*)
FIONA WATT

Bathtime PiggyWiggy
DIANE AND CHRISTYAN FOX

Bubbles, Bubbles
KATHI APPELT

Daniel's Duck
DEBBIE MACKINNON

Dirty Larry
BOBBIE HAMSA

Harry the Dirty Dog
   (Spanish: *Harry, el perrito sucio*)
GENE ZION

I Am Water
   (Spanish: *Soy el agua*)
JEAN MARZOLLO

Jesse Bear's Tra-La Tub
NANCY WHITE CARLSTROM

Maisy Takes a Bath
   (Spanish: *Maisy se bana*)
LUCY COUSINS

Max's Bath
ROSEMARY WELLS

Mrs. Wishy-Washy Makes a Splash
JOY COWLEY

No More Water in the Tub!
TEDD ARNOLD

Rub-a-Dub-Dub
PAGE EASTBURN O'ROURKE

Spot Goes Splash!
ERIC HILL

Sticky People
TONY JOHNSTON

Tiny's Bath
CARI MEISTER

Rhythms, Rhymes, and Fingerplays

Rub-a-Dub-Dub

Rub-a-dub-dub, one child in the tub.
   (rub knuckles lightly up and down on the chest)
Tell me what you see.
One foot with toes, *(point to parts of the body)*
A hand, a nose,
As clean as they can be. *(rub hands together)*

Rub-a-dub-dub, one child in the tub.
Tell me what you see.
Two ears, a cheek, *(point)*
So clean they squeak, *(rub cheeks gently)*
A chin, a tummy, a knee. *(point)*

Rub-a-dub-dub, one child in the tub.
Tell me what you see.
Legs and arms, *(extend legs and arms)*
So clean and warm, *(wiggle arms)*
Do they have a hug for me? *(cross arms
   over chest, giving "self" a hug)*

Washing   (tune: "Mulberry Bush")

This is the way we wash our face *(hands make
    washing motion over face)*
Wash our face, wash our face.
This is the way we wash our face,
Early in the morning.

[Verse 2]

. . . brush our teeth *(brushing motion)*
. . . after we eat breakfast.

[Verse 3]

. . . wash our hands *(hands make washing motion)*
. . . after we've been playing.

[Verse 4]

. . . take a bath *(rub knuckles on chest)*
. . . before we say "Good night."

Float My Boat   (tune: "Row, Row, Row Your Boat")

Float, float, float my boat,
In a soapy tub.
Together we are getting clean,
Rub-a-dub-a-dub.

Parents' Follow-Up Ideas

Take your children to a drive-through car wash to experience how
cars "take baths." Talk about the process before you go and take time
to watch other cars go in dirty and come out clean. Once inside, some
children may be frightened, so be prepared to offer reassurance and
talk about what is happening. You may find yourself washing the car
often once they decide it is safe and fun.

Put red, stick-on dots on hot-water handles to help your children
stay safe. Red means "hot" and "hands off," and only grown-ups
should touch red-dotted handles. Put dots on water faucets in bathrooms, the kitchen, and the laundry room. Also use them on stoves,
crock pots or other heated appliances, and other "hands off" areas.

To keep bath time fun, throw some Ping Pong balls with faces on
them into the bathwater. Add a few drops of food coloring to change
the color or float a couple of ice cubes in a warm bath. [*Note:* Some
toddlers develop urinary or vaginal infections from commercial bubble bath preparations. Save them for when they are older.]

A simple hand-washing routine in which your children help gather
items, prepare themselves, and put items away will give them pride in
their abilities and lessen struggles over getting cleaned up:

1. child gathers needed items (soap, towel, nail brush, chair, or low stool)
2. rolls up sleeves and steps up to sink on a chair or low stool
3. fills sink halfway with warm water (adult turns on the hot water)
4. wets hands and rubs soap on them, returning the soap to the soap dish
5. lathers hands well and gets the soap between fingers and on the backs of hands (If necessary, use a nail brush on nails and on tough spots.)
6. rinses hands well in basin and drains sink
7. dries hands, front and back, working one finger at a time
8. climbs down from stool
9. puts away towel, soap, stool, brush, etc.

Craft

Clean Clara (Clem), a Bath Mitt

You will need: 2 washcloths or an old hand towel

scissors and pins

needle and thread

yarn

small buttons

Photocopy or trace the mitt shape on page 32 to use as a pattern. With washcloths together, pin the pattern to the middle with the bottom edge (the opening) lined up along the edges of the washcloths so you don't have to hem them. Cut through both washcloths, and sew them together along the sides and top of the mitt. Turn it inside out. Sew several pieces of yarn to the top for hair and buttons on the front for eyes. Always monitor children around small objects like buttons.

When your child is taking a bath, show how Clara (Clem) can help her or him get clean. Put the mitt puppet on your child's hand and lather it with soap. Be sure the eyes are on the back of your child's hand so they do not scratch when washing. Your toddler can use Clara (Clem) to wash his or her face, legs, and arms, and you can wash the child's back. Clara (Clem) can also wash toys, friends, etc. For a no-sew version, use a child's mitten for a "one-armed" Clara (Clem).

Program Notes

Sign Language

BATH Rub your closed hands up and down lightly on your
chest as though washing the chest during a bath.

Have several towels, washcloths, a plastic tub, and a plastic
pitcher on hand. Between stories, talk with the storytime puppet
about how eating, playing, and other things can make us dirty or
sticky. With a plastic washtub, give the storytime puppet or some of
the library toys a "pretend" bath. Let the children help wash, rinse,
and dry them. As children are busy, talk about other things that get
"baths," such as cars, animals in the zoo, and pets, and mention that
some people take showers instead of sit-down baths. Use words and
phrases like "slippery," "still soapy," and "rinsing." Explain that baths
do more than make you clean; they help you get warm in the winter
and cool off in the summer.

Giveaways can be little soaps solicited from a motel chain and decorated with a colorful sticker.

Fingertaster "tastes" foods that must be washed, such as carrots,
cherries, apples, etc.

Children exit the story space singing the first verse to "Washing."

--- **Notes** ---

Bears

Books

Baby Bear's Chairs
JANE YOLEN

Bears, Bears Everywhere
(Spanish: *Osos, osos aqui y alli*)
RITA MILIOS

Bear's Busy Family
(Spanish: *La familia activa de oso*)
STELLA BLACKSTONE

Bear's Good Night
JANE CABRERA

Blueberries for Sal
ROBERT MCCLOSKEY

Can't You Sleep, Little Bear?
MARTIN WADDELL

I Love My Daddy
SEBASTIAN BRAUN

I Love You Just the Way You Are
VIRGINIA MILLER

If You Love a Bear
PIERS HARPER

My Brown Bear Barney
DOROTHY BUTLER

Sleepy Bear
LYDIA DABCOVICH

Ten Bears in My Bed
STANLEY MACK

This Is the Bear
(Spanish: *Yo soy el oso*)
SARAH HAYES

We're Going on a Bear Hunt
MICHAEL ROSEN AND HELEN OXENBURY

Where's the Bear?
CHARLOTTE POMERANTZ

You Are My I Love You
MARYANN K. CUSIMANO

Rhythms, Rhymes, and Fingerplays

Five Bears in Bed   (tune: "Ten in a Bed")

There were five bears in her bed, *(hold up five fingers)*
And the little one said,
"Roll over! Roll over!" *(roll hands over each other)*
So they all rolled over,
And one fell out. *(one hand rolls to one side)*

[Repeat with four, three, two, and one]

There were no bears in her bed, *(hold up fist)*
And the little one said,
"Good night!" *(lay head on hands and close eyes)*

Bears Everywhere

Bears, bears, bears everywhere! *(point in different directions)*
Bears climbing stairs. *(make climbing motion)*
Bears sitting on chairs. *(sitting motion)*

Bears collecting fares. *(reach out, as if taking money)*
Bears giving stares. *(eyes wide open, look around)*
Bears washing hairs. *(hair-washing motion)*
Bears, bears, bears everywhere! *(point)*

Going on a Bear Hunt

We are going hunting for a bear. *(shade eyes with hand and peer around)*
We will walk down the sidewalk; *(pat hands on knees for walking)*
Push our way through tall grass; *(alternately push hands away from body side to side)*
Swim a river; *(make swimming motions)*
And climb a tall tree. *("climb" as if pulling self up a rope, hands alternating)*

Keep looking!! *(shade eyes and peer all around)*
What do you see?? A bear???? *(act surprised)*
We have to get out of here! *(repeat above motions faster)*

Climb down that tree, and run!
Swim that river, and run!
Push through that grass, and run!
Now run up the sidewalk . . . and in the door . . .
And shut the door tight! *(clap hands loudly)*
Whew . . . I'm glad we are home safe!! *(wipe forehead with fingers and sigh)*

Parents' Follow-Up Ideas

A guess-what-I-am game uses the sounds and motions of different animals. Toddlers like to guess and act out the different animals with you. Start with a picture book about animals found on farms, in zoos, or at home. Initially choose animals that are familiar to your child. The book will give you ideas, and you can talk with your toddler about the animal's appearance, where it lives, and how it is different from others.

Watch for bears when shopping or traveling. This activity is fun because bears are plentiful. You will find them on clothing, linens, toys, and most products. Help your child become more observant by being on the lookout for bears. Name the different kinds of bears as your toddler finds them: polar bears, pandas, brown bears, etc. Examine displays of teddy bears in toy stores together. Can your child find the largest one? The smallest?

Cut pictures of bears out of magazines, catalogs, brochures, advertising flyers, and cereal boxes. Let your child sort them by size or color and then count them. Make a bear book, a bear mobile, or bear magnets for the refrigerator.

Craft

Kitchen Clay

You will need: 2 cups baking soda

1 cup cornstarch

1⅓ cups water

pinch of salt

saucepan

waxed paper

towel

plastic bag

This recipe feels almost like *real* clay. Put all the ingredients in a saucepan and mix well. Stir over medium heat until the mixture bubbles and thickens. Turn out onto a board or waxed paper and let cool. Knead until smooth. Wrap in a damp towel and place in the refrigerator for 10–15 minutes.

Help your child learn how to squeeze, roll, pat, and make balls from clay and to put them together to make many different objects.

Store the clay in a tightly closed plastic bag in the refrigerator, and add a few drops of water to the bag to keep it from hardening.

To preserve a special creation, let the object harden in the air for a day or two. Paint with tempera or acrylic paints and cover with shellac. The result: a work of art!

Program Notes

Sign Language

> BEAR   Cross your arms over your chest with hands on shoulders and scratch twice.

Introduce the theme using a picture of a bear or a teddy bear toy.

Use flannelboard bears for the song, "Five Bears in Bed." Place the bears in a row on the flannelboard, then remove them one at a time as you chant or sing the song. In more mature groups, children can help remove bears during the song.

A bear puppet or teddy bear can give "bear hugs" to children, and children pass the hugs along to their adults.

Giveaways are bear straw caddies, a bear picture with holes punched in the top and bottom and threaded on a straw.

Fingertaster "tastes" honey-related flavors: bread and honey, honey cake, honey pancakes, etc.

Children exit the story space like lumbering bears.

—————— **Notes** ——————

Bedtime

Books

Are You Sleepy Yet, Petey?
MARIE HODGE

Baby's Bedtime
(Spanish: *¡Felices sueños!*)
FIONA WATT

Bedtime, Maisy!
(Spanish: *Maisy se va a la cama*)
LUCY COUSINS

The Going to Bed Book
(Spanish: *Buenas noches a todos*)
SANDRA BOYNTON

Good Night!
CLAIRE MASUREL AND MARIE H. HENRY

Goodnight, Goodnight Sleepyhead
RUTH KRAUSS

Goodnight Moon
(Spanish: *Buenas noches, Luna;* and pop-up book: *Goodnight Moon Room*)
MARGARET WISE BROWN

How Many Kisses Do You Want Tonight?
VARSHA BAJAJ

How Will I Ever Sleep in This Bed?
DELLA ROSS FERRERI

Hush! A Thai Lullaby
MINFONG HO

A Nap in a Lap
SARAH WILSON

The Napping House
(Spanish: *La casa adormecida*)
AUDREY WOOD

Night-Night, Spot
(Spanish: *Buenas noches, Spot*)
ERIC HILL

Siesta (English/Spanish)
GINGER FOGLESONG GUY

Ten, Nine, Eight
(Spanish: *Diez, nueve, ocho*)
MOLLY BANG

Where Does the Brown Bear Go?
NICKI WEISS

Rhythms, Rhymes, and Fingerplays

Going to Bed

This little child is going to bed *(point to self)*
Down on the pillow he lays his head. *(rest head on hands)*
He wraps himself in covers tight, *(wrap arms across body)*
And this is the way he sleeps all night. *(close eyes, rest head on hands)*
Morning comes, he opens his eyes. *(raise head, eyes wide open)*
Off with a toss the covers fly. *(fling arms wide)*
Soon he is up, dressed, and away, *(bounce up and down)*
He's ready to play all day. *(clap hands)*

Japanese Lullaby

(chant softly while parents rock their children on laps; use soothing sounds)	*[translation]*
Nen-ne-n ko-ro-ri-yo [Nehn-neh-nnn koh-roh-ree-yoh]	*Please go to sleep, la-la-la*
O-ko-ro-ri-yo [Oh-koh-roh-ree-yoh]	*La-la-la*
Bo-ya-wa yo-i-ko-da [Boh-yah-wah yoh-ee-koh-dah]	*Baby is a good baby*
Ne-n-ne-shi-na [Neh-nnn-neh-shee-nah]	*Please go to sleep.*
Bo-ya-no O-mo-ri-wa [Boh-yah-noh Oh-moh-ree-wah]	*Baby's nursemaid*
Do-ko-e-i-ta [Doh-koh-eh-ee-tah]	*Where did she go?*
An-o Ya-ma Ko-e-te [Ahn-oh Yah-mah Koh-ee-teh]	*Over that mountain*
Sa-to Ko-e-te [Sah-toh Koh-eh-teh]	*Over to a village*
Sa-to-no Mi-ya-ge Ni [Sah-toh-noh Mee-yah-geh Nee]	*What present will she bring?*
Na-ni Mo-ro-ta [Nah-nee Moh-roh-tah]	*What will you get from her?*
Den-den Da-i-ko-ni [Dehn-dehn Dah-ee-koh-nee]	*A toy drum*
Sho-u No-fu-e [Shoh-oo Noh-foo-eh]	*And a toy flute*

Rock-a-Bye Baby   (song)

Rock-a-bye baby on a tree top. *(sway side to side, arms folded in a "cradle," as though holding a baby)*
When the wind blows, the cradle will rock. *(extend hands above head and keep swaying)*
When the bough breaks, *(clap hands on "breaks")*
the cradle will fall. *(hands, palm upward, move apart)*
And down will come cradle, baby, and all. *(slowly lower hands, returning arms to "cradle" motion)*

Parents' Follow-Up Ideas

Take a walk outside with your toddler near sunset. Talk about the sun moving lower in the sky and changes in the light: sky colors, amount of light, silhouettes, and stars appearing. Notice objects you can see clearly earlier but not later. Help your child recognize the various stages of dimming light and realize that the object is still there although you can no longer see it.

If you can see the horizon, encourage your child to watch the sun's final moments of descent. What are other changes as day becomes night? Talk about lights appearing in houses and buildings and on streets. Are there changes in the wind, sounds, or smells? What other changes show your neighborhood is preparing for night and for bedtime?

Examine the night sky with your child. Talk about the things you see there: the moon, stars, meteor showers, or aircraft lights. What shape is the moon? Can you see only a few stars or many? Are there other lights? Are they moving, blinking, or standing still? Let your toddler point to a bright star and make a wish upon it together. "Star light! Star bright! First star I see tonight. I wish I may, I wish I might, have the wish I wish tonight." All wishes are better when sealed with a kiss.

Bedtime is easier with a set routine. As in the story *Goodnight Moon*, toddlers need time to shift gears and settle down. A familiar routine, followed the same each night, will help your child feel more secure and relaxed, whether he or she is at home in bed or in a motel room. Baths; brushing teeth; putting on sleeping clothes; saying goodnight to family, pets, and toys; and sharing a book or two are all components of a good bedtime routine.

Craft

Bedtime Mobile

You will need: branch with several smaller twigs

string (several pieces 12″ long)

scissors

index cards

glue

pictures from magazines, photos, tinfoil shapes, small toys, or items from nature

Cut out pictures, photos, or shapes and glue to both sides of an index card. Trim around the edges, and punch a small hole in the top of the card. Push one end of a piece of string through the hole and tie

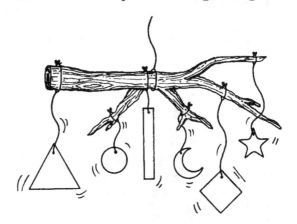

it in a knot. Tie the other end of the string to the branch and keep adding pictures, varying the length of the string and placement on the twigs. Hold the branch up often to see how it balances when hanging.

Find the center of the branch and tie a string there. Attach the mobile to the ceiling over your toddler's bed with a nail or plant hanger. It will move in the air currents, helping little ones fall asleep as they watch it. Change the items on the mobile or make a new one as seasons change or holidays approach. Use small objects (toys, pinecones, leaves, and so on) light enough to balance each other. Let your child help you accumulate the items to be added to a new mobile and decide where they will be placed.

Program Notes

Sign Language

SLEEP   With palms together, place your hands next to your cheek and lean your head against them as if on a pillow.

Introduce the theme with a sleepy storytime puppet. Provide a bed for the puppet (a pillow, box, or small blanket). The book *The Napping House* makes a good flannelboard or flip-chart story for toddlers. Between stories, the puppet can ask children to participate in its bedtime routine: changing clothes, brushing teeth, saying good night, etc. Share *Goodnight Moon,* and the puppet can give all children good night hugs, then they tuck it in bed. Place the "I'm Sleeping" doorknob hanger on the puppet's bed.

Giveaways are awake/asleep doorknob hangers made with index cards and yarn.

Fingertaster "tastes" bedtime snacks, such as milk, cookies, hot chocolate, etc.

Children exit the story space on tiptoe to keep from waking the puppet.

———————— Notes ————————

Birds

Books

Cheep! Cheep!
JULIE STIEGEMEYER

The Chick and the Duckling
MIRRA GINSBURG

The Chicken Book
GARTH WILLIAMS

Five Little Ducks
IVAN BATES

Goodnight, My Duckling
NANCY TAFURI

Good-Night, Owl!
PAT HUTCHINS

Hen on the Farm
LUCY COUSINS

Hoot! Hoot!
RICHARD POWELL

Little Bird
ROD CAMPBELL

Little Duck: Finger Puppet Book

Look Out, Bird!
   (Spanish: *¡Cuidado pajarito!*)
MARILYN JANOVITZ

Minerva Louise
JANET MORGAN STOEKE

My Goose Betsy
TRUDI BRAUN

Rosie's Walk
   (Spanish: *El paseo de Rosie*)
PAT HUTCHINS

This Little Chick
JOHN LAWRENCE

Your Personal Penguin
SANDRA BOYNTON

Rhythms, Rhymes, and Fingerplays

Five Little Red Birds

Five little red birds, *(hold up five fingers)*
Pecking at my door. *(mimic actions)*
One flew away, and
Then there were four. *(hold up four fingers)*

[Repeat with]
   Four . . . sitting in a tree. One pounced on
      a worm . . . three.
   Three . . . calling "Coo-coo-coo." One flew
      to a nest . . . two.
   Two . . . sleeping in the sun. One woke and
      hopped away . . . one.
   One . . . as lonely as could be. When it flew
      away, all that's left was me!

I'm a Little Chick

I'm a little chick who goes "Bawk, bawk, bawk!"
   (hands in armpits, flap arms like wings)
I dip my head when I walk, walk, walk.
   (lean front and back)
I scratch for a worm going "Bawk, bawk, bawk!"
   (one hand forms claw, make scratching motions)
Then I fly on home from my walk, walk, walk.
   (make flying motion)

I'm a little bird who goes "Peep, peep, peep!"
   (open and close fingers like a mouth)
I close my eyes when I sleep, sleep, sleep.
   (close eyes and rest head on hands)
I sing for my mommy going "Peep, peep, peep!"
   (open and close fingers like a mouth)
Then I ruffle my feathers and sleep, sleep, sleep.
   (close eyes and rest head on hands)

I'm a little duck who goes "Quack, quack, quack!"
   (open and close fingers like a mouth)
I waddle when I walk in the back, back, back.
   (put backs of hands on hips and wiggle side to side)
I swim in the water going "Quack, quack, quack!"
   (open and close fingers like a mouth)
Then I shake my tail in the back, back, back.
   (wiggle rear)

Six Little Ducks   (traditional folk song)

Six little ducks that I once knew,
Fat ones, skinny ones, they were, too.

[Chorus]
   But one little duck with a feather in his back
   Led all the others with a quack, quack, quack.
   Quack, quack, quack! Quack, quack, quack!
   He led all the others with a quack, quack, quack!

Down to the water they did go,
Wibble, wobble, wibble, wobble to and fro.

[Chorus]

Home from the water they did come,
Wibble, wobble, wibble, wobble ho-hum-hum.

[Chorus]

Parents' Follow-Up Ideas

Tossing or dropping beanbags into a container (laundry basket, large pan, wastebasket, or shoe box) is a good coordination exercise. Beanbags can be dropped from above by standing directly over containers, or they can be tossed from a short distance. To make beanbags, put a small amount of rice or beans in a plastic bag (newspaper bags work well) and tie the top closed. Slip the plastic bag inside a sock or mitten and sew the opening. Store beanbags inside a coffee can or shoe box.

Use cans with plastic lids (coffee, potato chip, or tennis ball containers) to make a bank for your child. Decorate the can with paint, photos, fabric, or contact paper, and cut a slot in the plastic lid. Show your toddler how to drop coins into the bank to "bank" any spare change. Keep the bank out of your child's reach, and supervise your toddler closely to prevent him or her from swallowing coins.

Compare real objects and animals with toys and pictures in books or magazines. Encourage your child to talk about the differences he or she sees in them. If you live in a city, visit a petting zoo to see real ducks and chickens and other farm animals.

Craft

Beanbag Chickens

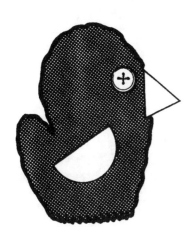

You will need: old mittens or hot mitts

buttons

fabric scraps or felt

glue

needle and thread

dried beans or rice

Hold the mitten up in front of you; the thumb will become the tail of the chicken and the opposite side is the chicken's head. Sew a button on each side for eyes and glue on a fabric triangle for a beak. Cut two semicircles of material for wings and glue them to each side of the body.

Fill a plastic bag loosely with dried beans or rice and close it securely. Slide the plastic bag in the mitten and sew the opening so that the beans will not fall out if handled roughly. Use scraps or yarn to create other animals or people out of other mitts.

Program Notes

Sign Language

BIRD   Pinch your index finger and thumb together and place them in front of your mouth, opening and closing them like a beak.

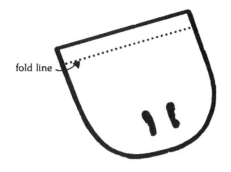 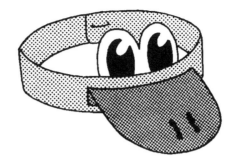 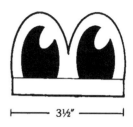

fold line

3½"

Storytime puppet introduces the theme wearing a duck headband and making quacking noises.

When using *Rosie's Walk*, make clucking noises throughout the book as Rosie walks. Good stories for flannelboards are *Good-Night, Owl!* and *The Chicken Book*.

Giveaways are duck headbands made with a strip of construction paper that has eyes and a beak glued to it. Distribute the duck headbands and then sing the "Six Little Ducks" song.

Fingertaster "tastes" things birds like to eat, such as corn, sunflower seeds, nuts, etc.

Children leave the story space flapping their "wings" like baby birds.

——————————— Notes ———————————

Birthdays

Books

Best Best Friends
MARGARET CHODOS-IRVINE

Birthday Monsters!
SANDRA BOYNTON

Birthdays
BRENDA HAUGEN

Dandelion
DON FREEMAN

¡Fiesta! (English/Spanish)
GINGER FOGLESONG GUY

Five Little Monkeys Bake a Birthday Cake
EILEEN CHRISTELOW

Happy Birthday, Sam
PAT HUTCHINS

If You Give a Pig a Party (Spanish: *Si le haces una fiesta a una cerdita*)
LAURA NUMEROFF

Jack—Happy Birthday
REBECCA ELGAR

Mary Wore Her Red Dress and Henry Wore His Green Sneakers
MERLE PEEK

Max's Birthday
ROSEMARY WELLS

Oscar's Half Birthday
BOB GRAHAM

Piñata! (English/Spanish)
REBECCA EMBERLEY

The Secret Birthday Message
ERIC CARLE

Spot's Birthday Party (French: *L'anniversaire de Spot* and Spanish: *El cumpleaños de Spot*)
ERIC HILL

Will It Ever Be My Birthday?
DOROTHY COREY

Rhythms, Rhymes, and Fingerplays

A Birthday

Today is *(insert child's name)* birthday
Let's make a birthday cake *(form circle with fingers)*
Mix and stir *(make stirring motions)*
Stir and mix,
Into the oven to bake. *(palm up, slide hand forward)*

Peeking through the window *(shade eyes with hands)*
I like to see it bake.
Sniff, sniff, sniff. It smells so good! *(sniff)*
Hurry, hurry, cake! *(clap hands sharply)*

Here's our cake so nice and round *(form circle with fingers)*
We'll frost it pink and white. *(make frosting motions)*
We'll put two candles on the top, *(hold up two fingers)*
And then we'll blow them out! 1, 2. *(blow on fingers)*

It's Your Birthday   (tune "Skip to My Lou")

It's your birthday, *(point to a child)*
What'll I do? *(point to self)*
It's your birthday, what'll I do? *(repeat actions)*
It's your birthday, what'll I do? *(repeat actions)*
What'll I do for you, dear? *(point to self and then to child)*

[Verse 2]

Share my cookie, *(both hands together, fingers
    curled and touching)*
Break it in two. *(make breaking motion)*
That's what I'll do for you, dear.

[Verse 3]

Wrap your present in ribbons blue. *(one hand
    circles around the other, as though wrapping
    ribbon around a present)*
That's what I'll do for you, dear.

[Verse 4]

Give you hugs and kisses, too. *(arms
    reach across body in hugging motion
    and blow a kiss)*
That's what I'll do for you, dear.

Balloon

This is the way we blow our balloon *(hold hands,
    palms together, in front of mouth)*
Blow!! Blow!! Blow!! *(blow into hands, pulling them
    apart slowly)*
This is the way we break our balloon *(hands wide apart)*
Oh!! Oh!! Oh!! *(clap hands three times)*

Parents' Follow-Up Ideas

Have a pretend birthday party (great for bad weather days). Invite pets, toys, or TV characters. Let your child help you put up decorations and set a "party" table. Wrap one of your child's old toys in Sunday comic pages or a decorated grocery sack. Devise a pretend birthday cake (sandwich, muffin, or cookie) and sing "Happy Birthday" to the lucky person or toy. Everybody helps blow out the pretend candles, and your child can open the gift.

Toddlers like to pretend. Sometimes this pretense helps them prepare for new situations, like taking a trip, Sunday school, parties, doctor visits, etc. When confronted with a new situation, try acting it out at home ahead of time to help your child feel more comfortable and know what is expected.

If your child has a birthday close to a major holiday like Christmas or Hanukkah, you can quietly celebrate on the actual date, then have an "unbirthday" party a few months later when the social calendar isn't as full.

One of the *best* presents you can give a toddler is a subscription to a magazine. Magazines are relatively inexpensive and arrive "new" every month, keeping reading material at hand and providing pictures to use in crafts. Besides, children love to get mail! There are many great magazines created especially for young children, such as *Your Big Back Yard* (nature topics) and *Sesame Street* (which comes with a separate parents' issue each month). Most libraries have *Magazines for Children,* a book that lists magazines and subscription information, grouping them by subject and age levels. Ask your librarian for help choosing the best magazines for your children.

Craft

Birthday Clown

You will need: scissors

colored paper

3 rubber bands (cut in half to make 6 pieces)

tape

glue

2 paste-on stars (for eyes)

From the colored paper, cut these shapes:

1 large heart (body)

2 small hearts (hands)

1 large circle (head)

3 small circles (pompoms)

1 small crescent (mouth)

2 small rectangles (shoes)

Using these shapes, assemble the head, hat, body, and pompoms to match the figure as shown. Glue a piece of rubber band to each shoe and hand, and then glue the other end to the back of the body as shown. Attach another rubber band to the top of the hat.

When you dangle the clown, it will dance for you! To make the clown more durable, reinforce each shape with light cardboard (3″ × 5″ card) before assembling. Watch that children don't put rubber bands in their mouths.

Program Notes

Sign Language

BIRTHDAY   With your right hand open on your chest, move your right hand out and down to lay, palm up, in open left hand.

Introduce the theme by singing "Happy Birthday" to the storytime puppet who is wearing a party hat. The puppet invites the children to join in its birthday celebration.

Use a flannelboard birthday cake with felt candles that can be added later. Let children take turns putting candles on the cake flannelboard, "blowing them out," and taking them down.

Although this theme lends itself to snacks, like cookies or cupcakes, some children have food allergies (to milk, flour, sugar, or peanuts). Check with parents the week before to see if you can offer a treat. If there is a child who cannot have the snack you've planned, cancel the snack or ask the parent for a suitable alternative for that child.

Giveaways are balloons, inflated and tied with ribbon or string. Put one balloon in a touch box (see appendix A), and invite children to reach inside to guess what is there.

Fingertaster "tastes" birthday party foods, such as cake, ice cream, raisins, etc.

Children exit the story space singing "Happy Birthday" to the puppet.

———————————— Notes ————————————

Boats

Books

Boats
BYRON BARTON

Boats
JAN PIEŃKOWSKI

Boats
ANNE ROCKWELL

Boats, Boats, Boats
JOANNA RUANE

Boats on the River
PETER MANDEL

Bobalong Boat
RICHARD POWELL

Go, Go, Boats!
SIMON HART

I Love Boats
FLORA MCDONNELL

Jack's New Boat
SARAH MCMENEMY

Little Boat
OPAL DUNN

Mr. Gumpy's Outing
JOHN BURNINGHAM

Noah's Ark
   (Spanish: *El arca de Noé*)
LUCY COUSINS

Row, Row, Row Your Boat
PENNY DANN

Ship Shapes
STELLA BLACKSTONE

Who Sank the Boat?
PAMELA ALLEN

Rhythms, Rhymes, and Fingerplays

Boats! Boats!

[Chorus]
   Boats! Boats! Lots of boats! *(clap hands in rhythm)*
   Watch them go! Watch them float!

Row! Row! *(rowing motion, both arms extended,*
   pull hands to chest together)
To and fro,
I am a ROW boat.

Toot! Toot! *(pretend to blow diesel horn)*
Chug-chug-chug, *(arms push and pull in piston motion)*
I am a TUG boat.

Come on wind *(blow air, hands form peak over head)*
Blow a gale!
I am a SAIL boat.

Going fast! *(hands alternately shoot across body)*
Whee! Whee!
I am a SPEED boat.

Back and forth, *("boat" sign; hands go right then left)*
People I carry
I am a FERRY boat.

Under water, *(make diving motion, palms together)*
Blub, blub, blub
I am a SUB-marine boat.

Row, Row, Row Your Boat (song)

Row, row, row your boat,
Gently down the stream.
Merrily, merrily, merrily, merrily,
Life is but a dream.

Parents' Follow-Up Ideas

Sit on the floor with your legs open and with your toddler sitting inside your legs facing you and holding your hands. Rock backward, gently pulling your child toward you. Then lean forward, having him or her rock backward. Sing "Row, Row, Row Your Boat" as you rock back and forth in a rowing motion. Do not rock so far backward that you pull your child's bottom off the floor. If necessary, move the child closer to you.

In the sink, bathtub, or wading pool, try floating different objects with your child to see which make good boats. Give your child lots of objects (plastic cup, jar lid, cork, and a rock). Experiment to see what floats and what doesn't. Styrofoam meat trays float well and can carry nonfloating cargo. After a rainstorm or washing the car, float boats made of paper or leaves on water streams and puddles. *Safety tip:* Never leave children alone with even a few inches of water nearby.

Go on pretend boat rides with your toddler. Help your child use blocks, boxes, or pillows to make a boat shape or designate a bed or the couch as today's boat. Decide where you will journey together and talk about the objects, animals, or people you "see" there. Take along a snack for a boat picnic, and remember to "swim" any time either of you leaves the boat.

Craft

Bathtub Boats

You will need: bottle cap or jar lid, bar of floating soap, cork, or empty walnut shell

         toothpicks

         dab of clay or clay dough

         scissors

         crayons

         paper

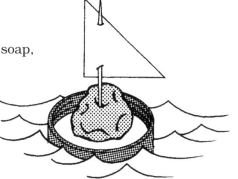

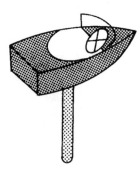

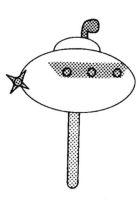

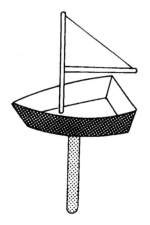

Cut a sail from the paper (triangle shape) and decorate it. Put your child's name on it. Poke a toothpick through the sail, through one side and out. Leave one end of the toothpick sticking down below the sail to anchor it to the boat. Stick a dab of clay inside the jar lid or shell, and press the toothpick into it. Your boat is now ready to sail.

If using cork or soap, the clay is not needed. Press the toothpick mast into the boat and set sail. If using a cork, cut a slit in one side and push a penny into it for balance.

Program Notes

Sign Language

> BOAT   Cup your hands at waist level. Raise and lower your hands slightly as you move them away from your body (like a boat on the waves).

Introduce the theme using a toy boat or pictures of boats. Or create stick puppets of different boats and, giving one to each child, let them float around the room before coming back to "port" and parking their boats in the "marina."

The "Boats! Boats!" rhyme and *Mr. Gumpy's Outing* work best as flannelboards.

Giveaways can be boat stick puppets made with craft sticks and pictures cut from magazines or photocopied and colored. Folded paper boats also make good giveaways.

Fingertaster "tastes" watery flavors: seawater, bathwater, fish, boiled potatoes, etc.

Invite children to carefully leave the story space in their favorite pretend boat. Remind them that even speedboats must go slower when other boats are around!

————————————————— Notes —————————————————

Bugs and Caterpillars

Books

Bugs! Bugs! Bugs!
BOB BARNER

Buzz
JANET S. WONG

Buzz! Buzz! Buzz!
BYRON BARTON

Five Little Ladybugs
MELANIE GERTH

Good Night, Sweet Butterflies
DAWN BENTLEY

Inch by Inch
LEO LIONNI

The Itsy-Bitsy Spider
ROSEMARY WELLS

The Itsy-Bitsy Spider
JEANETTE WINTER

Ladybug, Ladybug
RUTH BROWN

Little Bee: Finger Puppet Book

Little Ladybug: Finger Puppet Book

Oh My, a Fly!
JAN PIEŃKOWSKI

Spider on the Floor
RAFFI

Ten Flashing Fireflies
PHILEMON STURGES

The Very Hungry Caterpillar (French: *La chenille qui fait des trous;* Spanish: *La oruga muy hambrienta;* and Vietnamese: *Chu sau rom qua doi*)
ERIC CARLE

The Very Quiet Cricket
ERIC CARLE

Rhythms, Rhymes, and Fingerplays

Eency Weency Spider   (traditional song)

Eency weency spider went up the water spout,
　　(wiggle fingers upward in front of body)
Down came the rain and washed the spider out.
　　(sweep arms down and to one side)
Out came the sun and dried up all the rain,
　　(arms form circle over head)
And the eency weency spider went up the spout again.
　　(wiggle fingers upward again)

Baby Bumble Bee   (traditional song)

I'm bringing home a baby bumble bee.
　　(hold hand in front with fingers closed)
Won't my mommy be very proud of me?
I'm bringing home a baby bumble bee.
Buzzzz, buzzzzzz, buzzzzzzzzz . . .
Ouch! It stung me. *(open hand quickly and shake it)*

Caterpillar

This is the egg, found not far away.
   (point with index finger to center of other palm)

This is the caterpillar, who one sunny day,
   hatched from the egg, found not far away.
      (wiggle index finger like caterpillar)

This is the cocoon all snuggled away,
   that covered the caterpillar, who one sunny day,
   hatched from the egg, found not far away.
      (form fist, cup other hand over it, peek inside)

This is the butterfly, who did sashay
   out of the cocoon all snuggled away,
   that covered the caterpillar, who one sunny day,
   hatched from the egg, found not far away.
      *(palms toward you, hook thumbs together
      and wiggle fingers)*

These are the wings, on bright display
   worn by the butterfly, who did sashay
   out of the cocoon all snuggled away,
   that covered the caterpillar, who one sunny day,
   hatched from the egg, found not far away.
      (raise and lower arms at sides like butterfly wings)

Beautiful butterfly . . . Can I watch you play?
   ("fly" your butterfly up, down, and around)

Parents' Follow-Up Ideas

Make a butterfly sandwich for lunch. Cut one slice of bread diagonally, and lay the halves on a plate with the crust tips facing each other, forming wings. Spread jelly, cream cheese, or peanut butter on the bread and arrange cheese slices, carrot rounds, banana circles, or raisins to make the design on the wings. For the butterfly's antennae, cut celery or green pepper strips. Encourage your child to help think of other ways to decorate butterfly sandwiches or to make other "butterfly" lunches. How about a small pizza cut into quarters and re-arranged on a plate with a carrot as the butterfly's body?

Create a nesting game using different sizes of cans from mushrooms, soups, vegetables, etc. Cleanly cut open one end of the cans so there are no sharp edges. Remove the contents and the labels; wash the cans thoroughly and dry them. Cover the cut edges with adhesive or cloth tape to protect small fingers from accidental cuts. Cans may be stacked upside down on top of each other to build things or nested inside each other for storage. For more-colorful cans, cover them with bright contact paper.

To make a quick finger puppet, cut a finger from an old glove. Decorate it with markers, fabric, or yarn scraps to make ears, mouths, hair, etc. To make eyes, sew on buttons or glue on small wiggle eyes. Make a caterpillar finger puppet, then add some wings to turn it into a butterfly.

Craft

Colorful Butterfly

You will need: paper towels

newspapers

food coloring or tempera paint

sponge or small paintbrush

pipe cleaners

small containers (baby food jars, margarine containers, muffin pan)

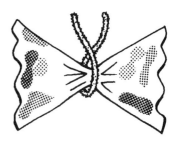

Cover the table with newspapers, several layers thick. Lay a paper towel flat on the newspapers. Pour food colors into separate containers for each color. With the sponge or paintbrush, help your child dab or drop each color on the paper towel. Point out how the colors spread through the towel. Where they mingle, new colors are created. Clear water can be sprinkled on the towel to lighten or spread the colors more. Hang the towel and let it dry thoroughly.

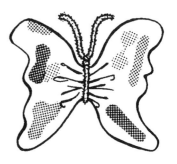

When dry, fold the towel lengthwise in accordion pleats. Pinch the pleats together at the center and twist a pipe cleaner around to hold them. Curve the ends of the pipe cleaner to look like antennae, and fluff out the paper towel on both sides of the pipe cleaner to form wings. Decorate your windows or room with beautiful butterflies.

Program Notes

Sign Language

BUTTERFLY   Cross your hands at the wrists, palms facing chest. Link your thumbs and wiggle your fingers like butterfly wings.

Storytime puppet introduces the theme with butterfly stickers or one of the storytime books about insects.

Use a finger puppet with *Inch by Inch*, having it measure the birds in the book. Following a stretching activity, the inchworm can measure children's arms, hands, etc.

Use stick puppets or a flannelboard of "Eency Weency Spider" and let children help the spider climb the spout.

After sharing *The Very Hungry Caterpillar*, introduce a sock puppet caterpillar that turns into a butterfly (instructions are in appendix A).

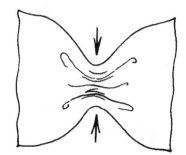

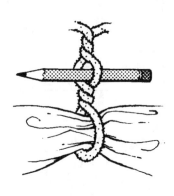

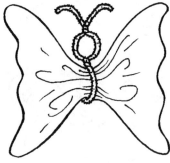

Shorten the number of insects in *The Very Quiet Cricket.* Giveaways are pipe-cleaner and facial-tissue butterflies. Fingertaster "tastes" foods from *The Very Hungry Caterpillar.* Children exit the story space as butterflies.

_____ Notes _____

Cats

Books

Cats Go . . .
ANNIE HORWOOD

The Cat's Meow
WARREN KIMBLE

Five Little Kitty Cats
JANET MORGAN STOEKE

Have You Seen My Cat?
ERIC CARLE

Katy Cat and Beaky Boo
   (Spanish: *La Gata Katy y*
   Piquito de Oro juegan)
LUCY COUSINS

Kitten for a Day
EZRA JACK KEATS

Kittycat Lullaby
EILEEN SPINELLI AND ANNE MORTIMER

My Big Dog
JANET STEVENS AND
SUSAN STEVENS CRUMMEL

No No, Jo!
KATE AND JIM MCMULLAN

Pat the Cat
EDITH KUNHARDT

Purrrrr
PAT CUMMINGS

Soft as a Kitten
AUDEAN JOHNSON

This and That
JULIE SYKES

Three Little Kittens
PAUL GALDONE

Where's the Kitten? Kote ti chat
la ye? (English/Haitian Creole)
CHERYL CHRISTIAN

Why Not?
MARY WORMELL

Rhythms, Rhymes, and Fingerplays

I Have a Cat

I have a cat *(one hand strokes the other)*
My cat is fat! *(arms form large circle)*
I have a cat. *(stroking motion)*
It wears a hat. *(hands on head)*
I have a cat. *(stroking motion)*
It caught a bat. *(make grabbing motion)*
I have a cat. *(stroking)*
Purrrrrrrrrrrr,
Meeeooowww!

Pretty Kitty   (tune: "Frere Jacques")

Pretty kitty. Pretty kitty.
Where are you? Where are you?
With your fur so silky,
And your tickly whiskers.
Meow, me—ow. Meow, me—ow.

Five Little Kittens

One, two, three, four, five *(count fingers on one hand)*
Five little kittens standing in a row. *(stand up straight)*
They nod their heads to the children, so. *(nod head)*
They run to the left, *(run in place, turning left)*
They run to the right, *(run in place, turning right)*
They stand and stretch in the bright sunlight.
    (stretch arms over head)
Along comes a dog, looking for some fun.
    (hunch shoulders)
Meowwww! Meowwww! *(fingers cupped, reach out
    quickly in scratching motion)*
See that doggie run! *(clap hands quickly)*

Parents' Follow-Up Ideas

Trace your children's hands and feet on a paper sack. Cut out the tracings and hang them where they can be admired. Indicate which cupboards or drawers your children are allowed to get into by taping one of their handprints to the outside. This works well for clothes and toy storage areas also. Trace hands from other members of the family and compare them. How are they alike and different? Write on handprints short notes dictated by your toddler or let your toddler decorate them and mail them to friends and relatives as impromptu greeting cards.

Our familiar house cats are part of a much larger family that includes lions, tigers, pumas, and panthers. Introduce your children to a neighbor's cat (if you do not have one at home), helping them learn how to treat animals smaller than they are. As a field trip, visit a pet store or humane shelter to observe cats. Watch how they move and what they do. Let your child mimic cats and talk about their behavior: cleaning, moving tails, stretching, jumping, etc. Visit the big cat exhibit at a local zoo or watch a nature program on television together and see if your child notices some of the same behaviors in the much larger cat cousins.

When your toddlers are in stubborn moods, chanting will help distract them and get them to cooperate. Start with a nursery rhyme, such as "Jack and Jill," "Humpty Dumpty," or "Little Boy Blue," and gradually change the words to what you want them to do: "Little Boy Blue, we're putting on your shoe; your shoe, shoe, shoe. There's two, two, two, shoes, shoes, shoes." Play with the words and the rhythms, keeping your voice lighthearted. Chanting often helps uncooperative and restless children refocus their attention.

Craft

Yummy Gelly Animals

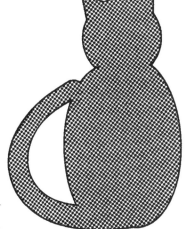

You will need: 2 envelopes of unflavored gelatin

2 small boxes of flavored gelatin (with or without sugar)

1½ cups cold water

1½ cups hot water

flat cake pan or cookie sheet with sides

cookie cutters

covered container for storage

Dissolve the unflavored gelatin in the cold water. Add the hot water to the flavored gelatin and stir until dissolved. Add flavored gelatin mixture to cold water mixture and stir until thoroughly mixed.

Pour gelatin into a flat cake pan or cookie sheets with rims. Chill in the refrigerator until firm, then cut with cookie cutters to make animals and shapes (or cut gelatin into blocks with a knife). Save all the scraps to nibble on later.

Store shapes in a covered container in the refrigerator. Although the mixture is as wiggly as traditional gelatin, it is easier to handle with fingers and fun to eat. Use some caution when your child is eating gelly animals; the coloring may stain some fabrics.

Program Notes

Sign Language

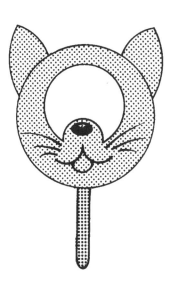

CAT Pinch your thumbs and index fingers together parallel to the edges of your mouth and move your hands outward, as though stroking a cat's whiskers.

Storytime puppet introduces the theme making purring and meowing noises and asking the children to guess what the animal is.

Three Little Kittens makes a good flannelboard story. *Pat the Cat* and *Soft as a Kitten* are good for children with visual difficulties since they can feel the kitten's fur. The rhyme "Five Little Kittens" can become a full action rhyme, as children act it out.

Giveaways are kitten masks made from paper plates and wooden sticks, making the ears out of the center of the plate that was cut away.

Fingertaster "tastes" foods cats enjoy, such as milk, tuna fish, melted ice cream, catnip, or catsup (ketchup).

Children exit the story space purring like cats.

——————————— Notes ———————————

Circus

Books

At the Carnival
KIRSTEN HALL

Bearymore
DON FREEMAN

Carousel
DONALD CREWS

Circus Opposites with Disappearing Animals: A Wacky Flaps Book

Circus Parade
HARRIET ZIEFERT

Clifford at the Circus
NORMAN BRIDWELL

Curious George's First Words at the Circus
MARGRET AND H. A. REY

Little Monkey Says Good Night
ANN WHITFORD PAUL

Maisy at the Fair
LUCY COUSINS

Minerva Louise at the Fair
JANET MORGAN STOEKE

Night at the Fair
DONALD CREWS

Peter Spier's Circus!
PETER SPIER

Spot and His Grandparents Go to the Carnival
ERIC HILL

Spot Goes to the Circus
ERIC HILL

Star of the Circus
MICHAEL AND MARY BETH SAMPSON

Up and Down on the Merry-Go-Round
BILL MARTIN JR. AND JOHN ARCHAMBAULT

Rhythms, Rhymes, and Fingerplays

Five Circus Elephants

Five circus elephants waiting near the door.
    (hold up five fingers)
One jumps through a hoop, *(jump in place)*
And now there are four. *(hold up four fingers)*

Four circus elephants looking up to see.
    (four fingers)
One walks around the ring, *(walk in place)*
And now there are three. *(three fingers)*

Three circus elephants waiting for their cue.
    (three fingers)
One dances to a song, *(dance in place)*
And now there are two. *(two fingers)*

Two circus elephants looking for some fun. *(two fingers)*
One bounced a yellow ball, *(bouncing motion)*
And now there is one. *(one finger)*

One circus elephant standing all alone.
    (one finger)
He waved his trunk to say good-bye,
    (wave arm side to side in front of body)
And slowly walked on home. *(walk in circle)*

Circus   (tune: "Sailing, Sailing")

Circus, circus,
Under the tent so high,
Prancing ponies and dancing dogs
Merrily go by.

Lions roaring,
Ladies flying high!
Elephants and silly clowns
All at the circus. Oh, my!

Five Little Clowns

Five little clowns all in a row, *(hold up five fingers)*
Wearing funny hats *(pat head)*
And polka-dotted bows. *(hands make motion
    like fixing a bow tie)*
One little clown hopped away, *(hop in place)*
Back to the circus to laugh and play.
    (wave "good-bye")

[Repeat with]
    Four . . . danced away *(dancing motion)*
    Three . . . somersaulted *(turn around)*
    Two . . . zoomed *(shoot hand quickly in
        front of body)*
    One . . . tiptoed *(tiptoe in place)*

Parents' Follow-Up Ideas

Draw three large circles on a sidewalk or driveway with chalk or arrange a hose in looping circles in the grass. Number each circle (or label them with colors, alphabet letters, shapes, etc.). Let your toddler become the performer as you play the part of the ringmaster describing the action. "In ring number one are prancing horses. See them march around the ring . . . and jump high . . . and turn 'round and 'round. Listen to them neigh!" This is a fun activity for play groups. For a change of pace, let a child be the ringmaster and you become one of the performers.

Draw a simple picture of a chubby clown or copy one from a coloring book. Give your child a page of colored dot stickers and let her decorate the clown's costume. When the costume is finished, count the number of dots of each color. As an alternative, make several clowns, one with red dots, one with blue, etc.

Tie a short piece of clothesline between the backs of two chairs, pulling the chairs apart until the line is taut. Using clip clothespins, show your child how to hang things on the line, to display artwork, favorite animal pictures, or pretend to hang some clothes out to "dry." *Safety tip:* Push the chairs up against a wall so no one will walk between them and get caught in the line.

Craft

Clown Poncho

You will need: a rectangular piece of fabric, an old
         pillowcase cut up two sides, or a bath towel

       scissors

       needle and thread or fabric glue

       fabric circles in bright colors

       pompoms

       ribbon (optional)

Fold the fabric in half, lengthwise. Fold it again, keeping the folded edges together, as shown. Cut a semicircle at the center fold and open the cloth. Cut a 2″ slit from the circle at the front of the poncho. (If circle is too small to go over child's head, fold the cloth again and cut a larger semicircle or make the slit longer.) Sew or glue pompoms down the front of the poncho and attach colored fabric circles randomly to the front and back. Do not use felt for circles if the poncho will be washed.

Optional: To make ties for the sides of the poncho, cut ribbon into four pieces. Sew two to the front sides and two to the back sides. Make other circus ponchos for lion tamers, circus master, acrobats, members of the circus band, etc.

Program Notes

Sign Language

     CIRCUS   Your left hand forms a curved "c" shape, palm down. Your right hand, fingertips together, touches the back of the left hand, then it moves out and around to create a circle, like a circus ring.

Mention the clown/circus connection during the opening routine as you assemble the clown-shape puzzle described in the opening routine. Storytime puppet can help introduce the theme wearing a clown hat or red nose. If there is a clown troupe in your town, invite a clown to come *at the end* of your program to make balloon animals

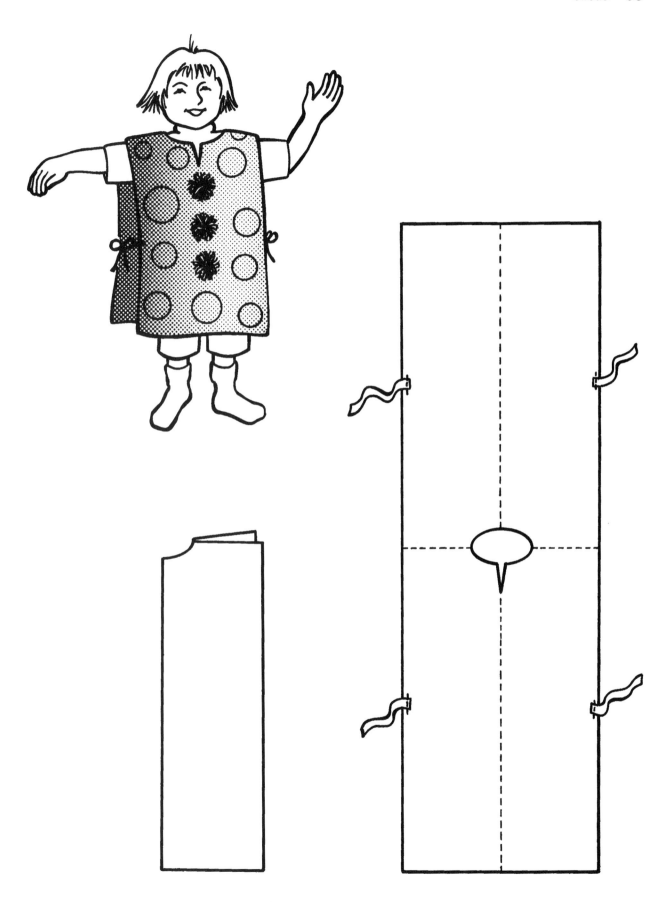

for children. Remember, most toddlers are afraid of clowns, so inter-view your clown visitor before to be certain the person has experience with this age and is sensitive to their needs. Before a clown visits, talk about clowns as people who like to dress up in silly clothes and put on makeup to make children laugh. Have the storytime puppet lead the contact with the clown, shyly approaching the clown, examining the makeup and costume, and finally taking a balloon or giving a hug. *Note:* No child should be forced to participate. Let the puppet be the intermediary for those who do not want to get near the clown.

The "Five Circus Elephants" and "Five Little Clowns" rhymes work well as flannelboard presentations.

Giveaways are clown stickers (or balloon figures if there is a clown visitor).

Fingertaster "tastes" foods from circuses or fairs, such as corn on the cob, cotton candy, corn dogs, popcorn, etc.

Children exit the story space prancing like circus ponies.

———————————————— Notes ————————————————

Colors

Books

Brown Bear, Brown Bear, What Do You See?
(Spanish: *Oso pardo, oso pardo, ¿qué ves ahí?*)
BILL MARTIN JR.

Cat's Colors
JANE CABRERA

Cows Going Past
BRUCE BALAN

Dog's Colorful Day
EMMA DODD

Eye Spy Colors
DEBBIE MACKINNON

Mouse Paint
ELLEN WALSH

My First Look at Colors

My Very First Book of Colors
ERIC CARLE

Purple Is Part of a Rainbow
(Spanish: *El morado es parte del arco iris*)
CAROLYN KOWALCZYK

Spot Looks at Colors
ERIC HILL

We'll All Go Sailing
MAGGEE SPICER AND
RICHARD THOMPSON

What Color? / ¿Que Color?
(English/Spanish)
ALAN BENJAMIN

What Color Is It? / ¿Qué color es éste? (English/Spanish)

What's in Grandma's Grocery Bag?
HUI-MEI PAN

White Rabbit's Color Book
ALAN BAKER

Who Said Red?
MARY SERFOZO

Rhythms, Rhymes, and Fingerplays

What Are You Wearing?
(tune: "Mary Had a Little Lamb")

Martin* has a red shirt on,
Red shirt on, red shirt on.
Martin has a red shirt on.
I see him here today.

[*Use the names of your children
and the colors of their clothes.]

Green Says Go

Green says, "Go!" *(march in place quickly)*
Go! Go! Go!
Yellow says, "Slow!" *(march slowly)*

Slow . . . slow . . . slow.
And red says, "Stop!" *(stop suddenly)*
Go, go, go! *(move fast)*
Slow . . . slow . . . slow. *(move slowly)*
And STOP! *(stop)*

[Repeat go, slow, stop instructions several times, giving children the opportunity to pretend they are cars driving down the street.]

Purple Song   (tune: "Twinkle, Twinkle Little Star")

Purple, purple
I see you.
Purple is a grape,
And a flower, too.
Part of the rainbow,
Up in the sky.
Purple's a color
On a butterfly.
Purple, purple,
I see you.
Purple is a grape
and a flower, too.

Parents' Follow-Up Ideas

It is a fact of life that crayons break, and the smaller pieces get scattered or worse (crushed under foot). Recycle broken crayons into multicolored "cookies" that are easy for small hands to hold and fun to use. Cut broken pieces into $\frac{1}{4}$" lengths and place three or four pieces in each section of a muffin pan. Bake at 250° for 5 minutes or until the pieces just start to melt together. Turn off the oven and let the muffin pan cool inside. Remove it when it is completely cooled and store the crayon cookies in a covered container.

Finger painting can be messy, so wear an old shirt for a smock and put newspaper under the surface where you'll be working.

To make finger paint combine:

liquid laundry starch or paste mixed with an equal amount of liquid dishwashing detergent

food coloring

Add the food coloring to the starch, dampen a piece of paper (shelf or butcher paper works best), and drop several teaspoons of finger paint on it. Use one or more colors. With fingers, hands, and wrists, encourage toddlers to swirl the paint around and around, making and changing the designs. Lay it on newspapers to dry. Monitor children during this activity.

For toddlers who don't like getting their hands messy, put the paint inside a zipping plastic bag and close it. Another idea is to let your toddler paint on a cookie sheet with a plastic spoon or paintbrush. The results are the same as above but without the mess.

Craft

Traffic Light

You will need: black construction paper or felt

green, yellow, and red construction paper or felt

scissors

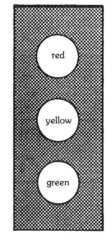

Cut a 4″ × 9″ rectangle from the black paper or felt. Using a can or glass as a pattern, draw circles on the green, yellow, and red construction paper or felt and cut them out.

Take turns with your toddler putting the colored circles onto the traffic light. As you do, talk about each color and what it means for safety.

Program Notes

Sign Language

STOP   Bring the edge of the right hand down sharply in the palm of the left hand.

Introduce the theme by naming the colors of the shape puzzle pieces in the opening routine. Point out matching colors in the room or children's clothing.

Storytime puppet can lead the "What Are You Wearing?" song as everyone stands and claps.

With the traffic light on the flannelboard, share the rhyme "Green Says Go," then have children be cars as you call out the colors (with hints like "Go! Go! Go!"). Repeat several times before "slowing" them down for the quiet activity.

Giveaways are colorful stickers or gummed stars.

Fingertaster "tastes" colorful foods, such as red apples, yellow bananas, purple grapes, etc.

Children exit the story space with the traffic light showing yellow so they are going slowly.

——————————— Notes ———————————

Counting

Books

Can You Count Ten Toes?
Count to Ten in Ten Different Languages
LEZLIE EVANS

Corduroy's Day
LYDIA FREEMAN

Counting Kids
KIM GOLDING

Fish Eyes: A Book You Can Count On
LOIS EHLERT

Max's Toys
ROSEMARY WELLS

Number One, Tickle Your Tum
JOHN PRATER

One Is a Drummer
ROSEANNE THONG

One, Two, Three!
SANDRA BOYNTON

1 2 3, Maisy
LUCY COUSINS

One Yellow Lion
MATTHEW VAN FLEET

Over in the Meadow
ANNIE KUBLER

Splash!
ANN JONAS

Spot Counts from 1 to 10
ERIC HILL

Ten Black Dots
   (Spanish: *Diez puntos negros*)
DONALD CREWS

Ten Red Apples
PAT HUTCHINS

Ten Red Apples
VIRGINIA MILLER

Rhythms, Rhymes, and Fingerplays

Inside the Space Shuttle

Inside the space shuttle *(crouch down low)*
Just enough room. *(pull hands close to body)*
Here comes the countdown,
1, 2, 3, 4, 5—
ZOOOOOOMMM! *(Jump up, throwing hands
   above head)*

A-Counting We Will Go   (tune: "A-Hunting We Will Go")

A-counting we will go. *(clap in rhythm)*
A-counting we will go.
1-2-3
4 and 5
A-counting we will go.

We're going to count our fingers. *(wiggle fingers)*
We're going to count our fingers.
1-2-3 *(count on fingers)*

4 and 5
A-counting we will go.

We're counting as we jump.
   (bounce up and down)
We're counting as we jump,
1-2-3 *(count as you bounce)*
4 and 5,
A-counting we will go.

Count with Me

Count with me in Spanish.
Count with me and see.
Counting in Spanish
Is as easy as can be!
One is uno [oo-no]
Two is dos [dose]
Three is tres [trace]
Four is quatro [kwa-tro]
Five is cinco [seen-ko]
Count with me in Spanish:
Uno, dos, tres, quatro, cinco.
It's as easy as can be!

[Verse 2]
   . . . Swahili.
   One is moja [mo-jah]
   Two is mbili [im-bee-lee]
   Three is tatu [tah-too]
   Four is nne [nah-nay]
   Five is tano [tah-no]

[Verse 3]
   . . . Japanese.
   One is ichi [ee-chee]
   Two is ni [nee]
   Three is san [sahn]
   Four is shi [shee]
   Five is go [goh]

Parents' Follow-Up Ideas

Counting in rhymes and listening to numbers and their sequence is vitally important for young children. Count everything! Don't expect or push your children to count with you. It is the sound of the number words and the sequence in which they are spoken that is important and entertaining for toddlers.

The strong rhythms in poetry and nursery rhymes help your children develop a sense of rhythm, which will make it easier for them to learn to count and to read later on. Recite favorite nursery rhymes, sing songs, and chant (even nonsense sounds) often to your child.

Identify the numbers 1–9 by name wherever you see them: in stores, on billboards or street signs, on price tags, etc. Don't push your children to understand the *math* that makes 2 into 3. Help them learn the word *two* means the numeral 2 and both of them represent two objects on the table.

Craft

Counting Balls

You will need: construction paper or colorful magazine pages

scissors

tape

string (optional)

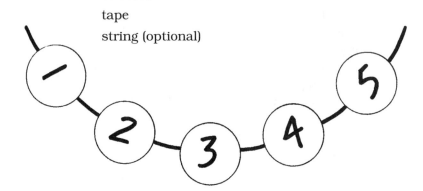

Trace around a glass or bowl to make five circles on different colors of paper. Cut out the circles and number them 1 to 5. Tape them to a door, refrigerator, or wall low enough that your child can touch them or make a mini-clothesline with a piece of string tied between two objects on which the circles are hung.

Each time you pass them, count the circles. Don't draw too much attention to yourself; just nonchalantly count, "1, 2, 3, 4, 5" and touch each circle as you pass by. Soon your child will be copying this activity and counting, too. Use these circles to talk about colors and line relationships (front, middle, and back).

Program Notes

Sign Language

ONE Your index finger is extended (the palm faces forward on all numbers).

TWO Your index and middle fingers are extended.

THREE Your thumb, index finger, and middle finger are extended.

FOUR Fingers extended, thumb folded across palm.

FIVE Your thumb and all fingers are extended.

Introduce the theme by counting the pieces of the shape puzzle in the opening routine before rearranging them into the clown. Point out the "two" stars and have the children find them on their name tags and count them. Encourage parents to count with you as you share today's books.

Put five objects on the flannelboard and use them as you recite "Count with Me." Count things in twos with children and adults standing. Count: eyes, ears, feet, knees, hands, etc. Then do actions and count them: two hops, two claps, two big steps, two little steps.

Giveaways are bee bookmarks made by copying the pattern on this page.

Fingertaster "tastes" small foods and includes numbers, such as three raisins, two grapes, one cookie, etc.

Children exit the story space counting in cadence: 1, 2; 1, 2 . . .

—————————— Notes ——————————

Dancing

Books

Baby Danced the Polka
KAREN BEAUMONT

Barnyard Dance!
SANDRA BOYNTON

Dance Away
GEORGE SHANNON

Dancing in My Bones
SYLVIA ANDREWS

Do Donkeys Dance?
MELANIE WALSH

Farmyard Boogie!
SALLY LLOYD JONES

Got to Dance
M. C. HELLDORFER

Jungle Jive!
SALLY LLOYD JONES

Maisy Likes Dancing
LUCY COUSINS

Rap a Tap Tap: Here's Bojangles—Think of That!
DIANE AND LEO DILLON

Red Dancing Shoes
DENISE LEWIS PATRICK

Skip to My Lou
NADINE BERNARD WESTCOTT

Sometimes I Like to Curl Up in a Ball
VICKI CHURCHILL AND CHARLES FUGE

Watch Me Dance
ANDREA AND BRIAN PINKNEY

Wiggle
DOREEN CRONIN

Word Bird's Rainy-Day Dance
JANE BELK MONCURE

Rhythms, Rhymes, and Fingerplays

Me and My Shadow   (tune: "Me and My Shadow")

Me and my shadow, *(sway side to side)*
Dancing down the avenue.
I raise my arms up, *(raise arms)*
And my shadow does it, too. *(raise arms again)*

I kick my legs out, *(kick legs)*
Then I bend down very low. *(bend down)*
My shadow's with me, *(sway)*
Dancing fast—*(sway fast)*
Or . . . dancing . . . slow. *(sway slow)*

My dancing partner *(sway)*
Is with me when the sun does shine. *(arms
    form circle over head)*
My shadow's dancing, *(sway)*
With me, and it's mine, all mine! *(hands on chest,
    sway side to side)*

Clap Your Hands

Clap, clap, clap your hands, *(clap hands
    in rhythm with words)*
Clap your hands with me.
Clap them fast! *(clap quickly)*
Clap—them—slow. *(clap slowly)*
Clap your hands with me. *(return to
    original rhythm)*

[continue with]

> Stomp, stomp your feet
> Pat your knees
> La-la, sing a song

Dancing Animals   (tune: "Mulberry Bush")

This is the way the horses prance,
    ("trot" in place, knees high)
The horses prance, the horses prance.
This is way the horses prance,
Dancing in the morning.

[continue with]

> ducks waddle
> bunnies hop
> worms wiggle
> cats stretch

Parents' Follow-Up Ideas

Dancing is a celebration of motion. Help your children discover the rhythms of the world around them by pointing out rhythm, movements, and cadences in familiar things. Imitate the movement of flags or a wind-tossed tree, the actions of machines (large and small), or dancers on television. Capture the rhythms of poetry and music using your feet, hands, arms, head, or whole body.

There are many opportunities to dance:

- Mirror dances: Dance and sing together in front of a full-length mirror. Toddlers love watching themselves and others as mirror images. Once your children have the hang of it, dance facing them, becoming their "mirror" and copying the things they do. Trade places, and let them "mirror" you.
- Shadow dances: In a place with a strong light source behind your children so that their shadows will be prominent, encourage them to dance, jump, skip, etc., and watch their shadows do it, too. Give them ribbon streamers, hoops, or a cape to make the shadow more intriguing. This is a good outside activity when the sunshine is bright and shadows can be seen on the ground or on a wall.

- Animal dances: Imitate the movement of animals, especially those that move fast or slow or have quick, jerky movements.

Save musical crib toys for dancing. Let children hold the toys and make the music as they move. If the toy is the type with a cord to make it play, let your toddler start it and both of you dance when the music plays. If the music slows down before stopping, encourage toddlers to slow their movements to match. When the music stops, stop dancing.

Crafts

Hand Streamers and Ankle Bells

You will need: 2 drapery rings (or other small circles like canning or shower curtain rings)

strips of colorful cloth, ribbons, or crepe paper streamers

yarn

2 pipe cleaners

small jingle bells

Hand Streamers (make two): Tie a bell to the eye of the drapery ring, forming the bottom of the hand streamer. Gather several strips of cloth together and tie them to one side of the drapery ring so the tails of the strips hang freely. Repeat on other side, leaving room at the top of the ring for the child's hand. Using materials of different weights (nylon, cottons, blends, tulle) or combining materials (cloth, plastic, paper) will make the streamers float and reflect light in different ways. Holding one ring in each hand, children can twirl and run with the streamers floating behind them.

Ankle Bells (make two): Thread several small bells on a pipe cleaner, and attach it around your child's ankle so it jingles with every step. Use these dancing props with some of the follow-up suggestions.

Program Notes

Sign Language

DANCE   Place your left hand, palm upward, with fingers toward right (becomes the dance floor); your right
hand, with the index and middle fingers extended
downward over your left palm, swings side to side
(as though dancing).

This is an excellent time to include music in your program. If you
do not play an instrument, bring a tape recorder or portable CD
player and play favorite children's songs between stories. Sing and
chant together as everyone dances. Between stories introduce shadow
dancing with a bright desk light or film projector aimed at a wall, or if
you have a full-length mirror, encourage children and adults to mirror-
dance.

Giveaways are small bells threaded on pipe cleaners.

Fingertaster "tastes" beverages, such as orange juice, Kool-Aid,
lemonade, etc.

Children exit the story space dancing.

——————————————— Notes ———————————————

December

Books

Claude the Dog: A Christmas Story
DICK GACKENBACH

The Great Hanukkah Party
SUZY-JANE TANNER

K Is for Kwanzaa
JUWANDA G. FORD

Kente Colors
DEBBI CHOCOLATE

Kwanzaa Kids
JOAN HOLUB

Let There Be Lights!
CAMILLE KRESS

Maisy's Snowy Christmas Eve
LUCY COUSINS

Max's Christmas
ROSEMARY WELLS

Messy Bessey's Holidays
PATRICIA AND FREDRICK MCKISSACK

On Kwanzaa
   (Spanish: *La Kwanzaa*)
JUDITH MAZZEO ZOCCHI

Rainbow Candles: A Hanukkah Counting Book
MYRA SHOSTAK

Spot's First Christmas
   (Spanish: *La primera Navidad de Spot*)
ERIC HILL

What Is Hanukkah?
HARRIET ZIEFERT

Where Is Christmas, Jesse Bear?
NANCY WHITE CARLSTROM

Where's My Christmas Stocking?
NOELLE CARTER

Word Bird's Christmas Words
JANE BELK MONCURE

Rhythms, Rhymes, and Fingerplays

Hanukkah Candles   (tune: "Ten Little Indians")

One little, two little, three little candles,
Four little, five little, six little candles,
Seven little, eight little Hanukkah candles,
Shining on my menorah.
Eight little, seven little, six little candles,
Five little, four little, three little candles,
Two little, one little Hanukkah candle,
Shining on my menorah.

[*Note:* This rhyme can also be used for Divali, the Indian Festival of Lights, which is also celebrated in December. Change "Hanukkah candles" to "candles for Divali," and the last line to "A festival of lights."]

Looking for Santa

We are looking for Santa *(arms form circle in front
  of belly and laugh "Ho, Ho, Ho!")*
Is the North Pole that way? Or that way? *(point in
  several directions)*
We will walk down the sidewalk, *(pat hands on knees)*
Don't fall on the ice! *(hands slide off knees left and right)*
We will swim across the ocean, *(make swimming motions)*
Climb up a snow bank, *(make climbing motions)*
And slide down the other side. *(hands slide from the
  knees down and away from the body)*

I see a little house. *(hand shades eyes)*
Knock on the door. Knock, knock, knock. *(make
  knocking motion)*
And there's Santa Claus! *(arms circle big belly and
  laugh "Ho, Ho, Ho!")*
Say, "Hi, Santa!" *(wave and call out greeting)*
Wait! He says we should hurry home to bed so he
  can come visit us.
Say, "Bye, Santa!" *(wave and say good-bye)*

We'd better run! *(pat knees quickly)*
Climb up that snow bank *(fast climbing motion)* and run!
Slide down the other side *(fast sliding motion)* and run!
Swim across the ocean *(fast swimming motion)* and run!
Careful not to fall on the ice. *(fast slipping motion)*

Run in the house and shut the door *(clap hands sharply)*
Jump in bed and go to sleep. *(lay cheek on hands)*
Merry Christmas, Santa, and good night. *(close eyes
  and snore)*

Merry Christmas   (tune: "We Wish
  You a Merry Christmas")

We wish you a merry Christmas,
We wish you a merry Christmas,
We wish you a merry Christmas,
It's that time of year.

We'll decorate our Christmas tree,
We'll decorate our Christmas tree,
We'll decorate our Christmas tree,
With ornaments dear.

We'll bake up some Christmas cookies,
We'll bake up some Christmas cookies,
We'll bake up some Christmas cookies,
To bring you good cheer.

We'll sing songs with fa-la-la's,
We'll sing songs with fa-la-la's,
We'll sing songs with fa-la-la's,
Christmas is near.

Parents' Follow-Up Ideas

Involve your toddlers in holiday preparations, such as shopping for foods and gifts and putting up decorations. Talk about the coming celebrations and take time to playact happenings for family or community ceremonies. Encourage them to be a part of appropriate activities but be aware that young children may become overwhelmed with the sights, sounds, and large crowds involved with holiday festivities. Help them focus on smaller components of the celebration. They will absorb and understand much of the broader traditions, but not in the same way as older children and adults do. That will come later.

Many cultures celebrate holidays in December. Use this opportunity and festive atmosphere to learn more about other people in your community and the holidays they celebrate.

Craft

Hanukkah Dreidel

You will need: cardboard egg carton

orange stick or pencil

small square of poster board

glue

poster paints

washable markers

beans, pennies, raisins, or counting pieces

Note: It is important to use *cardboard* egg cartons for this craft because they have four-sided dividers (pyramids) that separate the rows of egg cups.

Cut one of the divider pyramids from the egg carton and trim the edges so that the sides are the same length. Poke a hole through the narrow end of the pyramid and insert an orange stick or small sharpened pencil through the hole with the pointed end on the outside. Cut a square of poster board the same size as the open end of the pyramid. Punch a hole in the middle of the poster board for the blunt end of the stick to fit through snugly. Glue the poster board to the open end of the pyramid. Make certain the pointed end of the stick extends beyond the tip of the pyramid and the other end of the stick extends beyond the poster board far enough to make the dreidel twirl. Paint the dreidel. When it is dry, draw or paste one of the Hebrew symbols on each side. The four symbols represent the first letters in the phrase "A great miracle happened there," recognizing the event celebrated during Hanukkah.

Children play the dreidel game using beans, pennies, raisins, or any "counting" pieces. Children sit in a circle. Each child places one piece in the center. Children take turns spinning the top and following the directions that each symbol indicates:

Nun = do nothing; miss a turn

Gimel = take all the pieces

Hay = take half the pieces

Shin = put in two pieces

NUN

GIMEL

HAY

SHIN

When all pieces are gone, each child places one piece in the center again. The game is over when one child has all the pieces (or in a timed version, the winner is the one with the most pieces after a set amount of time). Toddlers may not have the patience to play the game to the end, but they like to participate.

Program Notes

Sign Language

CANDLE   Place the tip of the right index finger at the lips (as though blowing out a candle). Move it to the base of your outstretched left hand with palm facing out and fingers wiggling (like flickering candle flames).

Note: Be very relaxed at this time of year. Children are excited and can find it difficult to concentrate.

Flannelboard activities include the "Hanukkah Candles" song, adding candles as you sing; a plain pine tree, letting each child add a Christmas ornament; and round circles (enough so each child can participate) that become candleholders as each child adds a flannelboard candle.

Invite children to participate in "Looking for Santa." Introduce each action before beginning the activity. This is a perfect activity to lead into a surprise visit by a Santa impersonator. If you invite a Santa to your toddler program, plan for it to happen at the end of your program. Enlist another staff member to meet the Santa and to bring him into the story room just as the "Looking for Santa" activity is finished. Keep in mind that some toddlers are afraid of costumed characters. Let the storytime puppet act as a buffer between Santa and those children.

Giveaways are holiday stickers.

Fingertaster "tastes" holiday foods, such as candy canes, Christmas cookies, potato latkes, etc.

Children exit the story space singing a simple holiday song, like "We Wish You a Merry Christmas."

———————————————— Notes ————————————————

Dogs

Books

Big Dog and Little Dog
DAV PILKEY

Biscuit
ALYSSA SATIN CAPUCILLI

Busy Doggies
JOHN SCHINDEL AND BEVERLY SPARKS

Doggies
  (Spanish: *Perritos*)
SANDRA BOYNTON

Dog's Day
JANE CABRERA

Dogs Go . . .
ANNIE HORWOOD

Good Dog, Daisy!
LISA KOPPER

Hunky Dory Found It
KATIE EVANS

One Little Puppy Dog
JANET MORGAN STOEKE

Pat the Puppy
EDITH KUNHARDT

Scoot on Top of the World
ED BOXALL

Ten Dogs in the Window
CLAIRE MASUREL

What a Hungry Puppy!
GAIL HERMAN

Where's Al?
BYRON BARTON

Where's Spot?
  (French: *Où est Spot, mon
  petit chien?* and Spanish:
  ¿Dónde está Spot?)
ERIC HILL

Yip! Snap! Yap!
CHARLES FUGE

Rhythms, Rhymes, and Fingerplays

My Little Dog   (tune: "Where Has My Little Dog Gone?")

Oh, where? Oh, where has my little dog gone?
  (look all around)
Oh, where? Oh, where can he be? *(keep looking)*
With his ears cut short *(hands on ears)*
And his tail cut long. *(wave hand behind like a tail)*
Oh, where? Oh, where can he be? *(look all around)*

Here! Oh, here is my little lost dog! *(clap hands)*
He's here, right behind me! *(point over shoulder)*
With his ears cut short *(hands on ears)*
And his tail cut long. *(wave hand behind like a tail)*
He's here, right behind me! *(point over shoulder)*

Puppy's Doghouse

This is puppy's doghouse. *(hands form peak over head)*
This is puppy's bed. *(hands out in front, palms up)*
This is puppy's pan of milk, *(cup hands together
  like a bowl)*
Where he can be fed. *(make licking motion)*
This is puppy's collar *(encircle neck with fingers)*
His name is on it, too. *(nod)*
Take a stick and throw it! *(throwing motion)*
He'll bring it back to you. *(rapidly pat leg with hand)*

I See a Doggie   (tune: "How Much Is That Doggie in the Window?")

I see a doggie out the window, *(hands frame face
  as though peering out a window)*
In a box at the lady's yard sale. *(arms form large
  circle in front of body)*
I see a doggie out the window, *(hands frame face)*
And he has a waggily tail. *(arm sways side to side
  like a wagging tail)*

I wave to the doggie out the window, *(wave excitedly)*
And he wags his wiggily tail. *(arm sways side to side)*
I wave to the doggie out the window, *(wave)*
And he licks some milk from a pail. *(make
  licking motion)*

Mom hands me the doggie through the window,
  (arms outstretch as though receiving something)
She bought him at the lady's yard sale. *(arms
  folded across the chest)*
Together we are looking out the window, *(hands
  frame face)*
Just me and my dog and his tail. *(arm sways
  side to side)*

Parents' Follow-Up Ideas

Talk about animal safety to help your child understand caution when meeting unknown animals for the first time. Talk about the difference between wild animals and pets. Practice how the child will be "introduced" to someone's pet by pretending before this happens. *Note:* Animals are unpredictable; never leave children alone with animals. Check with the local animal shelter for guidelines for children (and adults) to avoid being bitten or frightened by dogs.

Toddlers tend to generalize animals. If your children are familiar with dogs, they may call all four-footed animals "dogs." Take every opportunity to help your toddlers learn there are many different kinds of animals. Some are called dogs even though they look very different from each other, and even more are not dogs (cats, cows, horses, etc.).

Gather pictures of dogs from advertising, magazines, and photographs. Make a dog book, letting your child sort the pictures by color, by height (dogs with long legs or short legs), long hair or short hair, pointy ears or droopy ears, long tails or short tails, etc. Practice dog noises: barking, whimpering, panting, growling. Examine your family dog, a neighbor's dog, or dogs in pet shops or humane shelters to see how they move, sound, smell, etc.

Craft

Dog Finger Puppets

You will need: paper

scissors

washable markers or crayons

tape

Trace these patterns, cut them out of paper, and color them. Wrap the tabs around your child's first and second fingers and tape the ends together. By moving these fingers, the puppies can walk, jump, run, and so on. With a small box you can make a doghouse in which your "pets" can live.

Make additional finger puppets by cutting pictures from magazines or greeting cards, leaving tabs on them to wrap around fingers.

Program Notes

Sign Language

DOG   Pat your leg with your hand, as if calling a dog to you.

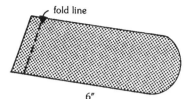

Storytime puppet introduces the theme with dog noises (barks, whimpers, panting) and asks children to guess what animal the stories are about that day.

Following the "My Little Dog" rhyme, "discover" a dog puppet or stuffed dog who likes to be petted, to lick fingers and noses, and to be hugged gently. The puppet teaches everybody how to swim doing the dog paddle (palms down, hands paddle in front of chest), and then it retires for a puppy nap.

Giveaways are puppy ears made by gluing construction paper ears to a headband that is tied on the child with string.

Fingertaster "tastes" things dogs would enjoy eating, such as hamburgers, hot dogs, dog biscuits, etc.

Children exit the story space by dog paddling.

———————————— Notes ————————————

Family

Books

Abuela's Weave
   (Spanish: *El tapiz de Abuela*)
OMAR S. CASTAÑEDA

Best-Ever Big Sister
KAREN KATZ

Brothers Are for Making Mud Pies
HARRIET ZIEFERT

Daddy All Day Long
FRANCESCA RUSACKAS

Daddy Cuddles
ANNE GUTMAN

I Love My Mommy Because . . .
LAUREL PORTER-GAYLORD

Jafta: The Homecoming
HUGH LEWIN

Just Like Daddy
FRANK ASCH

Just Like Me
BARBARA J. NEASI

Mama Zooms
JANE COWEN-FLETCHER

Mommy Mine
TIM WARNES

A Mother for Choco
KEIKO KASZA

One of Three
ANGELA JOHNSON

Spot Visits His Grandparents
   (French: *Spot chez papi et mamie*)
ERIC HILL

Twin to Twin
MARGARET O'HAIR

What Aunts Do Best / What Uncles Do Best
LAURA NUMEROFF

Rhythms, Rhymes, and Fingerplays

This Family

Mommy is working. *(hand open wide, point to thumb)*
Daddy's at the store. *(point to index finger)*
Little brother rides his bike. *(point to middle finger)*
Sister's on the floor. *(point to ring finger)*
This little one is me, me, me. *(hold and wiggle little finger)*
I hug my family, *(close hand)*
And they tickle me. *(open hand and tickle palm with finger of the other hand)*
We are happy as can be! *(wiggle all the fingers together)*

Am I Your Little One?

[rhyme to use with animal pictures]
Am I your little one? *(point to self)*
Look at you. *(point to animal picture)*
You have *horns,*

Do I have them, too?
You say *"Moo"* and it's *grass* you eat.
You're not my mommy,
You have cow's feet.

[Verse 2]

 . . . feathers . . . say "Quack"
  . . . bugs you eat . . . have duck feet.

[Verse 3]

 . . . whiskers . . . say "Meow"
  . . . mice you eat . . . have cat feet.

[Verse 4]

 . . . ten fingers . . . say "I love you"
  . . . pizza you eat.
You ARE my mommy! You can't be beat.

My Baby Bopping (tune: "Bye Baby Bunting")

My Baby Bopping.
Daddy's gone a-shopping,
To buy a little blanket warm
To wrap up Baby Bopping.

Parents' Follow-Up Ideas

Family and friends are very important to your toddlers as their awareness of the world gradually spreads outward from the immediate family. Knowing who their families are makes children feel more secure in the world. Helping them see relationships from different points of view is a good way to broaden their awareness.

Who's who in your family? Help your children learn how people in their families are related to your toddlers. Use photographs of family members. Before showing your children photos of adults as children, help them understand the time lapse by looking at their baby pictures, talking about how they used to look, and how much they have grown and changed. When talking about relatives, use family nicknames, such as "Nana," "Grammy," or "Da," but also explain kin names, like grandfather, cousin, or aunt. Help your children see that the same person can belong to several groups in the generations of a family.

Some of the most important stories your children will ever hear are stories of things that happened to you as a child. Everyone has stories to share, and the most interesting stories for your children are about the "little things" in life. Talk often about your memories from your childhood: pets, your room, favorite foods, chores, friends, toys, holidays, getting into trouble, visiting relatives, or taking vacations.

Share songs and rhymes you remember. Children are fascinated that adults were once children, too, and they gain a sense of security by knowing that you have been through similar trials and tribulations. Don't be surprised when they ask for a favorite story again and again.

Craft

Ping-Pong Family

You will need: 6–12 Ping-Pong balls

empty egg carton (cardboard preferred)

permanent markers

poster paints (optional)

Draw faces on the Ping-Pong balls to represent various family members (including pets). After letting the markers dry thoroughly, the Ping-Pong family is ready to move into their egg carton house, where they can be stored or transported. The "house" can be decorated inside and out with poster paints. Encourage your child to play with the Ping-Pong family and make up stories about them. The permanent markers allow the "family" in bathtubs and wading pools. New family or friends can be easily added.

Program Notes

Sign Language

FAMILY   Lightly pinch together your thumb and index finger on both hands and bring them together in front of your chest, palms facing and fingers up (looks like eyeglasses). Rotate your wrists until little fingers touch, forming a small circle.

Note: Be sensitive that families come in many different sizes and configurations.

This is a good program to include guests, such as grandparents, siblings, cousins, etc. Children who do not bring guests can bring a photograph of a family member.

Storytime puppet introduces another puppet or a stuffed animal as a sister, cousin, father, mother, etc.

Use flannelboard pictures of animals with the rhyme "Am I Your Little One?" Nesting dolls also fit well with this theme.

Giveaways are construction paper bracelets for child and adult made from strips of construction paper decorated with matching stickers. One sticker should be kept aside to hold the bracelet ends together around the wrist.

Fingertaster "tastes" different kinds of soups, such as chicken noodle, tomato, potato, etc.

Children exit the story space holding hands with the adults who brought them.

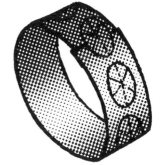

———————————————— Notes ————————————————

Farms

Books

Big Red Barn
(Spanish: *El gran granero rojo*)
MARGARET WISE BROWN

Carrot in My Pocket
KITSON FLYNN

Down on the Farm
MERRILY KUTNER

Maisy at the Farm
(Spanish: *Maisy en la granja*)
LUCY COUSINS

Millie in the Meadow
JANET PEDERSEN

Mrs. Wishy-Washy's Farm
JOY COWLEY

My Animals / Mis animales
(English/Spanish)
REBECCA EMBERLEY

My Piggy Book
SANDRA BOYNTON

Noisy Barn!
HARRIET ZIEFERT AND SIMMS TABACK

Old MacDonald Had a Cow
RICK BROWN

Old MacDonald Had a Farm
HOLLY BERRY

Open the Barn Door . . .
CHRISTOPHER SANTORO

Pat the Pony
EDITH KUNHARDT

Spot Goes to the Farm
(Spanish: *Spot va a la granja*)
ERIC HILL

This Is the Farmer
NANCY TAFURI

The Wonderful Feast
ESPHYR SLOBODKINA

Rhythms, Rhymes, and Fingerplays

Here Is a Farmer

Here is a farmer,
What does he do?
He feeds the cows
And milks them, too.

Chickens and pigs,
Horses and sheep,
He puts in the barn
To eat and sleep.

He drives the tractor,
Fields to sow.
Plants the seeds
So they will grow.

Here is the farmer,
At work or play.
He keeps busy
All through the day.

The Scarecrow

The old scarecrow is a funny
    old man.
He flaps in the wind as hard as
    he can.
He flaps to the right, *(lean right)*
He flaps to the left, *(lean left)*
He flaps back and forth *(lean
    forward and back)*
'Til he's 'most out of breath.
His arms swing out; *(swing arms)*
His legs swing, too. *(swing legs)*
He nods his head *(nod head)*
"How do you do?"
See him flippity flop *(swing arms
    and legs)*
When the wind blows hard,
That old scarecrow
In our backyard.

Old MacDonald   (traditional song)

Old MacDonald had a farm, E-I-E-I-O!
And on that farm he had a cow, E-I-E-I-O!
With a moo-moo here, and a moo-moo there.
Here a moo! There a moo! Everywhere a moo-moo.
Old MacDonald had a farm, E-I-E-I-O!

[Repeat using other farm animals and the sounds they make.]

Parents' Follow-Up Ideas

Make animal sounds with your toddler or sing "Old MacDonald Had a Farm." Some fun sounds are

chicken *(cluck)*	bird *(chirp)*	goose *(honk)*	cat *(meow)*
lamb *(baa)*	snake *(hiss)*	pig *(oink)*	donkey *(hee-haw)*
crow *(caw)*	duck *(quack)*	lion *(roar)*	
dog *(rruf)*	horse *(neigh)*	rooster *(cock-a-doodle-do)*	

Singing should be a part of your daily routine. Sing together to TV, the radio, or music from your stereo. Sing without accompanying music. Singing makes time go by faster: dressing, bathing, waiting in line, and riding in the car. You don't have to "carry a tune" to sing. No matter how good (or bad) you think your voice sounds, your voice is beautiful to your child. Ask your librarian to help you find books with children's songs in them or make up your own words to familiar tunes. Who cares if they don't rhyme or make sense? Your child will love it!

Create a farm animal sound game using a paper plate, clip clothespins, and pictures of farm animals. Cut pictures from magazines, brochures, advertising, etc. Find two pictures of each animal. Glue one picture of each animal around the rim of a paper plate. Glue the other picture to a clip clothespin. Help your child match the pictures and talk about the sounds the animals make, the foods they eat, where they live, etc. If you cannot find two animal pictures, color the clothespins with markers, and let your child match the color to the corresponding color behind the animal.

Craft

Old Scarecrow Flannelboard

You will need: felt pieces

scissors

markers

Cut the following pieces from different colors of felt:

> 1 stick, the length of the scarecrow
>
> 1 pair of pants
>
> 1 shirt
>
> 2 hands
>
> 1 hat
>
> 1 circle, for head

Draw a face on the circle and make patches, buttons, and pockets on the shirt and pants. Assemble the pieces, beginning with the stick and ending with the hat, using a flannelboard or a cushion from the sofa. Recite "The Scarecrow" rhyme with your child and act out the motions.

Program Notes

Sign Language

FARM   With your right hand open, palm facing left and thumb touching chin, drag the thumb across the chin from left to right.

Storytime puppet or the storyteller introduces the theme wearing a straw hat.

The "Old MacDonald" song works well as a flannelboard story or with stick puppet animals, which children can then return to the "barn" when finished.

Assemble the scarecrow on the flannelboard, beginning with the stick, and talk about how scarecrows flap their arms and legs to keep birds away from the farmer's seeds. After reciting "The Scarecrow" rhyme, repeat it for the children to act out.

Giveaways are farm animal finger puppets made by photocopying and enlarging this page and cutting them out, then taping the flaps in a circle.

Fingertaster "tastes" foods that farm animals eat, such as carrots, corn, oats, milk, hay, chicken feed, etc.

Children exit the story space making farm animal sounds.

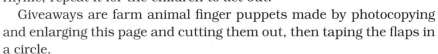

———————————— Notes ————————————

Feelings

Books

A Is for Angry
SANDRA BOYNTON

Glad Monster, Sad Monster
ED EMBERLEY AND ANNE MIRANDA

Goldie Is Mad
MARGIE PALATINI

How Do I Feel? / ¿Cómo me siento? (English/Spanish)

I Like It When . . .
MARY MURPHY

I Love It When You Smile
SAM MCBRATNEY

If You're Happy and You Know It
JANE CABRERA

I'm Feeling . . . Teaching Your Baby to Sign (Baby Fingers)
LORA HELLER

Jafta (Also in French)
HUGH LEWIN

Monster Faces
TOM BRANNON

No! No! No!
ANNE ROCKWELL

Shake My Sillies Out
RAFFI

Shy Charles
ROSEMARY WELLS

Smile, Lily!
CANDACE FLEMING

Spot Loves His Daddy
ERIC HILL

What Makes Me Happy?
CATHERINE AND LAURENCE ANHOLT

Rhythms, Rhymes, and Fingerplays

If You're Happy   (traditional song)

If you're happy and you know it, clap your hands.
  (clap hands twice)
If you're happy and you know it, clap your hands.
  (clap hands twice)
If you're happy and you know it,
Your face will surely show it. *(point to face)*
If you're happy and you know it, clap your hands.
  (clap hands twice)

[Repeat with]
  jump up high
  shout YA-HOO
  blow a kiss, etc.

[Once children are familiar with this song, change the emotions and add appropriate actions: sad = say "Boo-hoo"; silly = shake your head; grumpy = stamp your feet; scared = hide your eyes, etc.]

Old MacDonald Felt So Glad
  (tune: "Old MacDonald Had a Farm")

Old MacDonald felt so glad, HA-HA-HA-HA-HA
And when he's glad, he sounds like this:
    HA-HA-HA-HA-HA.
With a HA-HA here,
And a HO-HO there,
And a HEE-HEE-HEE-HEE everywhere,
Old MacDonald felt so glad, HA-HA-HA-HA-HA.

[Repeat with]
    grumpy, NO! NO! NO! NO! NO!
    sad, BOO-HOO-HOO-HOO-HOO.
    silly, NAH-NAH-NAH-NAH-NAH.
    shy, whisper-whisper-whisper-low.

Parents' Follow-Up Ideas

Everyone has emotions, and they are not "good" or "bad"; they are simply *feelings*. Feeling angry is perfectly normal, but throwing a temper tantrum is not the desirable way to express that anger. Helping your child identify and express emotions will make life easier for the entire family.

Talk naturally about your feelings so your children will learn emotions are something everyone experiences. Play with feelings using nursery rhymes: "Say 'Humpty Dumpty' with me and let's pretend like we are very sad . . . now happy . . . now grumpy." A brief burst of activity may help toddlers express strong emotions and change their moods: a twenty-second "angry dance" will let off steam and most likely become a "laughing dance."

Cut pictures from magazines, catalogs, newspapers, and advertising of faces (and bodies) showing emotions. Glue them on index cards and play a matching game with your toddler: "There is a picture of someone who is sad. Can you find another sad face?" Imitate the facial expressions in front of a mirror with your child or make a feelings book with the pictures. Glue happy-face pictures to one page and grumpy faces on another, etc.

Craft

Finger Circle Puppets

You will need: poster board
                    pill bottle (circle pattern)
                    scissors
                    washable markers
                    masking tape

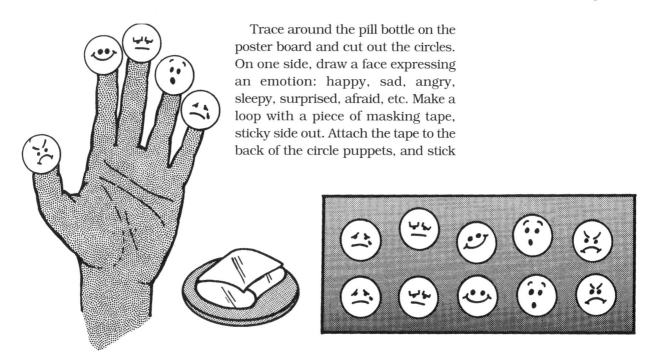

Trace around the pill bottle on the poster board and cut out the circles. On one side, draw a face expressing an emotion: happy, sad, angry, sleepy, surprised, afraid, etc. Make a loop with a piece of masking tape, sticky side out. Attach the tape to the back of the circle puppets, and stick them to your child's fingers. The tape can be easily replaced when it loses its tackiness. Circle puppets can be taped to the ends of straws or sticks if your child does not like having things stuck to fingers.

Other options: Glue pictures to circles instead of drawing faces on them. Make two sets of the circle puppets and play a matching game with them. Or use one puppet to help look for faces with the same expressions in magazines or books.

Program Notes

Sign Language

HAPPY   Bring the flat palm of the right hand, fingers pointing left, upward and outward on the chest.

Bring a mirror to the story space. When assembling the clown shape puzzle, show the children how the crescent smile can become a frown when turned upside down to introduce the theme for the day. Then let them practice making happy faces and sad (pouting) faces in the mirror.

The storytime puppet visits and leads children in the song "Old MacDonald Felt So Glad."

Giveaways are happy-face stickers.

Fingertaster "tastes" flavors that are pleasers, such as bubble gum, peanut butter, cookies, chocolate milk, etc.

Children exit the story space walking as "happy" as they can.

———————————— Notes ————————————

Firefighters

Books

All Aboard Fire Trucks
TEDDY SLATER

Clifford the Firehouse Dog
    (Spanish: *Clifford el perro
    bombero*)
NORMAN BRIDWELL

Corduroy Goes to the Fire Station
B. G. HENNESSY

*Curious George and the
Firefighters*
ANNA GROSSNICKLE HINES

Emergency!
MARGARET MAYO

Even Firefighters Hug Their Moms
CHRISTINE KOLE MACLEAN

Fire Engines
ANNE ROCKWELL

Fire Fighters
NORMA SIMON

Fire Truck
SALINA YOON

Firebears: The Rescue Team
RHONDA GOWLER GREENE

Firefighter
MICHAEL REX

Firefighter
KEN WILSON-MAX

Follow That Fire Truck
CHRISTOPHER NICHOLAS

Maisy's Fire Engine
    (Spanish: *El coche de
    bomberos de Maisy*)
LUCY COUSINS

Ten Men on a Ladder
CRAIG MACAULAY

Touch and Feel Fire Engine

Rhythms, Rhymes, and Fingerplays

Sirens

Fire engine, fire engine rolling down the street.
    (hands roll over one another)
With the siren blaring at everyone you meet.
Whoo-ooo! Coming through! *(hands frame
    mouth like megaphone)*
Whoo-ooo! Move aside!
Whoo-ooo, whoo-ooo!
On our way to save the day.
Whoo-ooo, whoo-ooo.

[Repeat with]
    police car
    ambulance

Down at the Station   (tune: "Down by the Station")

Down at the station
Firefighters waiting
Ready to come running
If there is a fire.

The alarm bell starts ringing,
Ding-ding, ding-ding, dinging.
Putting on their boots and hats,
They hurry out the door.

They jump upon the fire truck
Hear the siren wailing,
"Whoo-ooo-ooo-ooo-ooo,
Get out of our way!"

With ladders and hoses,
They put out the fire.
For our firefighters,
It's just another day.

The Firefighter

A firefighter's hat keeps her head and neck safe.
    (hands on head)
A firefighter's coat helps keep the flames away.
    (hands brush arms)
A firefighter's ladder helps her reach the windows high.
    (hands reach high)
A firefighter's boots keep her feet warm and dry.
    (point to feet)
A fire engine carries her quickly to the fire.
    (hands hold pretend steering wheel)
A cherry picker basket lets her reach above the wire.
    (one arm reaches high)
A firefighter's mask lets her see when smoke is thick.
    (hands frame face)
An ambulance is there in case someone's hurt or sick.
    (twist hand over head like emergency light)
A firefighter's hose, with water from its spout,
    (both hands hold pretend hose)
Sprays the fire and sprays the fire, *(point hands left and right)*
Until all the flames are out. *(hands fall away from each other)*
Inside the boots and hats, *(point to feet and head)*
Inside the coats and masks, *(touch arms and face)*
Brave men and women are *(hand on heart)*
Our friends, the firefighters! *(wave vigorously)*

Parents' Follow-Up Ideas

Put a *Tot Finder* sign on your child's window to guide firefighters in case of a fire in your home. They are available at most fire stations, and it is a fun trip with your toddler to see the fire trucks and meet firefighters while picking up the sign.

Every family should have a fire plan. To make certain all smoke detectors are working, test them once a month. Help your toddlers press the button so they will hear the alarm and know what it means. Keep fire extinguishers where they can be easily reached by adults, and check them regularly. Have a fire drill each season, complete with sounding the smoke detector alarm. Acting out emergency situations helps all family members understand what they should do and helps even the smallest child participate.

Keep matches and flammables (like candles and oil lamps) well out of reach of children. They are curious and fascinated by the flames they see when these items are used by adults. Their natural urge to explore for themselves can turn tragic when fire is involved. Put red-dot stickers on anything that could cause a burn, including stoves and irons, and teach your child that a red dot means "Hands off!" or "Will hurt!"

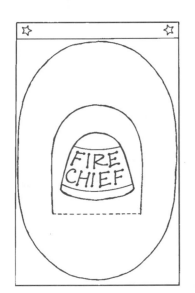

Craft

Firefighter's Hat

You will need: 11″ × 14″ poster board or heavy construction paper (yellow, red, or black)

pencil

scissors and stapler

washable markers

Cut a 1″ strip from the narrow side of the poster board, draw stars at each end, and set it aside. Draw an oval shape on the remaining paper and a semicircle toward the front of it (see the pattern). Cut out the oval, creating the hat brim, and cut along the semicircle making the top of the hat. Fold along the end of the semicircle so the top stands up. With markers, draw a badge and decorate it on the top of the hat. Staple one end of the 1″ strip to the top of the hat and the other end to the inside brim to stabilize the hat.

Program Notes

Sign Language

FIREFIGHTER   With your thumb and index finger curved into a *C* shape, put the thumb on the center of the forehead, fingers pointing upward. Keeping your thumb in place, rotate the hand to the left twice, as though the fingers were encircling the badge on a firefighter's hat.

Note: Invite a firefighter to arrive in the middle of your program. Let adults know in advance that there will be a guest because this program often runs long. Children want lots of time to touch and examine firefighting paraphernalia. Firefighters are happy to have the opportunity to talk with young children, acquainting them with the equipment used to fight fires and talking briefly to parents about fire safety. They will often bring pamphlets, stickers, or coloring pages to hand out.

The storytime puppet introduces the theme wearing a firefighter's hat or carrying a fire engine.

Toddlers love to make a siren sound, so give them the opportunity as you share stories or rhymes. If a firefighter is coming, use only one story and then get the children up to act out one of the rhymes.

Giveaways are stickers or coloring pages (get them from your fire department if no visitor is coming).

Fingertaster "tastes" foods commonly eaten by firefighters (cooked in quantity), such as chili, spaghetti, pizza, beef stew, etc.

Children exit the story space driving fire engines with sirens sounding.

—— Notes ——

Friends

Books

Bear's New Friend
KARMA WILSON AND JANE CHAPMAN

Biscuit Finds a Friend
ALYSSA SATIN CAPUCILLI

A Cat and a Dog
CLAIRE MASUREL AND BOB KOLAR

Do You Want to Be My Friend?
ERIC CARLE

The Doorbell Rang
    (Spanish: *Llaman a la puerta*)
PAT HUTCHINS

Fox Makes Friends
ADAM RELF

A Friend for Minerva Louise
JANET MORGAN STOEKE

Hello, Lulu
CAROLINE UFF

If You Give a Mouse a Cookie
    (Spanish: *Si le das una
    galletita a un ratón*)
LAURA NUMEROFF

Jambo Means Hello
MURIEL FEELINGS

Moonbear's Bargain
FRANK ASCH

My Friend Rabbit
ERIC ROHMANN

A Splendid Friend, Indeed
SUZANNE BLOOM

Swim, Little Wombat, Swim!
CHARLES FUGE

Uno, dos, hola y adiós
DAVID LE JARS

The Way to Wyatt's House
NANCY WHITE CARLSTROM

Rhythms, Rhymes, and Fingerplays

Hello!

Hello, hello, hello! *(wave hand enthusiastically)*
I see you. *(point to children)*
Hello, hello, hello! *(big wave)*
Do you see me, too? *(point to self)*
Hello! I see Danny* here. *(wave to each child,
    making eye contact and letting them wave back)*
Hello! I see Maria* here.
Hello! I see Keisha* here.
Hello, hello, hello! *(wave to everyone)*

[*Repeat until all children have been named. If it comes out uneven, say "Hello!" to the adults as a group, to a puppet, or to "my friends." Encourage parents and children to wave back to you and to each other as they are named.]

To Have a Friend (tune: "Pop Goes the Weasel")

To have a friend, we share our toys *(skip around)*
And happily we play.
It's your turn. And now it's mine. *(gesture to child, then to self)*
We're *friends* all the day. *(grasp hands and shake them up and down)*

[Repeat with other things to share]
    sandbox
    puzzles
    cookies

Good-bye (tune: "Good Night Ladies")

Good-bye José. *(wave goodbye to each child)*
Good-bye April.
Good-bye Meiko.
We'll see you all next week. *(wave to everyone)*

[Repeat until all children have been named. See note with "Hello!"]

Parents' Follow-Up Ideas

Use the magic of counting to reinforce sharing in everyday activities. When serving food at the table, help your children see how the meal is being "shared": "One for mommy. One for daddy. One for Susie." Let them help hand out the portions and pass plates or bowls around the table, taking care to help with hot or heavy plates. When playing together, take advantage of any opportunity to point out: "Your turn. My turn." or "You first . . . now me . . . now Max. . . ." Sharing does not come naturally to young children.

Toddlers are very interested in other children of all ages, but they may be shy around them. Help your children get to know other children by taking them places where there are children about the same age: library programs, playgroups, religious groups, mom's day out, and family gatherings. Talk about things your toddlers can do with other children, and talk about ways they can be a good friend to others. The old adage, "To have a friend, be a friend," is very true.

Reinforce sharing between children, even when it is accidental. When toddlers play together, provide toys that *share* well: balls, boats, blocks, a two-child rocking toy, etc. If possible, make sure there is more than one of a popular toy. Children will often share with mom when they won't share with others. Use these experiences to teach the value and fun of sharing with friends.

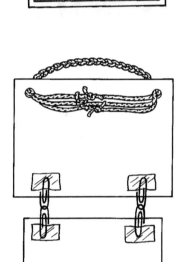

Craft

Welcome Sign with Special Greetings

You will need: 2 pieces of colorful poster board cut into rectangles 8″ × 12″ and 4″ × 10″

2 pieces of heavier cardboard cut the same as poster board

glue, pencil, and scissors or craft knife

cloth tape

3 24″ lengths of ribbons or yarn or 2″ strips of cloth

2 clip clothespins

4 large paper clips

washable markers or paints or contact paper

Reinforce the poster boards by gluing them to cardboard and letting them dry thoroughly under a board or books to keep them flat. Decorate the welcome and special greeting signs with paints, markers, or contact paper. Cover the edges of both signs with cloth tape to keep the edges from separating. On the welcome sign, mark two nickel-sized holes on the upper side. Carefully cut out the holes with a craft knife and spread a thin coat of white glue on the inside edges of the holes to reinforce them. While the glue is drying, put the craft knife safely away.

On the back of the welcome sign, glue two paper clips to the lower edge, with the double-loop end of the clip extending beyond the edge. Reinforce the glued clips with cloth tape to help hold them in place. Repeat this process on the back of the upper edge of the special greeting sign, making sure the clips match the distance between those on the welcome sign and being careful not to cover the *open* prong that allows the signs to be connected and changed.

Lay the ribbons evenly together, and clip them together about 4″ from one end with a clothespin. Braid the ribbons, leaving about 4″ at the opposite end unbraided. Thread the ribbon braid through the sign holes (ends in back) and secure them with a clothespin. Tie each of the ribbons together to form a continuous loop at the back of the sign. It is now ready to hang on the front door or in a special place inside the home.

Make other special greetings to use throughout the year: at holidays (Merry Christmas, Happy Hanukkah), welcoming special people (friends, relative, babysitter, Daddy when he's been out of town), or people making expected deliveries (Mail Lady or Pizza Guy). Keep extra greetings in a shoe box, and label the back of them with a drawing, magazine picture, or photograph to help your child identify them. Let your child locate the appropriate greeting and help attach it to the welcome sign.

Program Notes

Sign Language

FRIEND   Hook your right index finger (palm down) over your curved left index finger (palm down); repeat the action in reverse with your left finger on top. This indicates a close relationship.

Display the welcome sign on flannelboard. The storyteller or story-time puppet introduces the theme by greeting children with the "Hello!" rhyme (which can also be part of an opening routine). Substitute other languages: Spanish = "Hola" (Oh-la); Japanese = "Oyhyo" (Oh-hah-yo); or sign language = "Hi" (a salute with the right hand, palm facing out) and sing it again throughout the program.

Giveaways are friendship bracelets made from loops of braided yarn. (These usually can be bought in bulk quantities at a carnival supply house.)

Fingertaster "tastes" foods that are easily shared, such as pizza, orange slices, Popsicles, raisins, etc.

Sing the "Good-bye" song, and encourage children to exit the story space waving good-bye. (The "Good-bye" song can also become part of a closing routine.)

—————————————— Notes ——————————————

Frogs and Turtles

Books

Can You Hop?
LISA LAWSTON

The Caterpillar and the Polliwog
JACK KENT

Flora the Frog
PHILIPPE DUBARLE-BOSSY

Frog
FIONA WATT

Hop Jump
ELLEN STOLL WALSH

Hoptoad
JANE YOLEN

Hurry Home, Hungry Frog
CARLA DIJS

I Love Daddy
LIZI BOYD

Icky Sticky Frog
DAWN BENTLEY

Jump, Frog, Jump!
  (Spanish: *¡Salta, ranita, salta!*)
ROBERT KALAN

Jumping Frog
AMANDA LESLIE

Little Quack's New Friend
LAUREN THOMPSON

Moonbear's Pet
FRANK ASCH

Tarquin's Shell
SALLY CHAMBERS

To the Tub
PEGGY PERRY ANDERSON

The Wide-Mouthed Frog
KEITH FAULKNER

Rhythms, Rhymes, and Fingerplays

The Little Frog

I am a little frog *(point to self)*
Sitting on a log *(hands on knees)*
Listen to my song *(hand to ear)*
I sing it all day long: *(cup hands to mouth)*
Ribbit! Ribbit! Ribbit! Ribbit! *(sway side to side)*
If hungry, I eat flies, *(hand to mouth)*
And I can blink my eyes. *(blink)*
I hop, and hop, and hop *(bounce up and down)*
And then, I stop! *(sit still)*

Little Turtle (by Vachel Lindsay)

There was a little turtle *(make fist, cover with other hand)*
Who lived in a box. *(form circle, fingers touching)*
He swam in the water, *(thumbs together, flutter fingers)*
And climbed on the rocks. *("walk" one hand over the other)*
He snapped at a mosquito, *(grabbing motion, up high)*

He snapped at a flea, *(grabbing motion, in front)*
He snapped at a minnow, *(grabbing motion, down low)*
And he snapped at me! *(grabbing motion, under chin)*
He caught the mosquito, *(clap hands up high)*
He caught the flea, *(clap hands in front)*
He caught the minnow, *(clap hands down low)*
But he didn't catch me! *(point to self, shake head)*

Five Little Froggies   (tune: "Ten Little Indians")

One little, two little, three little froggies.
   (hand open, point to fingers)
Four little, five little, *(point to fingers)*
Green little froggies *(wave hand side to side)*
Splashing, *(hands splash)*
Croaking, *(hands cup mouth)*
Hopping froggies, *(bounce)*
Living in my pond. *(point to self)*

Five little, four little, three little froggies.
   (repeat appropriate actions)
Two little, one little,
Green little froggies.
Hopping, croaking, splashing froggies,
Living in my pond.

Parents' Follow-Up Ideas

Teach your child the game of leapfrog using a favorite stuffed animal or a friend. Show your toddler how to crouch low on the floor and jump the stuffed animal over your child. Put the toy on the floor in front of your child and help him or her jump over it. Play in a carpeted area where falls are softened. Leap in a circle or from one point to another (sofa to doorway). Once your children understand the concept of taking turns, they are ready to play this game with friends and with you.

Make a "turtle salad" for lunch using a peach half for the shell, a nut or grape for the head, and carrot sticks for legs and a tail. Serve your turtle on a lettuce-leaf lily pad.

Have fun with a frog friends counting game. Make five "frogs" using pieces of celery or green pepper. A bowl of slightly salted water becomes a pond. Have your toddler hop the first frog up to the bowl and into it. Let him or her play with the frog in the water, swimming round and round, jumping in and out, swimming fast and slow, above and below water, etc. Talk about what the frog is doing. When the frog gets lonely, introduce a second one: "Now there are two." Don't rush this. Let your child explore how two frogs play together (leapfrog, taking turns in and out of the water). As you talk, use number words (1, 2, 3, more, less, some, all). When all the frogs have been introduced, let your child become a hungry bird and gobble the frogs down one at a time. *Hint:* When toddlers are faced with many items, they find it hard to concentrate. Keep extra frogs out of sight until it is time to use them.

Craft

Turtle Marionette

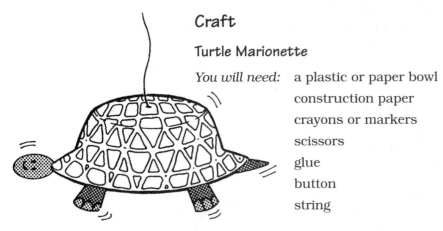

You will need: a plastic or paper bowl

construction paper

crayons or markers

scissors

glue

button

string

Let your child decorate the outside of the bowl, which will become the turtle's shell. Cut from construction paper: one circle (head), four small rectangles (legs), and one triangle (tail). Draw a face on the circle and glue the paper shapes to the edge of the bowl.

Poke a hole in the center of the bowl and thread the string through it. Thread the button onto the string and tie it securely. This helps to keep the string from pulling out of the bowl.

Hold the string, and the turtle will dangle above the floor. It can be made to walk slowly, jump, dance, or even fly.

Program Notes

Sign Language

TURTLE   Cup the left hand over your right fist, extend the right thumb, and wiggle it like a turtle peeking from under its shell.

Note: Avoid using live turtles in your program due to the risks of their carrying salmonella.

Introduce the theme with a frog or turtle puppet or stuffed animal, talking about how they move and turtle's shell or frog's sound.

The "Five Little Froggies" rhyme and the story *Jump, Frog, Jump!* make good flannelboard presentations. "The Little Frog" rhyme can be either a lap-sitting or jump-around-the-room activity. Children enjoy jumping and croaking like frogs, as well as crawling slowly and ducking their heads like turtles. The storytime puppet can lead the way.

Giveaways are frog puppets made by sealing an envelope and folding it lengthwise, then cutting a slit in the front of it and gluing on the eyes and body copied from the next page.

Fingertaster "tastes" things frogs and turtles might eat, such as mosquitoes, flies, leaves, little fish, etc.

Children exit the story space jumping like frogs.

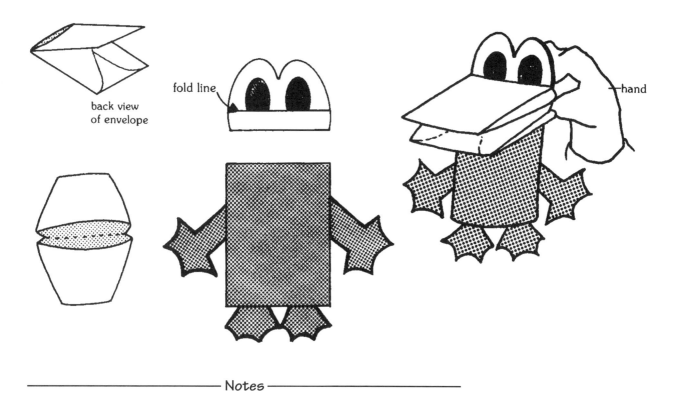

back view
of envelope

fold line

hand

— Notes —

Gardens

Books

Apples and Pumpkins
ANNE ROCKWELL

The Carrot Seed
   (Spanish: *La semilla de
   zanahoria*)
RUTH KRAUSS

Flower Garden
EVE BUNTING

Garden Animals
LUCY COUSINS

The Great Big Enormous Turnip
ALEX TOLSTOY

Growing Vegetable Soup
   (Spanish: *A sembrar sopa
   de verduras*)
LOIS EHLERT

Inch by Inch: The Garden Song
DAVID MALLETT

*Mrs. McNosh and the Great Big
Squash*
SARAH WEEKS

My Father's Hands
JOANNE RYDER

My Garden / Mi jardín
(English/Spanish)
REBECCA EMBERLEY

One Bean
ANNE ROCKWELL

One Little Seed
ELAINE GREENSTEIN

So Happy!
KEVIN HENKES

*Spot's Little Book of Fun in
the Garden*
ERIC HILL

Ten Seeds
RUTH BROWN

This Is the Sunflower
LOLA M. SCHAEFER

Rhythms, Rhymes, and Fingerplays

My Garden

This is my garden *(hands in front, palms up)*
I'll rake it with care *(rake fingers of one hand
      over other palm)*
And then some flower seeds *(twist index finger
      of one hand into center of palm)*
I will plant there. *(pat palm with other fingers)*

The sun will shine *(make circle with arms
      over head)*
And the rain will fall, *(wiggle fingers down
      in front of body)*
And my garden will blossom *(make fists, open
      fingers slowly)*
Growing straight and tall. *(reach hands high
      above head)*

Grow, Grow, Grow   (tune: "Row, Row, Row Your Boat")

Grow, grow, growing tall. *(hands raise slowly)*
Flowers growing tall. *(raise hands over head)*
I water my garden *(mimic actions)*
And pull the weeds
And flowers grow from little seeds.
   (cupped hands unfold like blossoms)

Grow, grow, growing wide. *(hands spread outward)*
Pumpkins growing wide. *(arms outstretched at sides)*
I water my garden *(mimic actions)*
And pull the weeds
And pumpkins grow from little seeds. *(cupped hands*
   move outward like a pumpkin growing)

Grow, grow, growing deep. *(hands lower slowly)*
Carrots growing deep. *(hands on the floor)*
I water my garden *(mimic actions)*
And pull the weeds
And carrots grow from little seeds. *(cupped hands*
   move away vertically, like elongating carrot)

I Dig, Dig, Dig

I dig, dig, dig *(digging motion)*
And plant some seeds. *(planting motion)*
I rake, rake, rake *(raking motion)*
And pull some weeds. *(pulling motion)*
I wait and watch *(hands on hips)*
And soon I know, *(point to self)*
My garden sprouts *(hands low, palms down)*
And starts to grow. *(raise hands toward ceiling)*

Parents' Follow-Up Ideas

Plant seeds from the fruits you eat (oranges, grapefruits, tangerines, and others). Rinse the seeds and blot them dry with a paper towel. Plant them in a container (flowerpot or paper cup) filled with potting soil, labeling each pot with the name of the plant or a picture cut from a magazine. Put the pots in a warm place and keep the soil moist. Let your child feel the differences in the soil before and after you water it. When shoots begin to appear, move the pot to a sunny window and continue to water it regularly. Talk with your child about how seeds grow and how they need light and water to survive. If one wilts slightly, let your child give it water and notice the change when the plant revives later.

Talk about things that grow in gardens when doing grocery shopping. The produce department is the ideal place to start with fresh vegetables and fruits, but also point out similar canned foods or those that begin as seeds. See if you can find foods that grow above and below ground. Name each item as you pass by. If you are unsure, ask the produce manager, showing your toddler that you are learning something new together. Identify items as part of a larger group (fruits, vegetables, above- or below-ground growers, colors, and shapes) and compare the items with others, helping your child be observant and creative in how she or he sees things. "A carrot is a vegetable and an orange is a fruit, but they are the same color. What color is that? Can you find something else that color?"

Make a sponge planter with a piece of sponge. Soak the sponge in water, and sprinkle birdseed or grass seed on it. Put it in a container that holds water, and set it—or hang it with string—in a sunny window. Soak the sponge every day, and soon it will be filled with lovely green plants.

Craft

Funny Potato Face

You will need: 1 large raw potato

cotton balls

grass seed or birdseed

a knife and a tablespoon

7–8 whole cloves

a small dish of water

Scoop some of the pulp out of the top of the potato. Moisten the cotton balls with water and place them in the hollow of the potato. Slice off the bottom of the potato so it will stand by itself; place it in the dish of water. Let your child sprinkle the seed over the cotton. Stick the cloves in the side of the potato to make eyes, nose, and mouth. Keep the cotton moist, and in a few days the potato will sprout a wonderful head of green hair!

Program Notes

Sign Language

GROW   The left hand forms a cup, palm facing you. With tips of fingers together, your right hand comes up through the cupped left hand, with the fingers slowly opening as if a flower were emerging and opening its petals.

Introduce the theme with a plastic watering can and toy garden tools, giving children the opportunity to touch them as you talk about the theme.

When using the story *The Carrot Seed,* bring out a garden box (a large box with a stuffed carrot hidden inside) early in the program. Let children help "rake" or "water" your garden at various stages throughout the program. After sharing the story, insert a green feather duster in the top of the hidden carrot. The feathers become the carrot's leaves. Encourage the children to help you pull the carrot out. Keep your hands *firmly* on the carrot and its "leaves" until time for it to POP out and allow lots of time for them to look and touch the carrot after it has been "harvested." *The Great Big Enormous Turnip* makes a good flannelboard or glove puppet story.

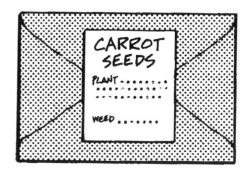

Giveaways are seeds (carrot or other) divided into small envelopes with instructions for planting glued to them. (Radish seeds grow quicker than carrots and are almost foolproof to grow.) Keep a few seeds in a plastic bag so children can see what they look like and how small they are.

Fingertaster "tastes" things grown in gardens, such as carrots, celery, watermelon, corn, tomatoes, etc.

Children exit the story space singing the "Grow, Grow, Grow" song.

───────────────── **Notes** ─────────────────

Getting Dressed

Books

All Sorts of Clothes!
HANNAH REIDY

Ella Sarah Gets Dressed
MARGARET CHODOS-IRVINE

How Do I Put It On?
SHIGEO WATANABE

Jamaica and Brianna
JUANITA HAVILL

Maisy Dresses Up
   (Spanish: *Maisy se disfraza*)
LUCY COUSINS

Max's Dragon Shirt
ROSEMARY WELLS

Mrs. McNosh Hangs Up Her Wash
SARAH WEEKS

My Clothes / Mi ropa
(English/Spanish)
REBECCA EMBERLEY

My Very First Look at Clothes
CHRISTIANE GUNZI

A Pocket for Corduroy
   (Spanish: *Un bolsillo para
   Corduroy*)
DON FREEMAN

Red, Blue, Yellow Shoe
TANA HOBAN

*Snap! Button! Zip! Sesame
Street*
ABIGAIL TABBY

Where Does It Go?
MARGARET MILLER

Whose Clothes Are Those?
SHAHEEN BILGRAMI

Whose Socks Are Those?
JEZ ALBOROUGH

*You'll Soon Grow into
Them, Titch*
PAT HUTCHINS

Rhythms, Rhymes, and Fingerplays

Early in the Morning   (tune: "Mulberry Bush")

This is how we wear our pants, *(mime putting on pants)*
Wear our pants, wear our pants.
This is how we wear our pants,
So early in the morning. *(march in place)*

[Repeat with]
   shirts
   shoes
   hats

Dressed to Play   (tune: "Three Blind Mice")

Hat, gloves, coat.
Hat, gloves, coat.
Warm socks and boots.
Warm socks and boots.

I'm staying warm while
    I'm out to play
On this cold and snowy day.
I'll have fun as long as I stay
With hat, gloves, coat.

[Verse 2]
    Shorts and sandals. Sunscreen, too.
        . . . staying cool . . . bright and sunny day.

[Verse 3]
    Boots and umbrella. Raincoats and hat.
        . . . staying dry . . . wet and rainy day.

[Verse 4]
    Sweater and jacket. Zipped up tight.
        . . . staying warm . . . cold and windy day.

Look at Me!

Look at me! *(point to self)*
Upon my head
I wear a hat of brightest red.
    (hands on head)
Look at me! *(point to self)*
Don't I look neat
With shiny shoes upon my feet?
    (point to feet)
Look at me! (point to self)
Hip hip hooray! *(clap hands)*
With shirt and pants *(point to clothing)*
I'm dressed to play. *(jump up and down)*

Parents' Follow-Up Ideas

Set aside definite places in the home for your children's clothes. Put hooks or hangers low enough for children to hang up their own clothes. Store folded clothes in drawers where they can be easily reached. Your children can help put laundry away and make their own selections when getting dressed.

On laundry day ask your children to remember which of their dirty clothes need washing. Give hints ("What do you wear on your legs?"), and help them give names to specific items of clothing ("Those are called leggings."). Talk about the sequence of laundry actions (gathering, sorting, washing, drying, folding, and putting away). Let your toddlers help sort the laundry by type: underwear, towels, shirts, etc. Help them measure the soap or fabric softener into the washing machine or tear off a softener sheet to put in the dryer. Let them feel a wet sock and a dry one, and talk about the differences in weight, texture, or temperature.

Your children can match socks from the dryer and separate large and small underpants. Use laundry words *(folding, smoothing)*, and talk about colors, shapes (rectangle pillowcases), and parts of clothing (corners, sleeves, collars, buttons). *Safety tip:* Never leave children unattended in a laundry room where they might climb into appliances or "sample" cleaning products.

A good way to avoid right and left shoe mix-ups is to use a waterproof marker or laundry pen. Draw a dot inside each shoe along the inner edges. When shoes are sitting next to each other correctly, the dots are lined up side by side.

Craft

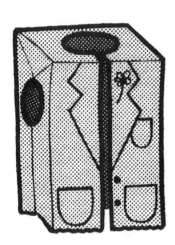

Paper Bag Costume

You will need: paper grocery sack

crayons or washable markers

paper or cloth scraps

glue

scissors

With the sack upside down, cut three holes in it: one on the bottom for the head and one on each side for the arms. Cut in a line from the neck hole down the front of the sack to make it easier to get on and off.

Decorate the sack with crayons, markers, or scraps. Add buttons, pockets, collar, belt, sash, or fringe. The costume can look like everyday clothes or be exotic: superheroes, wild creatures, and so on. Hang these costumes from hangers in an area where your child has access to them for fun and pretend play. Don't be surprised if older brothers or sisters want to be part of this, too.

Program Notes

Sign Language

SHIRT   Pinch clothing at the shoulders and pull gently.

Introduce the theme by remarking on the different kinds of clothing worn by adults and children, using clothing words (dress, jumper, overalls, blouse) as well as descriptors (warm, cool, long sleeves, ruffles, etc.).

A simple stretching activity between stories is to pretend to get dressed together to go out to play. The story *How Do I Put It On?* is excellent as a flannelboard presentation, and the clothing can be adapted to cooler weather by making the sleeves and pant legs longer and turning the shoes into boots.

The storytime puppet arrives carrying clothing easy to put on it (hat, collar, scarf) and asks for help getting dressed. Children can help, with the puppet directing them to put the clothing in the wrong places. The storyteller encourages children to help the puppet get dressed correctly.

Giveaways are paper doll bears and clothes, copied from this page.

Fingertaster "tastes" foods appropriate to the season, such as hot soups or frozen yogurt and watermelon.

Children exit the story space marching. Focus their attention on their shoes.

――――――――――― Notes ―――――――――――

Growing Up Safe

Books

All by Myself
ALIKI

All by Myself
(Spanish: *Yo solito*)
MERCER MAYER

*Big Enough for a Bike: A Sesame
Street Book*

Big Like Me
ANNA GROSSNICKLE HINES

Corduroy Goes to the Doctor
LISA MCCUE

Doctor Maisy
(Spanish: *La doctora Maisy*)
LUCY COUSINS

Felix Feels Better
ROSEMARY WELLS

Grow Up!
NINA LADEN

Guess What I'll Be
ANNI AXWORTHY

I Used to Be the Baby
ROBIN BALLARD

Minerva Louise at School
JANET MORGAN STOEKE

My Big Boy Bed
EVE BUNTING

Sam's Potty
BARBRO LINDGREN

Sara's Potty
HARRIET ZIEFERT

Spot Sleeps Over
ERIC HILL

Te Amo, Bebé, Little One
(Spanish/English)
LISA WHEELER

Rhythms, Rhymes, and Fingerplays

I Can!

I can! I can! I can! *(clap hands)*
Roll a ball. *(make rolling motion)*
I can! I can! I can! *(clap hands)*
Roll a ball. *(make rolling motion)*
I can! I can! I can! *(clap hands)*
Roll a ball. *(make rolling motion)*
Come roll a ball with me.

[Repeat with]

throw a ball
bounce a ball
jump up high
turn around
run so fast
tippytoe

Stop, Look, and Listen!

Stop! *(hands in front, palms out)*
Look! *(hands shade eyes)*
And listen! *(hands cup ears)*
Before you cross the street,
   (look both ways)
Use your eyes, *(point to eyes)*
Use your ears, *(point to ears)*
And then use your feet. *(point to
   feet and nod head)*

Growing Up Healthy   (tune: "Paw-Paw Patch")

We eat good food,
We're growing up healthy.
We eat good food,
We're growing up healthy.
We eat good food,
We're growing up healthy.
Growing up big and strong.

[Repeat with]

   We help Mommy
   We play outside
   We look both ways
   We get lots of sleep

Parents' Follow-Up Ideas

Children are always in a hurry to "grow up," to be big enough to do things older children do. Help your toddlers realize how much they have already grown. Look at baby pictures together and talk about when they could not eat, crawl, walk, or talk. If there is something they want to do but their skills are not yet good enough, help find things they can do now that will lead into that activity. For example, if they want to ride a two-wheel bike, they need to learn to pedal, and steer, and balance. Those are skills they can work on now.

Introduce your children to a ruler or cloth measuring tape and show them how to "measure" two objects to see which is larger. Point out the numbers on the ruler to reinforce the concept of counting. Using pictures from magazines, make a chart of the biggest and smallest objects you measure. Remember that sizes in photographs can be confusing; the picture of a refrigerator may look smaller than one of a toy. Make a growth chart for your children and mark their growth progress on it. Use it to compare their height (growth) with others, including smaller pets, toys, and younger children as well as larger examples of different sizes.

Talk about how all living things grow and change. Young children are beginning to notice similarities between themselves and the rest of the world. Notice how flowers bud and then blossom. Visit the petting zoo often to see the progress young animals make over time. Talk about changes in abilities of babies in your home or neighborhood.

Craft

Growth Chart

You will need: a strip of paper, 4–6′ long by 6″ wide

ruler

permanent marker

glue

photo of child at birth or as a young infant

clear contact paper

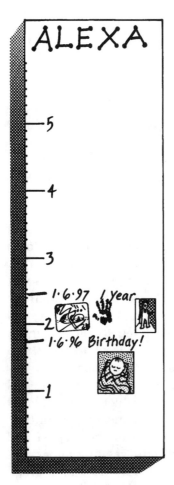

Along the left side of the paper strip, and starting at the bottom, mark inches and feet the length of the paper. Make a large mark at your child's birth length and write the date. Next to it, glue a photo of your child as an infant. Using a baby book or doctor's records, mark growth at various ages and attach a picture of your child taken at that age.

Laminate the growth chart or cover it with clear contact paper on both sides. Mount it on a wall in your child's room where she or he can see it to study the growth rate. Mounting it across from a full-length mirror allows your child to check progress and allows you to introduce the seemingly magical concept of perspective: stand close to the mirror and look taller than the growth chart. Continue to mark growth at milestones, documenting with dates, ages, and photos. Cover additions with clear tape to preserve them and to create a keepsake.

Program Notes

Sign Language

TALL   The left hand is open, palm forward, fingers upward.
Lay the right-hand index finger horizontally across
the left palm and slide it upward.

The storytime puppet introduces the theme by telling children some of the things it wants to do when it "grows up." The storyteller points out to the puppet some of the things it can do now that it could not do before, such as talking, picking up things, dancing, walking, etc. Make a growth chart for the puppet, marking estimated heights for different "ages" and making it large enough to measure the children against. Mount the growth chart on a nearby wall and invite children to be measured in comparison to the puppet. Focus attention on how much taller each of them is compared with the puppet. Avoid comparing them with each other.

Use flannelboard figures of babies, toddlers, and older children to help toddlers better understand the changes in their growing bodies. Make flannelboard figures from pictures in magazines to illustrate the rhyme "I Can" or the song "Growing Up Healthy."

Giveaways are toothbrushes that you can get free from a local dentist.

Fingertaster "tastes" fruits, such as oranges, bananas, apples, peaches, strawberries, etc.

Children exit the story space walking "tall."

Notes

Hats

Books

Blue Hat, Green Hat
   (Spanish: *Azul el sombrero,
   verde el sombrero*)
SANDRA BOYNTON

Caps for Sale
   (Spanish: *Se venden gorras*)
ESPHYR SLOBODKINA

Do You Have a Hat?
EILEEN SPINELLI

*A Frog Inside My Hat: A First Book
of Poems*
FAY ROBINSON

A Hat for Minerva Louise
JANET MORGAN STOEKE

Hats, Hats, Hats
ANN MORRIS

Jennie's Hat
EZRA JACK KEATS

Mrs. Honey's Hat
PAM ADAMS

Old Hat, New Hat
STAN AND JAN BERENSTAIN

Red Hat! Green Hat!
LOUISE GIKOW

*This Is the Hat: A Story
in Rhyme*
NANCY VAN LAAN

*Who Took the
Farmer's Hat?*
JOAN L. NODSET

Who's Under That Hat?
DAVID A. CARTER

Whose Hat Is That?
PETER TRUMBULL

Yellow Hat, Red Hat
BASIA BOGDANOWICZ

Zoe's Hats
SHARON LANE HOLM

Rhythms, Rhymes, and Fingerplays

Hats

A cowboy wears a cowboy hat *(hands
   encircle head)*
As he gallops on his horse. *(galloping
   motion)*
A firefighter's hat keeps her safe *(hands
   encircle head)*
As fires run their course. *(spraying motion
   as with hose)*
A clown wears a pointy hat *(hands form
   point on head)*
And a smile upon his face. *(smile broadly)*
And astronauts wear helmets, *(encircle
   face with hands)*
When blasting into space. *(palms together,
   shoot hands up to sky)*

Paper Hat

Fold the paper just in half, *(arms wide apart,*
   bring hands together over head)
And turn the corners down. *(drop first one hand*
   in front, then the other)
Fold up the edges like this . . . and that. *(elbows in,*
   raise one hand to shoulder; repeat on other side)
Now put it on. *(hands move to head)*
It's a paper hat! *(hands form point on head)*

Mary Has a Blue Hat On
(tune: "Mary Had a Little Lamb")

Mary has a blue hat on,
Blue hat on, blue hat on.
Mary has a blue hat on
She'll wear it today.

[Repeat with other names and colors.]

Parents' Follow-Up Ideas

Make a simple strip-hat using a 2″-wide strip of paper, measuring the length around your child's head and securing the ends with tape. Decorate the front with crayons or markers or add a picture of a hat cut from magazines, advertising, or catalogs. Encourage your child to wear the cowboy (police, sports, or Easter) hat when pretending. To better preserve the hat, untape it and cover it with clear contact paper before reassembling it. Store strip-hats on stuffed animals or un-taped and lying flat in a box.

Create a hat game using pictures of all kinds of hats cut from magazines, advertising, or catalogs and mounted on index cards. Your child can play a matching game, sort the hat collection by colors or sizes, and put hats on people (or animals) in other books or magazines. Talk about the different kinds of hats (sizes, colors, shapes) and who wears them for work or play. Encourage your toddler to be silly sometimes: "This boy doesn't wear his hat on his head; he wears it on his foot!" Keep the hat collection in a "hat box" made from a plastic container with a lid or a shoe box.

Tired of looking for missing hats and mittens at home? Attach a strip of Velcro (the scratchy, hooked side) along the wall behind the door. When children come home, they'll enjoy pressing their knitted mittens or hats to the strip to hold them in place. Mount the Velcro strip away from high-traffic areas because it also sticks to sweaters, scarves, and other fabrics as they pass by.

Craft

Helmets

You will need: plastic milk gallon jug, washed thoroughly

scissors and packing knife

adhesive or cloth tape

glue

permanent markers

cloth and paper scraps

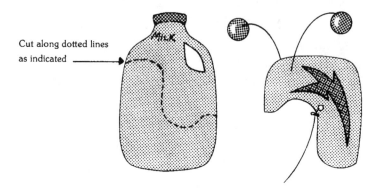

Cut along dotted lines as indicated ⟶

Cut the milk jug in one continuous movement, removing the spout and lid, handle, and top of jug. What is left is a piece of bowl-shaped plastic that will form the body of the helmet. Place it over your child's head and mark where it should be cut away so it does not rub against shoulders, ears, or neck. You may have to stuff a small towel inside it to make it sit right on your child's head. Cover the edges with tape to avoid scratches.

When the helmet fits comfortably, decorate it with markers or scraps to create a motorcycle, football, or astronaut helmet.

Program Notes

Sign Language

HAT   Pat the top of your head with the right hand.

Note: At the end of the previous week, invite children to wear hats to the next program. Have paper hats available for children who come without them, letting them decide whether or not they want to participate.

Reinforce the theme when assembling the clown-shape puzzle: the triangle is the clown's hat.

The story *Caps for Sale* can be used several ways: with the book, as a flannelboard story, and as a play with the children being the monkeys and using baseball caps, paper, or pretend hats. The rhyme "Mary Has a Blue Hat On" makes a good flannelboard presentation using different-colored hats and a smiling felt face.

Giveaways are paper hats folded from newspaper or wrapping paper with children's names printed on them. Be sure to tape the corners so they don't come unfolded, and if it is windy, remind children to "hold on to your hats" as they leave.

Since some bakers wear chefs' hats, fingertaster "tastes" things made in bakeries, such as bread, muffins, cake, cookies, etc.

Children exit the story space wearing their hats.

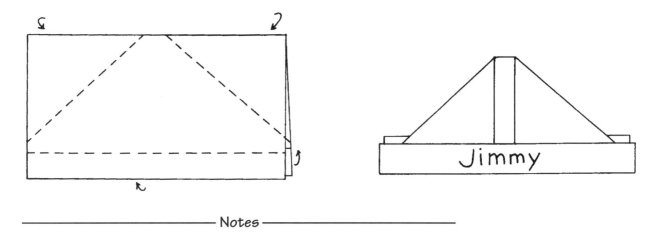

—————— Notes ——————

Helping

Books

Big Help
ANNA GROSSNICKLE HINES

Brave Bear
KATHY MALLAT

Clifford's Good Deeds
   (Spanish: *Las buenas*
   acciones de Clifford)
NORMAN BRIDWELL

Five Little Monkeys Wash the Car
EILEEN CHRISTELOW

How Kind!
MARY MURPHY

Hurray for Elephant!
JANET ALLISON BROWN

The Little Red Hen
PAUL GALDONE

Maisy Cleans Up
LUCY COUSINS

My Apron
ERIC CARLE

Pizza Party!
GRACE MACCARONE

Sophie's Window
HOLLY KELLER

Spot Helps Out
ERIC HILL

Tidy Titch
PAT HUTCHINS

What Do I Do?
(English/Spanish)
NORMA SIMON

What's the Magic Word?
KELLY DIPUCCHIO

You and Me, Little Bear
MARTIN WADDELL

Rhythms, Rhymes, and Fingerplays

Clean Up Song   (tune: "Mary Had a Little Lamb")

We can help pick up the toys,
   (mimic the action)
Up the toys, up the toys.
We can help pick up the toys,
To make things nice and neat.

[Repeat with]
   wipe off the chair
   sort the clothes
   dust the house
   sweep the floor
   pick up rug spots (carpet squares)

I Can Help

Push the button
On the elevator door.
  (mimic actions)
Pick up toys
Lying on the floor.
Feed the dog,
Water the cat.
Take off my shoes,
Put on my hat.
Pour a drink,
Wipe up my mess.
Turn off the light,
Get undressed.
There are lots of ways
Throughout the day
  (hands spread wide)
I help Mommy *(point to self)*
As we work and play.

One, Two, Buckle My Shoe

One, two, buckle my shoe.
  (touch shoe)
Three, four, shut the door.
  (bring hands together)
Five, six, pick up sticks.
  (pretend to pick up objects)
Seven, eight, lay them straight.
  (pretend to lay objects in a row)
Nine, ten, do it again.

[Repeat once]

Parents' Follow-Up Ideas

Make cleaning up and putting away toys into a game by cutting sil-houettes of toys or common items out of contact paper (or use pic-tures from magazines). Apply the pictures to shelves or outsides of drawers where the items should be stored. By putting the correct item in the right place, your child is cleaning up and practicing matching skills at the same time.

Toddlers can pick things up and put them in the trash, put things away, carry light objects, help set the table, wash and dry their own hands, empty a small trash can, sponge off the table, help dust, feed some pets, sort laundry by colors and types of clothes, and put away unbreakable, reachable groceries or dishes.

Have child-sized tools or similar toys (a toy lawn mower will double as a vacuum cleaner) for your toddlers to use and encourage them to mimic you as you do chores. This will improve their physical coordination, observation, and sequencing skills. Talk about the kind of help you need with a job and describe step-by-step how you will do it, using "first we . . . , then we . . ." Keep instructions simple and review them at each step, admiring your child's assistance and progress, as well as the result of a job well done together. Name all the tools you are using, such as a vacuum cleaner, broom, rake, or wheelbarrow, and talk about how you are working, "dust under the table . . . pick up the leaves behind the bush . . ." Keep mock cleaning tools (sponge, bucket, small broom) in the child's play area.

Craft

Refrigerator Magnets

You will need: pictures (cut from magazines,
                     advertising flyers, food labels, or catalogs)

      index cards

      glue

      magnetic strips (available in craft stores)

      scissors

      clear contact paper (optional)

Using pictures of your child's favorite foods, glue them to index cards to make them more durable. (Optional: cover with clear contact paper to make them cleanable.) Cut a piece of magnetic strip and peel the paper from the adhesive side. Attach the magnetic strip to the back of the food picture. They will now stick to any metal appliance.

Let your child use the food magnets to help decide what to have for breakfast or lunch, creating picture menus on the refrigerator. Or play a sorting game naming the food and the food group to which it belongs ("Apple is a fruit"). Help your toddler create a meal plan by suggesting, "pick a vegetable to go with that," or "what fruit do you want for dessert?" Food magnets can also create lists for the grocery store or picnic basket.

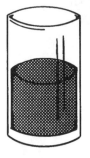

Store magnets in a box or can near the refrigerator, or make a magnetic storage box out of a sturdy box (Velveeta cheese), applying long magnetic strips to the back.

Make other refrigerator magnets of people, shapes, objects, animals, and activities. A set of household-chore magnets can be used on the washing machine or dryer to entertain your toddler while you are working or to plan chores you can both do together. Take the magnets on the road using a cookie sheet (with a rim so the magnets don't slide off) or a large coffee can (covering the rim with cloth tape to protect little fingers).

Program Notes

Sign Language

HELP   Lay your left fist in the palm of the right hand and raise them both upward, as though your right hand were giving assistance to the left.

This is a fun theme because toddlers *love* to help. The storytime puppet introduces the theme by announcing it is time to clean something (a small portion of the story space, a table, chair, the flannelboard, or the lap stage). Have several small cleaning tools on hand (cloths, pails, brooms, etc.), and let the children help with pretend cleaning. They can dust, sweep, wipe, and brush the space or object until you or the puppet declares it clean. Make sure to praise them for their assistance and the great job they do.

Throughout the program, make opportunities for children to "help" with the stories or their props, moving pieces on the flannelboard or holding objects. Singing the "Clean Up Song," the storyteller and the children pick up the carpet squares or put books in a box at the end of the program.

Giveaways are "helper" aprons (similar to nail aprons obtained free or inexpensively from lumberyards). They can be made by folding a pocket into a rectangle of fabric, then folding the upper edge over a ribbon and gluing the edges with fabric glue.

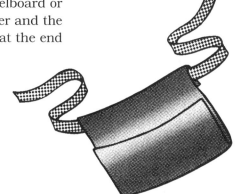

Fingertaster "tastes" condiments, such as ketchup, mustard, chocolate sauce, etc.

Children exit the story space "sweeping" the floor.

———————————————— Notes ————————————————

Homes

Books

Animal Homes
SONIA BLACK

Building a House
BYRON BARTON

Do Lions Live on Lily Pads?
MELANIE WALSH

Goodbye House
FRANK ASCH

Houses and Homes
ANN MORRIS

Little House, Little Town
SCOTT BECK

Moving Day
ROBERT KALAN

Moving from One to Ten
SHARI HALPERN

My House / Mi casa
(English/Spanish)
REBECCA EMBERLEY

My Very First Look at My Home
CHRISTIANE GUNZI

Nicky Upstairs and Down
HARRIET ZIEFERT

Nonna's Porch
RITA GRAY

There's a Cow in the Cabbage Patch
   (Spanish: *Hay una vaca entre las coles*)
CLARE BEATON

This Is My House
   (Spanish: *Ésta es mi casa*)
ARTHUR DORROS

Where Does Maisy Live?
   (Spanish: *¿Donde vive Maisy?*)
LUCY COUSINS

Whose House Is This?
CHARLES REASONER

Rhythms, Rhymes, and Fingerplays

Houses

This is a nest for a bluebird. *(cup hands together)*
This is a hive for a bee. *(close hands together)*
This is the hole for a bunny rabbit *(arms form circle)*
And this is a house for me! *(peak fingers over head)*

Do You Know Where I Live?
   (tune: "Did You Ever See a Lassie?")

[Chorus]

Do you know where I live?
Where I live, where I live?
Do you know where I live?
Where I make my home?

I live in a red barn,
A red barn, a red barn.
I live in a red barn,
And I am a cow.

I live in a big tree,
A big tree, a big tree.
I live in a big tree,
And I am a squirrel.

I live in a little hole,
A little hole, a little hole.
I live in a little hole,
And I am a rabbit.

I Shut the Door

I shut the door.
   (clap hands sharply)
I locked it tight,
   (turn wrist in locking motion)
And put the key out of sight.
   (pretend to put in pocket)
I went to play in the bright sunlight.
   (wave hands over head)

I found the key to open the door,
   ("pull" key from pocket)
And turned, and turned, and turned
   some more. *(repeat locking motions)*
And then I opened the door! *(move
   hands apart)*

Parents' Follow-Up Ideas

Help your child learn the different names for places where people live: houses, town houses, duplexes, condos, apartments, mobile homes, travel trailers or motor homes, motels, etc. Point out the various parts of buildings where people live and the names for them: structures (windows, doors, walls, stairs, porches), rooms (kitchens, bathrooms, bedrooms, closets), and furnishings (chairs, sofas, beds). Talk about others' homes you have visited—those of friends and relatives. Do the same with animal homes, encouraging children to be creative: "Do you think a dog would live in a tree?"

Create "homes" for stuffed animals, puppets, or dolls using different sizes of boxes, baskets, grocery sacks, etc. Help children make their own villages by cutting doors and windows for them so the residents can go in and see out. Talk about where different kinds of people or animals might live and why. Even if a toy is "homeless," you can talk about the kind of places it would like to live in.

Homes are where people receive letters, and *all* children love to get mail. Help children "write" to friends or relatives who will correspond with them. Cut the fronts off old greeting cards and use them as postcards (the postage is less expensive). Your children can draw a picture or dictate a message to put on them. Let your children choose colorful stamps at the post office, attach them, and post them through mail slots or mailboxes. Talk about how mail carriers help take messages from one place to another. Make a pretend mailbox at home with a slot and a back door, and set aside all the "junk" mail for your children, giving them stickers for stamps.

Craft

Bird Feeder

You will need: peanut butter

Styrofoam cup

piece of string

birdseed

Tie a knot in one end of the string. Make a small hole in the bottom of the cup and thread the string through the hole with the knot on the inside. Cover the cup, inside and out, with peanut butter and roll it in birdseed until it is well covered. Hang the cup outside near a window so you can watch the birds eat!

Program Notes

Sign Language

HOUSE   Peak your hands over the head, separate hands and move them sideways and down, like a roofline.

Introduce the theme with the storytime puppet or stuffed animal talking about where it lives: in a closet, in a pocket, etc. If stories about "moving" will predominate, the puppet brings a box and asks the children to help pack some of its stuff (books, hat, clothes, etc.). Follow up at next week's program with the puppet mentioning its new home and unpacking all its favorite things.

For the song "Do You Know Where I Live?" put different animal pictures on the flannelboard and extend the song into an activity by having the children make animal sounds or move like the animals. Using a shoe box with a slot in the lid, let children "mail" letters to a buddy-puppet or absent friend. Gather unopened "junk" mail, giving one envelope to each child who then puts it in the mailbox. Distribute your program handouts as "letters" from this same mailbox.

Giveaways are key bookmarks made by copying this page.

Fingertaster "tastes" flavors in the kitchen, such as bread, cheese, peanut butter, etc.

Children exit the story space carrying pretend boxes for the puppet who's moving, which they can "leave" in the children's area.

———— Notes ————

Love (Valentine's Day)

Books

Ask Mr. Bear
MARJORIE FLACK

Corduroy (Also in Spanish)
DON FREEMAN

Counting Kisses
KAREN KATZ

The Cuddle Book
GUIDO VAN GENECHTEN

Guess How Much I Love You
    (Spanish: *Adivina cuanto
    te quiero*)
SAM MCBRATNEY

Honey Baby Sugar Child
ALICE FAYE DUNCAN

I Love You! A Bushel and a Peck
FRANK LOESSER AND ROSEMARY WELLS

I Love You All Day Long
FRANCESCA RUSACKAS

I Love You as Much . . .
LAURA KRAUSS MELMED

I Love You Like Crazy Cakes
ROSE A. LEWIS

Kiss Kiss!
MARGARET WILD AND BRIDGET
STREVENS-MARZO

On Mother's Lap
    (Spanish: *En las piernas de
    Mamá*)
ANN HERBERT SCOTT

Snuggle Puppy!
SANDRA BOYNTON

What Is Valentine's Day?
HARRIET ZIEFERT

Won't You Be My Hugaroo?
JOANNE RYDER AND MELISSA SWEET

*Word Bird's Valentine's
Day Words*
JANE BELK MONCURE

Rhythms, Rhymes, and Fingerplays

Skinna-Marinky   (tune: "Skinnamarink")

Skinna-marinky dinky dink, skinna-marinky doo.
    (sway gently)
I *(point to self)* love *(cross arms across chest)* you!
    (point to child)
Skinna-marinky dinky dink, skinna-marinky doo.
I *(point to self)* love *(cross arms across chest)* you!
    (point to child)
I love you in the morning, and in the afternoon.
    (sway side to side, arms crossed over chest)
I love you in the evening, and underneath the moon.
    (arms open wide)
Oh, skinna-marinky dinky dink, skinna-marinky doo.
I *(point to self)* love *(cross arms across chest)* you!
    (point to child)

Make a Valentine

Snip, snip, snip. *(move index fingers
    close and apart)*
Paste, paste, paste. *(brush fingers
    of one hand on other palm)*
And press the paper together.
    (press palms together)
Look and see, *(open palms and peek inside)*
It's from me! *(point to self)*
A valentine just for you! *(pretend to pick up card
    from palm and hand to child)*

I Have a Little Heart

I have a little heart *(hand over heart)*
And it goes thump, thump, thump
    (pat chest with fingers)
It keeps right on beating
When I jump, jump, jump. *(jump in place)*

I get a special feeling *(hug shoulders)*
When I look at you. *(point to children)*
It makes me want to give you
    (shrug shoulders shyly)
A kiss or two! *(storyteller blows kisses
    to child, parent kisses child on cheek)*

Parents' Follow-Up Ideas

Everyone likes to know they are loved. Tell your children often that you care. Especially when disciplining them or dealing with stressful situations, help them understand that you can dislike something they've done while continuing to love them. Touching is an important way to show children that they are loved. Make sure your toddlers get lots of hugs, kisses, and tender touches every day. It makes you feel good, too.

Hearts are a universal symbol of love. Cut folded heart shapes from different colors and textures of paper (sandpaper, tissue paper, aluminum foil, embossed wallpaper, etc.). Vary the sizes. Let your children sort them by sizes and colors or line them up with large ones on one end and small ones on the other. Talk about the different textures and how they look and feel. Make two sets of textured hearts, putting one set in a box or sack. Your child can hold one heart in his or her hand and reach into the box to locate the other by feel.

Cut the fronts from old greeting cards and make a colorful book with them. Punch a hole in the upper left corner and thread the cards together on ribbon or yarn. Loosely tie a knot in the ribbon so the "pages" of the book can be easily turned. Make up stories about the pictures on the cards. Use the card book as a counting book, counting hearts, bears, or any common objects.

Craft

Ribbon Bookmark

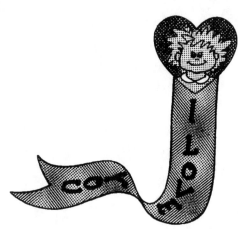

You will need: a photograph (that can be cut)

scissors

a 6″ piece of ribbon (or colored paper)

glue

felt-tipped marking pen

Cut the photograph into the shape of a heart with the person's face in the center of the heart. Glue the heart photo to one end of the ribbon and let it dry thoroughly.

With a marking pen, write a special message on the bookmark like "I Love You," "Best Grandma," "Big Sister," or the name of the person in the picture or the one receiving the bookmark.

Program Notes

Sign Language

LOVE   Cross your arms over the chest with hands on shoulders, like a hug.

The storytime puppet introduces the theme by bringing a paper heart to the storyteller.

The book *Ask Mr. Bear* works well as a flannelboard story; finish it by having the children give big "bear" hugs to their adults.

Giveaways are construction-paper hearts made by folding the paper and cutting an arc along the fold line.

Fingertaster "tastes" sweet things, such as honey, jelly, sugar, etc.

Children exit the story space after giving the fingertaster or storytime puppet a big hug.

———————————————————— Notes ————————————————————

—————— Mealtimes (Thanksgiving) ——————

Books

The Best Mouse Cookie
LAURA NUMEROFF AND FELICIA BOND

Crunch Munch
JONATHAN LONDON

Hunky Dory Ate It
KATIE EVANS

*I Know an Old Lady Who
Swallowed a Fly*
COLIN HAWKINS AND JACQUI HAWKINS

I Like a Snack on an Iceberg
IRIS HISKEY ARNO

Let's Eat / Vamos a comer
(English/Spanish)
ALAN BENJAMIN

Lunch
DENISE FLEMING

Maisy Makes Gingerbread
LUCY COUSINS

Max's Breakfast
ROSEMARY WELLS

My Food / Mi comida
(English/Spanish)
REBECCA EMBERLEY

Ruby's Dinnertime
PAUL AND EMMA ROGERS

Sam's Cookie
BARBRO LINDGREN

Spot's Thanksgiving
ERIC HILL

What Is Thanksgiving?
HARRIET ZIEFERT

Who Eats?
EDWINA LEWIS

Yummy Yucky
LESLIE PATRICELLI

Rhythms, Rhymes, and Fingerplays

Yummy Lunch   (tune: "Little Drummer Boy")

I'll have some pizza. Yummy-yum-yum.
Some crunchy carrots. Yummy-yum-yum.
A glass of milk, please. Yummy-yum-yum.
Grapes for dessert now. Yummy-yum-yum,
Yummy-yum-yum, yummy-yum-yum.
Fill up my tum! *(rub hand on tummy)*

The Apple Tree

Away up high in the apple tree *(point up)*
Two red apples smiled at me. *(point to self)*
I shook that tree as hard as I could,
    (shaking motion)
And down they came . . . *(point down)*
Mmmmm, they were good! *(rub tummy)*

Doughnut

Here is a doughnut *(form circle with*
    thumbs and forefingers)
Round and fat.
There's a hole in the middle *(hold finger-*
    circle up and look through it)
But you can't eat that!! *(shake head)*

It's Almost Thanksgiving

Run, turkey, run! *(pat knees)*
Run, turkey, run!
It's almost Thanksgiving.
Run, turkey, run!

Roll, pumpkin, roll! *(roll hands)*
Roll, pumpkin, roll!
It's almost Thanksgiving.
Roll, pumpkin, roll!

Grow, corn, grow! *(raise arms above head)*
Grow, corn, grow!
It's almost Thanksgiving.
Grow, corn, grow!

Eat, children, eat! *(make eating motion)*
Eat, children, eat!
It is now Thanksgiving.
Eat, children, eat!

Parents' Follow-Up Ideas

Cut pictures from magazines or labels from cans or boxes. Glue them to index cards to make a matching game. You will need two pictures of each food. Turn all the cards facedown on the table or floor. Take turns with your child, turning over two cards at a time. Examine the pictures and name the food. Do the cards match? If so, remove them. If not, turn them facedown and put them back in the same place. Talk with your child as you turn over the first card to demonstrate how you identify the picture and remember if you've seen one like it before: "Here is a banana! I remember seeing another banana before. Where was that? You are right! It was in the top row." This game helps toddlers develop their memories and learn more words about foods, colors, shapes, and spatial concepts.

Make a food book by gluing pictures to notebook or typing paper. Start with your child's favorite foods. (*Hint:* Glue sticks are easier for toddlers to handle than bottles of glue.) Staple pages together or put them in a three-ring binder. Group pictures together in larger food groups: vegetables, fruits, breads, meats, etc. Encourage your child to put foods together to make pretend meals or create meal pages.

Gather pictures of foods together on one page for breakfasts, lunches, snacks, and dinners.

Before taking your children to eat in a restaurant, playact the experience at home. Let them help you make a menu of lunch choices using the food pictures (above). Take turns pretending to be the customer and the waitstaff. Unlike home, where children can play until called to a meal that is ready and waiting for them, there are always delays in restaurants. Help your children understand the reasons they (and everybody else) must wait until the meal is served. Plan things you can do at the restaurant while waiting for the food to come.

Craft

Fingertasting Sock Puppet

You will need: an old sock with toe and heel intact

needle and thread

notions for features (buttons, pompoms, yarn)

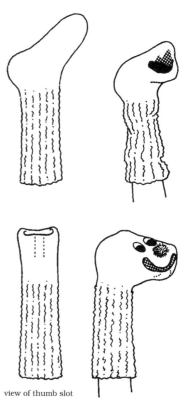

Place the sock over your hand with the heel over your knuckles. Open your fingers wide inside the sock and tuck the toe into the palm of your hand. With needle and thread, sew the underside of the sock "mouth," forming a slot into which your thumb can slide.

Sew on eyes, keeping them close to the mouth opening. Add nose, hair, clothes . . . whatever you want to make the puppet real. Please, no teeth, however. Keep the puppet nonthreatening. Features can be made with any scraps or odds and ends you have around. Avoid using materials that cannot be washed. The puppet can be thrown in the laundry with the family clothes.

Sock puppets are very flexible, "make faces" easily, and can be used by adults or children. Practice moving your fingers inside the puppet to make happy faces, sad faces, and silly faces.

To taste fingers: Have the puppet gently suck or lick the fingers of children with a slurping sound, and then tell each child what his or her finger tasted like. Use flavors with which the children are familiar.

view of thumb slot

Program Notes

Sign Language

EAT   With the tips of your thumb and fingertips together, tap your mouth twice.

Note: Snacks lend themselves to this theme, but take care since some children have food allergies (milk, flour, sugar, peanuts). Check with adults the previous week, and if there are children who cannot have the planned snack, cancel it or ask the adult for a suitable alternative that will work for all program participants.

Introduce the theme by putting a bib on the storytime puppet who is going out to dinner. Between stories children pretend mealtimes: washing hands, setting the table, eating, drinking, and washing dishes. Use simple felt shapes for a flannelboard table setting, letting children help: large circle = plate, small circle = glass, rectangles = spoon and fork.

A sack puppet version of the song "I Know an Old Lady Who Swallowed a Fly" with a window stomach (pattern in appendix A) is always popular.

Giveaways are place mats made of large pieces of construction paper. Each has a child's name written on it and table-setting shapes glued on. The place mats will last longer if they are laminated.

Fingertaster "tastes" restaurant foods, such as French fries, hamburgers, and pizza, or traditional Thanksgiving foods, such as turkey, pumpkin pie, corn on the cob, etc.

——————————————— Notes ———————————————

Monkeys

Books

Busy Monkeys
JOHN SCHINDEL AND
LUIZ CLAUDIO MARIGO

Curious George
　(Spanish: *Jorge el curioso*)
H. A. REY

Don't Be Pesky, Little Monkey
RONNE RANDALL

Eight Silly Monkeys
　(Spanish: *Ocho monitos*)
STEVE HASKAMP

*Five Little Monkeys
Sitting in a Tree*
　(Spanish: *En un árbol están los
　cinco monitos*)
EILEEN CHRISTELOW

Good Night, Gorilla
PEGGY RATHMANN

Hug
JEZ ALBOROUGH

I'm a Little Monkey
TIM WEARE

Little Gorilla
　(Spanish: *Gorilita*)
RUTH BORNSTEIN

Monkey See, Monkey Do
MARC GAVE

Monkey's Play Time
JANE CABRERA

Okomi Enjoys His Outings
HELEN AND CLIVE DORMAN

One Monkey Too Many
JACKIE FRENCH KOLLER

Tom and Pippo's Day
HELEN OXENBURY

*What Do You Say When a
Monkey Acts This Way?*
JANE BELK MONCURE

Who Is Coming?
PATRICIA MCKISSACK

Rhythms, Rhymes, and Fingerplays

Five Little Monkeys

Five little monkeys *(hold up five fingers)*
Swinging in a tree. *(swing hands over head)*
Teasing Mr. Crocodile *(shake one finger)*
"You can't catch me. *(point to self, shake head)*
You can't catch me!"
Up comes Mr. Crocodile quiet as can be.
　(palms together, move hands upward)
Snap! *(clap hands, sharply)*

[Repeat with]
　　Four
　　Three
　　Two
　　One

Pop Goes the Weasel   (traditional song)

All around the mulberry bush *(turn in circle)*
The monkey chased the weasel. *(make grabbing motions)*
The monkey thought 'twas all in fun. *(shake one finger)*
Pop! *(clap hands)* goes the weasel.

Monkey See, Monkey Do

When you clap, clap, clap your hands *(clap hands)*
The monkey clap, clap, claps his hands. *(clap hands)*
Monkey see *(shade eyes with hands)*
Monkey do *(repeat first motion)*
Monkey does the same as you. *(point to child)*

[Repeat with]

stamp, stamp, stamp your feet
jump, jump, jump up high
make, make, make a funny face
turn, turn, turn around

Parents' Follow-Up Ideas

Monkey see, monkey do is a simple version of "Simon Says" that teaches your child to listen and follow directions. Begin with small actions ("touch your nose"; "reach up high"; "clap your hands") and save bigger actions for out-of-doors or places with lots of room ("run fast"; "jump high"; "twirl around").

Inexpensive painting books are available at department stores with the colors imbedded into the pages. When you add water with a paintbrush, the colors come out. These books will not promote artistic ability in your child, but they are good for learning to work with a small tool like a paintbrush.

Another way to paint with water in warm weather is to fill a can with water and let your child "paint" the house, the sidewalk, or driveway. Talk about evaporation as the water dries and becomes invisible.

Craft

Clown-Shape Puzzle

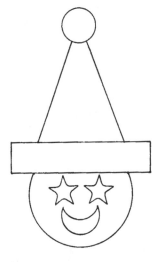

You will need: brightly colored pieces of felt in the following shapes:

1 rectangle

1 triangle

1 large and 1 small circle

2 small stars

1 crescent (for smile)

For circles, trace around objects (margarine tubs or salt shakers) onto the felt. Use a ruler to draw the rectangle and triangle. Do not worry about pencil marks since the pieces can easily be flipped over when used. Draw the stars and crescent freehand.

Talk with your child about the shapes of these puzzle pieces and their colors. Take turns arranging and rearranging them on a table, sofa cushion, or flannelboard to form a clown's face. Make additional pieces and see what other designs or pictures you can create.

Program Notes

Sign Language

MONKEY   Curl your hands under your arms and make a scratching motion along the sides of the body.

The storytime puppet introduces the theme with a stuffed or toy monkey, teaching children to "chatter" like monkeys.

The "Five Little Monkeys" rhyme works well with flannelboard figures or glove puppets as well as an action rhyme. After all the monkeys have been taken by the crocodile, have the crocodile put them back into the tree again as everyone counts. (This is reassuring to young children, and they love to count.)

Giveaways are paper sack monkey puppets made with lunch sacks, photocopied monkey faces, and yarn for a tail.

Fingertaster "tastes" things made with bananas, such as banana pudding, banana sandwiches, banana pie, etc.

Children exit the story space chattering like monkeys.

———————————————— Notes ————————————————

——————— Morning ———————

Books

Early Morning in the Barn
NANCY TAFURI

Good Morning, Baby
CHERYL WILLIS HUDSON

Good Morning, Chick
MIRRA GINSBURG

Good Morning, Sam
MARIE-LOUISE GAY

Greetings, Sun
PHILLIS AND DAVID GERSHATOR

The Grumpy Morning
PAMELA DUNCAN EDWARDS

Hey! Wake Up!
SANDRA BOYNTON

Maisy's Morning on the Farm
LUCY COUSINS

Milton the Early Riser
ROBERT KRAUS

Moo in the Morning
BARBARA MAITLAND

My Day / Mi día
(English/Spanish)
REBECCA EMBERLEY

Now It Is Morning
CANDACE WHITMAN

On a Wintry Morning
DORI CHACONAS

Sunshine
JAN ORMEROD

Wake Up, Big Barn!
SUZANNE TANNER CHITWOOD

Wake Up, Sun!
DAVID L. HARRISON

Rhythms, Rhymes, and Fingerplays

Good Morning   (tune: "Good Morning")

Good morning! Good morning! *(sing very slowly,
    as though waking up)*
Wake up and stretch today. *(stretching motion)*
Good morning . . . good morning . . . to you!
    (continue stretching)
Good morning! Good morning! *(say a little faster:
    wave hand slowly)*
Wake UP and then we'll say, *(eyes closed,
    then they pop open on* up*)*
Good morning, GOOD MORNING to you.
    (wave slowly)
It's the top of the morning, *(arms sweep over
    head and open wide)*
And I'm here to say, *(point to self)*
We're going to make this *(gesture to group)*
A grand . . . new . . . day! *(clap)*

Good morning! Good morning! *(wave hand energetically)*
   energetically)
Jump UP and start the day! *(jump)*
Good morning, good morning to you . . .
   (point to child)
And you . . . and you and you and you.
   (point to different children)
GOOD MORNING! *(call loudly, clapping hands)*

Today   (Clapping Rhyme)

Today is Monday,
   (insert current day of the week)
Today is Monday,
Today is Monday,
What'll we do today?
Wake up, sleepy head.
Wake up, sleepy head.
Wake up, sleepy head.
It's a brand-new day!

Looking Out the Window   (tune: "Paw-Paw Patch")

In the morning looking out my window.
In the morning looking out my window.
In the morning looking out my window.
What do I see today?

[Additional verses]

   I see sunshine, looking out my window.
     (insert current weather)
   I see cats and dogs, looking out my window.
   I see people, looking out my window.

Parents' Follow-Up Ideas

A successful way to gently wake sleeping children is to tickle their ears while softly calling their names. This technique is successfully used by child-care professionals.

For a child who wakes up early, bundle up and go outside (or to an east-facing window) to watch the sun rise. Once it begins, a sunrise happens quickly. Talk about the changes happening as the sky gets lighter and objects go from being invisible to silhouettes to being recognizable. What other changes can you notice? If you live in the city, streetlights may turn off. Does the wind change? Are there new sounds? New smells? When the sun is bright enough, dance with your shadows.

Weather predicting is difficult (even for the experts), but weather watching is easy. Pick a window through which your toddler can see the outdoors, and help your child determine what kind of weather is occurring each morning. Talk about obvious signs, such as the sun shining, thunder, or snow on the ground. Also discuss other clues you see: people dressed warmly, flags blowing, or umbrellas. Use weather words and phrases to help your child learn. Keep a weather calendar or weather wheel nearby. Let your toddler mark the calendar with stickers or a simple drawing. When weather changes during the day, talk about how it changed and how you know it changed.

Craft

Weather Wheel

You will need: 2 paper plates

sharp pencil

brass fastener

scissors

washable markers or weather
pictures cut from magazines

Punch a hole in the center of both plates. Divide one plate into six or eight pie-shaped pieces. Draw (or glue) pictures in each section to represent normal weather conditions. Label each picture with descriptive words. Using the other paper plate, cut out a wedge the same size as one of the sections so that the pictures will show through the opening when the plates are placed together. With the cut plate on top, attach both plates together using the brass fastener. The bottom plate will rotate, displaying one weather picture at a time in the window. Let your child make a weather observation each morning and turn the bottom plate until the corresponding weather picture shows. When weather patterns change, encourage your child to change the picture again. To hang the weather wheel, glue or tape a string to the back of the top plate. To change weather pictures, remove the brass fastener and make a new bottom plate.

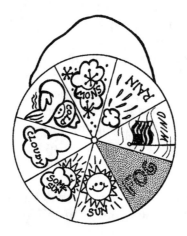

Program Notes

Sign Language

MORNING   With the fingers of the open left hand in the crook of the extended right arm, bring the right palm upward toward the face, like the rising of the sun.

The storytime puppet introduces the theme by arriving very sleepy with a blanket in tow and asking for help waking up. Children can call its name, tickle it under the chin, "ring" like an alarm clock, or come up with their own ideas of how to help the puppet wake. If there is a window nearby, encourage children to look outside to determine the weather so the puppet can get dressed.

Children enjoy making the morning noises of farms, starting with crowing roosters. Make one story a flannelboard farm morning and encourage children to contribute the sounds.

Giveaways are window stickers made by sandwiching a large sticker or magazine picture between two layers of plastic wrap. The wrap sticks to the window and can be easily removed.

Fingertaster "tastes" breakfast foods, such as cereal, toast, pancakes, orange juice, etc.

Children exit the story space singing the "Good Morning" song.

————————————— Notes —————————————

My Body

Books

Belly Button Book
SANDRA BOYNTON

Bright Eyes, Brown Skin
CHERYL WILLIS HUDSON AND
BERNETTE G. FORD

Busy Toes
C. W. BOWIE

Eyes, Nose, Fingers, and Toes
JUDY HINDLEY

Feet Are Not for Kicking
ELIZABETH VERDICK

Hand, Hand, Fingers, Thumb
AL PERKINS

Hands Are Not for Hitting
MARTINE AGASSI

Hands Can
CHERYL WILLIS HUDSON

Hello Toes! Hello Feet!
ANN WHITFORD PAUL

My First Body Board Book / Mi primer libro del cuerpo
(English/Spanish)

One Little Spoonful
ALIKI

Rainbow Is Our Face
LAURA PEGRAM

Teeth Are Not for Biting
ELIZABETH VERDICK

Toes, Ears, and Nose!
MARION DANE BAUER

Where Is Baby's Belly Button?
KAREN KATZ

Wiggle Your Toes
KAREN KATZ

Rhythms, Rhymes, and Fingerplays

Head and Shoulders   (song)

Head and shoulders, knees and toes.
  (touch each)
Knees and toes, knees and toes.
Head and shoulders, knees and toes.
Eyes and ears and mouth and nose.

[Repeat, starting slowly and getting faster.]

I Have a Nose

On my face I have a nose, *(point to nose)*
And way down here I have ten toes. *(point to toes)*
I have two eyes that I can blink. *(blink eyes)*
I have a head to help me think. *(hands on head)*
I have a chin and very near, *(point to chin)*
I have two ears to help me hear. *(hands on ears)*
I have a mouth I use to speak, *(point to mouth)*
And when I run, I use my feet. *(point to feet)*

Here are my arms I hold up high, *(raise arms high)*
And here's my hand to wave good-bye. *(wave)*

We Can Jump

We can jump, jump, jump.
   (follow the actions)
We can hop, hop, hop.
We can clap, clap, clap.
We can stop, stop, stop.
We can nod our heads for "yes,"
We can shake our heads for "no."
We can bend our knees a little bit
And sit . . . down . . . slow.

Parents' Follow-Up Ideas

Toddlers need lots of experience hearing words and language. The more you talk to them, the better their language skills will be. Talk through daily routines ("now we let the water go down the drain"), name *everything:* objects ("here's a hammer, a screwdriver, and pliers"), body parts ("your fingers, nails, knuckles, wrist"), animals ("I see a cricket, a robin, an earthworm"), and vehicles ("that truck is a front-loader, and there's a crane"). If you don't know what something is, say so . . . and go to the library together to find a book about it so you both can learn.

Touching different parts of their bodies with their eyes closed is a challenge for toddlers. This is a game that can be practiced anywhere, even in the car when your child is getting restless. "Close your eyes and touch your knee. Open your eyes to see if you found it."

Trace around your child's hands and feet on poster board. Use these patterns to create a mobile out of a hanger or small branch, tying on each foot or hand shape with string. Cut another set out of different colors of paper and let your child match them. Trace hands and feet of family members and compare them with each other.

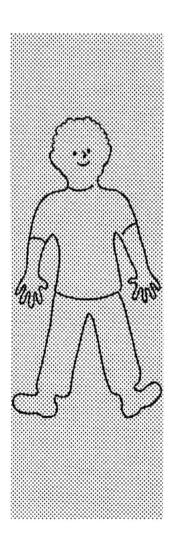

Craft

A Me Picture

You will need: a large grocery sack or wide shelf paper

a pencil

scissors

crayons or washable markers

Cut the bottom from the sack and cut up one side so it will lie flat. Have your child lie down on the sack and quickly trace around him or her. Draw on the features and talk about parts of the body and the clothes that cover them. Color the picture and hang it on a door or the refrigerator or send it as a special card to a grandparent or friend. When you make this activity part of a birthday celebration, you can compare it with last year's picture.

A change of clothes could be made from newspaper or another paper sack and paper-clipped or taped to the picture as situations or weather changes.

Program Notes

Sign Language

ME   Point to yourself with your index finger.

Note: Be sensitive to differences in children with disabilities, pointing out how they are the same as the others, not how they are different.

Introduce the theme by pointing out the facial features on the clown-shape puzzle. Make note of the similarities in people's bodies: two hands, two feet, eyes, hair, noses, etc.

Explore the senses using different musical instruments (bells, drums, horn) for sounds, colors for sight, scents (cinnamon, chocolate, banana) for smell, and textures (sandpaper, fur, terry cloth) for touch, giving each child the opportunity to experience each. A flannelboard face with removable features is a good activity. Let children take turns placing eyes, nose, mouth, ears, hair, eyebrows, etc., on the face.

Giveaways are the traced hands. Provide each adult with paper and pencil to trace his or her hand and then their child's hand inside it.

Fingertaster "tastes" foods with strong smells, such as chocolate, banana, oranges, etc.

Children exit the story space clapping their hands.

———————————————— Notes ————————————————

Parades

Books

Animal Music
HARRIET ZIEFERT

Animal Parade
JAKKI WOOD

The Best Bug Parade
STUART J. MURPHY

Bing: Make Music
TED DEWAN

Clifford and the Big Parade
NORMAN BRIDWELL

Curious George at the Parade
MARGRET AND H. A. REY

The Dancing Dragon
MARCIA VAUGHAN

Gossie and Gertie
OLIVER DUNREA

Here Comes the Big Parade
JANE BELK MONCURE

I Make Music
ELOISE GREENFIELD

Maisy Likes Music
LUCY COUSINS

Our Marching Band
LLOYD MOSS

Parade
DONALD CREWS

Shake Shake Shake
ANDREA AND BRIAN PINKNEY

Spot's Marching Band
ERIC HILL

Thump, Thump, Rat-a-Tat-Tat
GENE BAER

Rhythms, Rhymes, and Fingerplays

Old MacDonald Had a Band   (tune: "Old MacDonald")

Old MacDonald had a band, E-I-E-I-O.
And in that band he had some horns, E-I-E-I-O.
With a toot-toot here,
And a toot-toot there,
Here a toot, there a toot,
Everywhere a toot-toot!
Old MacDonald had a band, E-I-E-I-O.

[Repeat with]
    drums . . . bang, bang
    cymbals . . . crash, crash
    hands . . . clap, clap
    feet . . . stomp, stomp

The Finger Band   (tune: "Mulberry Bush")

The finger band is coming to town,
   (wiggling fingers, move hands from
   behind back to front)
Coming to town, coming to town.
The finger band is coming to town,
So early in the morning.

This is the way they wear their hats,
   (hands form pointed hats on heads)
Wear their hats, wear their hats.
This is the way they wear their hats,
So early in the morning.

[Repeat with]

   This is the way they wave their flags
      (hands above head, wave back and forth)
   This is the way they beat their drums
      (beating motion with hands)
   This is the way they blow their horns
      (hands cup mouth like horn)
   This is the way they clash their cymbals
      (clap hands together)
   This is the way they march along *(stand tall,*
      march lifting feet high)

The finger band is going away, *(wiggling fingers,*
   move hands from front to behind back)
Going away, going away.
The finger band is going away,
So early in the morning.

Here Comes the Parade!

Clap your hands! *(clap hands)*
Stamp your feet! *(stamp feet)*
The parade is coming down the street.
   (march in place)
Bum, bum, bum, *(motion beating a drum)*
A great big drum.
Root-a-toot-toot, *(hands to mouth like*
   blowing a horn)
A horn and flute.
Bang! Bang! Bang! *(clap hands together)*
Cymbals clang.
Ding-ding-ding, *(small ringing motion)*
Triangles ring.
Clap your hands! *(clap hands)*
Stamp your feet! *(stamp feet)*
The parade is coming down the street.
   (march in place, swinging arms high)

Parents' Follow-Up Ideas

Playing "follow-the-leader" teaches your children to be observant, to copy another's movements, and to be a leader. Tie several pull toys together and let your toddlers lead a parade through the house or the yard. Take turns being the parade leader, starting out by having them simply follow where you go. As your children grasp this concept, add actions to be copied while following your lead . . . and vice versa.

Playing with objects (blocks, toys, or boxes) in a line is a lot of fun for toddlers, and it teaches them about sequencing, an important skill for learning to read. Encourage your children to put the objects in a line. Use phrases such as "first, middle, last, between, in front of, and at the end." Play with other space-related concepts, such as on top of, beside, under, and through, to help your children understand how objects relate to each other.

When you read stories to your children, talk about the sequencing: what has already happened, what is happening now, and "what do you think will happen next?" Putting children down for a nap or to bed at night is the perfect opportunity to "sequence" the events of the day. Remember what you've done together and plan something you will do when they wake up. Reviewing the day helps children remember things that happened and reinforces new words they might have heard that day.

Craft

Homemade Musical Instruments

Homemade musical instruments are a lot of fun. Many things in the home can be turned into music makers. Use them to create a parade around the house, to accompany television programs, or while listening to the radio or a record.

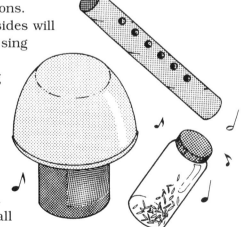

Drums:	Use empty oatmeal boxes, metal pans, or wooden bowls. Beat them with hands or wooden spoons.
Horns:	Cardboard tubes with holes poked in the sides will produce different notes as children hum or sing through one end to create music.
Tambourine:	Use a ring of keys or metal measuring spoons. Shake them away from the body. Also, tie bells on a small aluminum pie tin for a good effect.
Cymbals:	Use two metal lids or aluminum pie pans. Bang them together.
Shaker:	Use a small container with a tightly fitting lid that is half-filled with beans or macaroni. Tape the lid securely in place to keep small items inside. Shake it fast or slow.
Rhythm sticks:	Use two wooden spoons. Bang them together.

Program Notes

Sign Language

DRUM   Make motions like playing a drum.

The storytime puppet introduces the theme with an oatmeal-container drum and lets children take turns beating it. Between stories children can march around the room acting out the "Finger Band" rhyme. The puppet distributes paper plates, which children put on the floor to use as drums. They follow the puppet's lead in beating their drums fast, slow, loud, and quiet. Between two stories, form children into a parade to march around the story space, waving to adults still seated. Marching slower and slower and more and more quietly will prepare them to sit down for the next story.

Put pictures of musical instruments on the flannelboard. Imitate the sound each instrument makes.

Invite children to make the sounds as you point to the instruments.

Giveaways are parade flags made from straws and paper triangles with children's names printed on them.

Fingertaster "tastes" festive foods, such as hot dogs, cotton candy, nachos, etc.

Children exit the story space marching in their own parade.

——————————————— Notes ———————————————

—— Peek, Peek . . . Hide and Seek ——

Books

Find the Teddy
STEPHEN CARTWRIGHT

Five Little Monkeys Play Hide-and-Seek
EILEEN CHRISTELOW

Guess What I Am
ANNI AXWORTHY

Hide and Seek
JEZ ALBOROUGH

Hide and Seek
JANET MORGAN STOEKE

Moongame
FRANK ASCH

Peek! A Thai Hide-and-Seek
MINFONG HO

Peekaboo!
JAN ORMEROD

Peek-a-Who?
MOIRA BUTTERFIELD

Ready, Set, Go!
NINA LADEN

Spot's Treasure Hunt
ERIC HILL

The Surprise
GEORGE SHANNON

Treasure Hunt
ALLAN AHLBERG

Where Is Maisy?
   (Spanish: *¿Donde se esconde Maisy?*)
LUCY COUSINS

Who's at the Door?
JONATHAN ALLEN

You're Just What I Need
RUTH KRAUSS

Rhythms, Rhymes, and Fingerplays

Where Are the Baby Mice?

Where are the baby mice? *(make a fist)*
"Squeak, squeak, squeak!"
I cannot see them *(peer into fist)*
Peek! Peek! Peek!
Here they come from their hole in the wall
1, 2, 3, 4, 5 . . . *(point to fingers)*
And, that's all! *(point to empty palm)*

Someone Is Creeping

Someone* is creeping *(two fingers tiptoe up other forearm)*
Shhhhhhhhhhhhhhh! *(index finger to lips in hushing motion)*
Someone is creeping *(repeat)*
Shhhhhhhhhhhhhhh!

He does not make a sound *(tiptoe finger again)*
As his feet touch the ground.
Someone is creeping.
Shhhhhhhhhhhhhh!

[*insert children's names or animals]

Who's That Knocking?
(tune: "Who's That Knocking at My Door?")

Who's that knocking at my door?
  (make knocking motion)
Who's that knocking at my door?
Who's that knocking at my door?
Guess who is out there?

[chant] KNOCK, KNOCK! *(chant and clap in rhythm)*
  WHO'S THERE?
  MEOW!
  MEOW WHO?
  IT'S A CAT!

[Repeat with other animals, singing the song between
the chants and prompting children for the answer to
the riddle.]

Parents' Follow-Up Ideas

Look out a window with your children and ask, "What do you see?"
Help your children talk about the weather: sunny, snowy, raining.
Are there birds or animals or people? What are they doing? Are there
trucks, bicycles, cars, airplanes? Do the same thing at night, looking
for dark places, lights (stationary, moving, or blinking), the moon,
and the stars. Window watching helps your children become more
observant and increases vocabulary.

Play hide-and-seek using a stuffed animal or a toy. Hide the toy
(not too well) someplace in the house, keeping it within range of your
children's eyesight and reach. Give hints such as, "Look by the lamp
where Daddy likes to sit." Once the toy is found, have your children
hide it and you search. Ask for a hint, even though it may be in plain
sight. The important thing is to have fun and help your children learn
to follow (and give) directions.

Children like having a "hideout" as a pretending place or just to get
away from things once in a while. Inside the house, drape a blanket
over a small table or over two chairs facing away from each other, or
screen a corner of a room with kitchen chairs and a sheet. Outside, a
blanket over a clothesline or a sturdy bush creates a tent. Appliance
boxes are usually large enough for a door to be cut in them. Encourage
children to make their hideouts large enough for a friend (or you) to
visit, and stay aware of what they're doing by peeking in occasionally.

Craft

Touch Box

You will need: cardboard box with flaps or lid
that closes it completely

an old sock

glue

scissors or box cutter

straight pins

contact paper or paint

Cut a hole in one side of the box (not the side that opens). The hole must be large enough to insert your hand. Cover the box with contact paper or paint.

Cut the ribbed edge (top) off the sock and glue one end around the hole on the *inside* of the box. Pin with straight pins to hold the sock in place until the glue dries thoroughly, then remove the pins.

Put an object in the box and close the lid. As the children reach through the sock, they feel the object. Ask the children to name the object or describe what it feels like, rather than trying to pull it out of the hole. Ask questions: "Is it soft or hard? little or big? warm or cold?" and so on. This activity is good for language development.

Open the lid and take out the object, naming it and describing the way it looks or feels. Children learn to discriminate between objects by the way they feel and look based on descriptions learned from others. Put the same object back in the box or use a different object. Also let the children put something in the box for you to feel.

Program Notes

Sign Language

SURPRISE Place your hands at the temples in loose fists, palms facing each other. Quickly flick index fingers and thumbs open as the hands are pulled away from the temples and the eyes open wide in surprise.

Introduce the theme by playing "peekaboo" while putting name tags on children. Bring a touch box to the program and put something familiar to the children inside. Show them how to reach inside to feel what is there, but remind them not to pull the object out. *Note:* Don't let children be pushed into putting their hands in the touch box. When everyone who wants to participate has had a turn, open the top of the box and let them peek inside to see what's there.

The book *The Surprise* works well as a flannelboard story, and children enjoy the present-inside-present idea.

 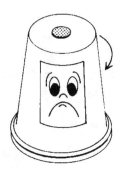

Giveaways are turn-around faces made of two plastic cups nested together. The outer cup has an opening cut in it, and the inner cup has faces on opposite sides that are visible through the outer opening when the inner cup is turned. Secure them together with a brass fastener through the cup bottoms.

Fingertaster "tastes" crunchy foods, such as carrots, celery, pretzels, etc.

Children exit the story space playing peekaboo.

―――――――――――――― Notes ――――――――――――――

Picnics

Books

Bailey Goes Camping
KEVIN HENKES

Bing: Go Picnic
TED DEWAN

Blue Tortoise
    (Spanish: *La tortuga azul*)
ALAN ROGERS

Curious George Goes Camping
MARGRET AND H. A. REY

Fun at the Park
LARA JONES

In a Minute!
VIRGINIA MILLER

Maisy Goes Camping
LUCY COUSINS

Maisy Goes to the Playground
LUCY COUSINS

Mr. Bear's Picnic
DEBI GLIORI

Spot Goes to the Park
    (Spanish: *Spot va al parque*)
ERIC HILL

Spot's First Picnic and Other Stories
ERIC HILL

This Is the Bear and the Picnic Lunch
SARAH HAYES

Tiny Goes Camping
CARI MEISTER

A Tree Is Nice
    (Spanish: *Un árbol es hermoso*)
JANICE MAY UDRY

We're Going on a Picnic
PAT HUTCHINS

Zigby Camps Out
BRIAN PATERSON

Rhythms, Rhymes, and Fingerplays

On a Picnic   (tune: "London Bridge")

On a picnic, spread the blanket,
Spread the blanket, spread the blanket.
On a picnic, spread the blanket.
Picnic in the park.

[Repeat with]
    open the basket
    eat the sandwich
    drink the juice
    run and play
    pack it up
    walk on home

Picnic Baskets

Five picnic baskets,
Waiting by the door.
One went to the park,
And then there were four.

[Additional verses]

Four . . . As full as they can be,
    One went to the lake . . . three.

Three . . . Yellow, red, and blue;
    One went to the backyard . . . two.

Two . . . Sitting in the sun, One's for
    Bobby who's sick today . . . one.

One picnic basket.
I think it should be
Taken on a picnic
By you and me!

Picnic Basket   (tune: "A Tisket, a Tasket")

A tisket, a tasket,
A green and yellow basket.
I packed a picnic for my friend,
And on the way I lost it . . .
I lost it, I lost it.
And on the way I lost it.
I packed a picnic for my friend,
And on the way I lost it.

Parents' Follow-Up Ideas

On a cold or rainy day, have a picnic inside the house with your children. Pack a picnic lunch of small sandwiches or finger foods (cheese cubes, crackers, grapes, carrot or celery sticks, apple slices, animal crackers, etc.) into a small basket or grocery bag. Add a wet washcloth in a plastic bag, napkins, a favorite book, and something to drink. Dress in special "picnic clothes": summer hats, sunglasses, and sandals. Carrying a blanket, search the house with your toddlers for a good "picnic spot." Spread the blanket on the floor, sit on it, and unpack the lunch together. Put sandwiches on napkins or paper plates or give your children a paper cup filled with finger foods. Eat your lunches on the blanket and talk about picnics you have taken together in the past or plan one for the future. Talk about some things you may see on your next outdoor picnic: other children, playground equipment, a lake, insects, or animals. After eating, clean up your lunch debris, returning it to the basket or sack. Wipe sticky fingers on the washcloth and curl up together to read a book. Then play some picnic games on the blanket or in the surrounding area. Practicing picnic activities will help your toddlers know what to expect before encountering the excitement of a real outdoor picnic in the park.

Look for interesting places for picnics around your community. If you live in the city, keep your eyes open for a park or a small plaza far enough from pedestrians where you can sit on the ground. Also consider picnicking on the steps of the library or a museum. Ask the managers inside if they have any objections. Other good picnic places are zoos, botanical gardens, school yards (when school is not in session), or in the backyard. While warm weather is preferred for picnics, pack a picnic and go for a rainy-day walk in the spring, finding a sheltered place, or have a quick snow picnic in the winter.

Craft

Mini Picnic Basket

You will need: plastic berry basket (quart)

strips of fabric, ribbons, or yarn

masking tape

Wash and dry a berry basket. To make weaving easier, wrap one end of the fabric strip, ribbon, or yarn with masking tape. At one corner of the basket, tie one end of the fabric strip through the top square. At a neighboring corner, thread the fabric strip through the top square of the basket, leaving a loop large enough for a handle, and tie it off. Repeat with the remaining corners so that you make two handles on opposite sides of the basket.

Weave the sides of the basket by tying another strip to a bottom corner of the basket. Show your children how to weave the ribbon in, out, and around the sides of the basket. When your children reach the end of the strip, tie on another ribbon (with the knot on the inside) and let them continue. Your toddlers may need help weaving over the fabric ends where handles attach to the top row. When complete, tie the end securely to the basket and weave the fabric tail into the basket on the inside. To make the basket more sturdy, weave across the bottom.

Line the basket with a washcloth or paper towel, and let your children pack it with a juice box, plastic spoon or fork wrapped in a napkin, yogurt, fruit, and a sandwich or finger foods in zipping plastic bags or a paper cup. Help them balance the load so it doesn't spill when they pick up the basket.

Program Notes

Sign Language

PICNIC   Use both hands, left hand behind right, with all fingers pointing at the mouth. Move your hands toward the mouth twice, as though pushing a lot of food in your mouth.

If possible bring a picnic basket or a basket with a napkin cover to the program. Inside have a paper plate for each child with food pictures glued to it or let them pretend the food is there. The storytime puppet invites children to have a picnic, and children help spread out a blanket (pretend or not) so they can all sit together to listen to stories and have their picnic. After eating, pass a paper plate with animal stickers on it and invite each child to take a pretend "animal cracker" for dessert.

The flannelboard rectangle becomes the inside of a picnic basket. Let children help "pack" the basket with flannelboard picnic item figures. The rhyme "Picnic Baskets" makes a good flannelboard activity, too.

Between-story activities can include pretending to play on playground equipment found in parks.

Giveaways are a plastic spoon and fork wrapped in a napkin and sealed with a colorful sticker.

Fingertaster "tastes" picnic foods, such as peanut butter sandwiches, apples, raisins, cookies, etc.

Children exit the story space pretending to swing a picnic basket.

 Notes ───────────────────

Playing

Books

All Fall Down
HELEN OXENBURY

Can You Make a Piggy Giggle?
LINDA ASHMAN

*Five Little Monkeys
Jumping on the Bed*
    (Spanish: *Cinco monitos
    brincando en la cama*)
EILEEN CHRISTELOW

Let's Be Animals
ANN TURNER

Let's Play / Vamos a jugar
(English/Spanish)
ALAN BENJAMIN

Lulu's Busy Day
CAROLINE UFF

Maisy's Big Flap Book
    (Spanish: *Diviertete y
    aprende con Maisy*)
LUCY COUSINS

Millie Wants to Play!
JANET PEDERSEN

My Toys / Mis juguetes
(English/Spanish)
REBECCA EMBERLEY

Play with Me
MARIE HALL ETS

Please, Baby, Please
SPIKE AND TONYA LEWIS LEE

Sam's Ball
BARBRO LINDGREN

Spot's Toy Box
    (Spanish: *Los juguetes
    de Spot*)
ERIC HILL

Ten Tiny Tickles
KAREN KATZ

When We Play Together
NICK BUTTERWORTH

*Yay, You! Moving Out,
Moving Up, Moving On*
SANDRA BOYNTON

Rhythms, Rhymes, and Fingerplays

Playing   (tune: "Mulberry Bush")

Let's throw a ball to play today,
Play today, play today.
Let's throw a ball to play today.
Inside and outside, we play.

[Repeat with]

    do a puzzle to play today
    ride a bike
    paint a picture
    build a castle
    play with puppets

Bounce the Ball

Bounce the ball to Billy.* *(make bouncing motion)*
Bounces it back to me. *(make catching motion)*

Bounce the ball to Tran. *(repeat)*
Bounce it back to me.
Bounce the ball, bounce the ball, *(bouncing motion)*
Bounce the ball with me.

[*insert children's names]

Five Little Monkeys

Five little monkeys *(hold up five fingers)*
Jumping on the bed. *(jump in place)*
One fell off and bumped his head. *(pat head)*
Mama called the doctor *(motion talking
    into a phone)*
And the doctor said, *(nod head)*
"No more monkeys jumping on the bed!"
    (shake finger as though scolding)

[Repeat with four, three, two, one.]

Parents' Follow-Up Ideas

Storing toys in a jumbled toy box is a mess, and things are always getting broken. Keep similar toys together in smaller, more manageable containers, and your children can use their sorting skills while keeping their toys neat. Put little cars in a shoe box, snap beads in a tin can with taped edges, etc. Store small containers of toys on a closet shelf (put seldom-used toys on top shelf), in a dresser drawer, or in a cardboard filing cabinet (light enough to take on a trip or to a friend's house).

Children often receive several toys on birthdays or holidays. They may play with them briefly, then set them aside. Put away some of the ignored toys, and bring one out again in a few weeks. It will appear new to your child, who can better enjoy the toy when it is not lost amid many others. "New-again" toys can be brought out as a special treat when children are left with a babysitter or when they go to visit relatives.

Small toys, like little cars or blocks, seem to multiply as you pick them up to put away. Buy a plastic dustpan and your children can scoop those little toys into a storage container. You can make a scoop by cutting the top off a milk or fabric softener bottle. Cut it at an angle, with the handle on top. Scooping up toys is fast and easy. Best of all, your toddler will enjoy doing this activity alone.

Craft

Clothespin Bird Toss: a game played by Eskimo children

You will need: wooden clothespins (not the clip kind)
                    lightweight cardboard, cut into wing shapes
                    washable marking pen
                    2 colors of poster paint

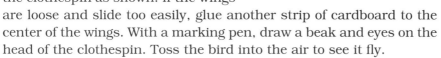

Paint one side of the wings one color and the other side a different color. Let the paint dry, then slightly bend the wings in the middle so they form a wide V shape. Bend them so that the same color is on the inside of them all. Slide the cardboard wings into the slot of the clothespin as shown. If the wings are loose and slide too easily, glue another strip of cardboard to the center of the wings. With a marking pen, draw a beak and eyes on the head of the clothespin. Toss the bird into the air to see it fly.

Toddlers will enjoy making the birds fly. They can toss them at a laundry basket or empty wading pool trying to make them land inside. The game played by Eskimo children counts the number of times the bird lands up (wings angled toward ground) and down (wings angled toward sky). When some of the novelty of making the bird fly wears off, encourage your child to keep track of what color is facing upward when the bird lands. If the birds are painted red and yellow, get one red cup and one yellow cup. Each time the bird lands, the child drops a raisin or cereal O into the appropriate cup. When the game is finished, count the goodies to see which color appeared most often, then eat them.

Program Notes

Sign Language

PLAY   Use both hands and have palms facing up. Fold the middle fingers into the palms, leaving the thumbs and little fingers extended. Rotate the hands so the palms face downward a couple of times.

The storytime puppet introduces the theme by inviting everyone to play.

Between stories, say "Let's play!" introducing the action rhymes. Use a pretend ball for the rhyme "Bounce the Ball."

"Five Little Monkeys" works well on a flannelboard, and it can be used as an action rhyme, too.

Giveaways are paper airplanes folded from typing paper.

Fingertaster "tastes" fun foods, such as pudding, popcorn, cookies, raisins, etc.

As children are getting ready to leave, the storytime puppet can ask them how they are going to play the rest of the day.

Children exit the story space jumping.

———————————— Notes ————————————

Rabbits

Books

Bing: Something for Daddy
TED DEWAN

The Bunny Hop
TEDDY SLATER

Carry Me!
ROSEMARY WELLS

Curious George and the Bunny
H. A. REY

Little Rabbits' First Word Book
ALAN BAKER

Mr. Rabbit and the Lovely Present
   (Spanish: *El señor Conejo y el hermoso regalo*)
CHARLOTTE ZOLOTOW

Pat the Bunny
DOROTHY KUNHARDT

Rabbit Pie
PENNY IVES

Rabbits and Raindrops
JIM ARNOSKY

The Runaway Bunny
   (Spanish: *El conejito andarín*)
MARGARET WISE BROWN

So Many Bunnies
(also in braille)
RICK WALTON AND PAIGE MIGLIO

Sweet Dreams, Sam
YVES GOT

That's Not My Bunny . . . Its Tail Is Too Fluffy
FIONA WATT

Tickle Tum
NANCY VAN LAAN AND
BERNADETTE PONS

Too Many Bunnies
TOMIE DE PAOLA

What Can Rabbit See?
   (Spanish: *¿Qué puede ver Blas?*)
LUCY COUSINS

Rhythms, Rhymes, and Fingerplays

Little Rabbit

I saw a little rabbit go hop, hop, hop.
   (jump in place)
I saw his long ears go flop, flop, flop.
   (hands above head, "flop" wrists over and back)
I saw his little eyes go wink, wink, wink.
   (blink eyes)
I saw his little nose go twink, twink, twink.
   (wiggle nose)
I said, "Little Rabbit, won't you stay?"
   (make beckoning motion)
He looked at me and . . . hopped away!
   (jump quickly)

Hop, Hop, Hoppy   (tune: "Peter Cottontail")

Hop, Hop, Hoppy cannot wait, *(bounce in place)*
Jumping near my garden gate.
Hippity, hoppity,
Carrots on his mind. *(pretend to eat carrot
    with little noises)*
Floppy ears are flipping high, *(hands alternately
    flip-flop on top of head)*
Big feet jumping. My, oh my! *(lift one foot and
    then the other)*
Hippity, hoppity, *(bounce in place)*
No carrots left behind. *(shake head sadly)*

Here Is a Bunny

Here is a bunny with ears so funny. *(hands
    above head to make ears, flop wrists)*
Here is his hole in the ground. *(arms create
    circle in front of body)*
When a noise he hears, *(clap hands sharply)*
He pricks up his ears *(hands above head,
    held straight up)*
And jumps in his hole in the ground. *(jump
    into a crouching position)*

Parents' Follow-Up Ideas

Animal riddles are good for times when you are waiting for things to happen (such as being called into the doctor's office). Try these:

I eat grass.	I gallop.	I have feathers.
I say moo.	I trot.	I peck and peck.
What am I?	My hooves go	I say cluck, cluck.
	clip, clop.	What am I?
	What am I?	

Plant a "rabbit garden," even in the middle of winter, by cutting pictures from magazines, food labels, and advertising of garden vegetables: carrots, lettuce, beans, corn, etc. Tape each picture to one end of a coffee stirring stick or straw. Insert the opposite end of the stick into a Styrofoam block or an empty box. Arrange them in a line, as though they were growing in the garden. You be the farmer, and let your child be a hungry bunny, sneaking into your garden to eat the goodies there. When the bunny gets caught (only occasionally), the farmer gets to tickle it and hug it, and together you "replant" the garden. Ask your "bunny" to help you choose which vegetables to serve for lunch or dinner.

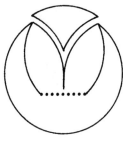

Craft

Rabbit Cup Puppet

You will need: a paper cup

a straw

tape

a picture of a rabbit small enough to fit
inside the cup (draw one or cut from
magazine or greeting card)

Poke a hole in the bottom of the cup large enough so that a straw can easily slide through. Tape the rabbit picture to one end of the straw and slide the other end of the straw down through the hole in the bottom of the cup. Operate the puppet by sliding the straw up and down. While reciting the rhyme "Here Is a Bunny," let your child operate the rabbit puppet, making it appear and disappear at the proper times.

Program Notes

Sign Language

RABBIT   Cross your hands at the wrists, palms facing away
from each other. Extend your index and middle
fingers of each hand (fingers kept together) and
quickly bend the fingers twice, like a rabbit's ears
twitching.

Introduce the theme with a toy rabbit, rabbit puppet, or storytime puppet wearing rabbit ears. Invite children to jump around the story space before settling in their rabbit holes (rug spots).

Use a basket and artificial fruit for *Mr. Rabbit and the Lovely Present.* Give children the opportunity to touch the fruit when the story is finished, inviting them to "hop" up to the basket. Between other stories children can jump fast and slow, crouch down to hide, and hurry quickly home (to their adults).

Giveaways are bunny ears made from a paper plate: cut, folded, and stapled and ready to be tied on children's heads.

Fingertaster "tastes" carrot flavors, such as carrot cake, carrot soup, carrot milk shakes, etc.

Children exit the story space hopping like bunnies.

——————————————— Notes ———————————————

Rain

Books

Hi, Clouds
CAROL GREENE

In the Rain with Baby Duck
AMY HEST

It Looked Like Spilt Milk
CHARLES G. SHAW

Just a Rainy Day
MERCER MAYER

Moonbear's Skyfire
FRANK ASCH

Mushroom in the Rain
MIRRA GINSBURG

Rain
ROBERT KALAN

Rain
MANYA STOJIC

Rain Feet
ANGELA JOHNSON

Rainbow of My Own
DON FREEMAN

The Rainy Day
   (Spanish: *Un dia de lluvia*)
ANNA MILBOURNE AND SARAH GILL

Rainy Day
JANET MORGAN STOEKE

Spot at Home
   (Spanish: *Spot en casa*)
ERIC HILL

Umbrella
TARO YASHIMA

Up the Mountain
CHARLOTTE AGELL

Water, Water
ELOISE GREENFIELD

Rhythms, Rhymes, and Fingerplays

Walking in the Rain   (tune: "London Bridge")

Let's go walking in the rain,
In the rain, in the rain.
Let's go walking in the rain,
Early in the morning.

[Repeat with]

   jump puddles in our boots
   walk under umbrellas
   feel the raindrops, splash, splash, splash
   see the rainbow, shining bright

Eency Weency Spider   (traditional song)

Eency weency spider went up the water spout.
   (wiggle fingers upward in front of body)
Down came the rain and washed the spider out.
   (sweep arms down and to one side)
Out came the sun and dried up all the rain,
   (arms form circle over head)
And the eency weency spider went up the spout again.
   (wiggle fingers upward again)

Busy Windshield Wipers

*(hold arms up in front of body and
   move them from side to side)*
Busy windshield wipers go
A-dash, a-dash, a-dash.
Wiping all the drops away
Splash, splash, splash.

Parents' Follow-Up Ideas

Playing in water is educational for toddlers. Stay close by and play with your children whenever they are near even a small amount of water. Help them learn safety rules (stay away from hot water; don't throw water; keep objects out of the mouth). The kitchen sink, a bathtub, or a wading pool are good places for water play. When clean-up time comes, toddlers can be good helpers.

Good water toys are sponges, plastic containers (some with holes), measuring cups, eyedroppers, funnels, jar lids, or anything unbreakable. Add interest with a squirt of shaving cream or food coloring.

This is a great language-building time. "Pour, spill, sprinkle, splash, spurt, squirt, dribble, flow, flood, trickle, and spray" all describe different ways that water behaves. Each word sounds like what it describes. Use these words to increase your children's vocabulary and the way they think about water.

Pry the ball off an empty roll-on deodorant jar and wash the bottle out. Fill it with tempera paint and push the ball back on. Presto: you have a giant ballpoint pen that paints. Cover a table with newspaper and let your children create pictures on shelf paper or paper sacks.

Craft

A Rainbow

You will need: a paper plate   a craft stick

colored paper streamers   tape or a stapler

scissors   a marker

Cut a pie-shaped wedge from the paper plate and draw a face near the outer edge. Attach colored streamers along the outer edge, and staple the inner edge to the stick. When your child holds the stick, the rainbow colors will move over and around him or her like a flexible rainbow!

Program Notes

Sign Language

RAIN   Place your hands at the shoulders, palms facing outward and fingers curved slightly. Bend your wrists twice, like rain falling.

Introduce the theme with an umbrella (if you are not superstitious, an open one). Let each child come to sit or stand under the umbrella with you.

It Looked Like Spilt Milk is good for flannelboard sharing. Use "Eency Weency Spider" as an action rhyme, standing and stretching high as the spider climbs and sweeping hands to the floor when it rains. Repeat it more than once, saying it loudly with lots of action, and then again with smaller actions and quiet voices. The rhyme can also be used as a flannelboard presentation.

Giveaways are paper rain hats or fluttering rainbows (see craft).

Fingertaster "tastes" colorful foods, such as green peppers, red cherries, oranges, purple plums, etc.

Children exit the story space wearing their rain hats or waving their rainbows over their heads.

———————————— Notes ————————————

Read to Me!

Books

Chinese Mother Goose Rhymes
ROBERT WYNDHAM

Here Comes Mother Goose
IONA OPIE

Hey Diddle Diddle
JAMES MARSHALL

*Jaha and Jamil Went Down the Hill:
An African Mother Goose*
VIRGINIA KROLL

Listen! Peter Rabbit
BEATRIX POTTER

The Little Red Hen
   (Spanish: *La gallinita roja*)
BYRON BARTON

Maisy Goes to the Library
LUCY COUSINS

Old Mother Hubbard
JANE CABRERA

*Pat-a-Cake and Other
Play Rhymes*
JOANNA COLE AND
STEPHANIE CALMENSON

Read to Your Bunny
ROSEMARY WELLS

Teddy Bear, Teddy Bear

Three Bears
BYRON BARTON

Tiny Goes to the Library
CARI MEISTER

Tom and Pippo Read a Story
HELEN OXENBURY

*Tomie's Baa, Baa, Black
Sheep and Other Rhymes*
TOMIE DE PAOLA

Where the Wild Things Are
MAURICE SENDAK

Rhythms, Rhymes, and Fingerplays

Hickory Dickory Dock

Hickory, dickory, dock . . . tick, tock. *(swing
   arms in front of body like pendulum)*
The mouse ran up the clock. *(make climbing motion)*
The clock struck one, *(clap hands once)*
The mouse ran down. *(reverse climbing motion)*
Hickory, dickory, dock . . . tick, tock. *(repeat
   first motion)*
Hickory, dickory, dock.

Mary Had a Little Lamb   (song)

Mary had a little lamb,
Little lamb, little lamb.
Mary had a little lamb,
Its fleece was white as snow.

And everywhere that Mary went,
Mary went, Mary went.
Everywhere that Mary went,
That lamb was sure to go.

Jack and Jill   (chant)

Jack and Jill went up the hill *(clap in rhythm,
   four times each line)*
To fetch a pail of wa-ter.
Jack fell down and broke his crown,
And Jill came tumbling af-ter.

<u>Jack,</u> <u>Jack,</u> <u>Jack</u> and <u>Jill,</u> <u>Jill,</u> <u>Jill,</u> *(clap on
   underlined words)*
Went <u>up,</u> <u>up,</u> <u>up</u> the <u>hill,</u> <u>hill,</u> <u>hill.</u>
Up the hill, went Jack and Jill, *(clap in rhythm)*
To fetch a pail of water.
<u>Jack,</u> <u>Jack,</u> <u>Jack</u> fell <u>down,</u> <u>down,</u> <u>down,</u> *(clap on
   underlined words)*
And <u>broke,</u> <u>broke,</u> <u>broke</u> his <u>crown,</u> <u>crown,</u> <u>crown.</u>
Jack fell down and broke his crown *(clap in rhythm)*
And Jill came tumbling after.

[The strong rhythm in this rhyme makes it a fun one
to play with. Changing the cadence and repetitions
creates a new chant. Try it with: Jack, Jack (pause)
Jack-Jack.]

Parents' Follow-Up Ideas

Read to your children every day. Change your voice as you read, from
high to low, fast to slow, soft to loud. Keep the story interesting and
be prepared to read favorites over and over again. If your children will
not sit still for an entire book, the book may be too long or their listening skills are still too limited. Instead of reading the words in the
book, try "reading" a few pictures at a time. Here are some questions
you might ask about a picture to encourage discussion with your
child:

1. What do you see in the picture? (Children need to know
   the names of objects as well as people and animals.)
2. What is happening?
3. What are the people (animals) doing?
4. Do you see something funny (sad, silly, dangerous, and so
   on) in this picture? What do you think will happen next?

5. Do you see someone who is angry (happy, sad, frightened) in this picture? Why do you think he or she is feeling that way?

6. How many _____ do you see? (Children enjoy counting objects in pictures.)

7. What is over (under, beside, behind) the _____ in this picture?

8. I see something that is red (or any color). What do you see that is red in this picture? (or) What color is the boy's shirt?

9. What shapes can you find in this picture? (circles, squares, stars)

10. What do you see that is big? Little?

11. What do you think the girl is saying?

12. What sounds could you hear if you were in this picture? (or) What sound does this cat make?

Reading pictures acquaints children with books, demonstrating how the story progresses from beginning (front of the book) to end. They also learn that there is a pattern of reading left to right as they look at the pages of a book and you slide your finger under the words while reading.

Reading pictures allows greater flexibility for using books with children of all ages. The story can change with each encounter as new things are discovered in the illustrations. Children become an active part of the story by helping to create it.

Listening skills are learned, and it takes time. To help your toddlers lengthen their attention spans, start with short sessions and take your cues from your children. When they get restless, stop.

When you read a book or tell stories to your children, sit close enough so you are touching. Touching children as you read (an arm around the shoulders, sitting on your lap, and stroking or patting their arms) increases brain activity and helps the children learn more and remember better. Besides, it is another gesture of how much your toddlers mean to you. Remember, when you hear, "Read it again," your children are asking for more than hearing the words another time. Your time and attention are very valuable to them.

A good way to teach values is through stories, but they should not be heavy-handed with the ending "And the moral to that story is. . . ." Even young children can tell right from wrong when presented in a story form. When children are struggling with an issue (like jealousy, sharing, or biting), it helps enormously for them to listen to a story about characters with similar problems. Ask your librarian to help you find appropriate books, or simply start with "Once upon a time . . ." and create your own story using a favorite toy as the main character. Encourage your children to help you tell the story and to find solutions for the character's problem.

Craft

Zipping-Bag Books

You will need: reclosable plastic bags (sandwich size)

poster board pages, cut to fit easily inside
the bags; one page per bag

magazine pictures, photographs, or children's
artwork

permanent marker (optional)

hole punch

yarn

Decide what kind of book you will make. You can make theme
books (things with wheels, red things, favorite foods, animals), books
about family members, counting pages with stickers, or make up stories with randomly chosen pictures. Select enough pictures or photographs so there will be one picture on each side of the poster board
page. Glue pictures to both sides of the poster board and let them dry
thoroughly. If you wish, label under each picture with a permanent
marker.

Slide one page into each bag and close the zipping seal, getting the
extra air out of the bag. Stack the bags on top of each other with the
resealing edge at the top. Punch two holes in the left side of each bag
and tie them together with yarn. Encourage your child to "read" the
pictures. These books can be used over and over again. Wipe them off
with a damp cloth when they become sticky and change the pictures
inside when you are both ready for something new.

Program Notes

Sign Language

BOOK   Put your palms together with fingers pointing forward; open your hands, keeping the little fingers together, as though opening a book.

This is a great time to introduce children's classics and nursery rhymes to toddlers and their parents. If your library does not have an age requirement for library cards, encourage parents to get cards for their toddlers at this program. The storytime puppet can produce its own library card and bring favorite books to the storyteller to be shared with everyone. Share at least one story about the library to reinforce where you are. Nursery rhymes work well when they are introduced as flannelboard activities followed by chanting them as the group claps or marches in a circle.

Giveaways are book bags. If your library does not have access to "real" book bags, collect enough plastic grocery bags and tie colorful ribbons to the handles.

Fingertaster "tastes" dinnertime foods, such as meat loaf, green beans, catfish, etc.

Children exit the story space chanting "Jack and Jill."

—————————————————— Notes ——————————————————

Sizes and Shapes

Books

Bear in a Square
STELLA BLACKSTONE

Big and Little
MARGARET MILLER

Big and Little on the Farm
DOROTHY DONOHUE

Big Dog . . . Little Dog
   (Spanish: *Perro grande . . .*
   perro pequeño)
P. D. EASTMAN

Big Little
LESLIE PATRICELLI

Blue Sea
   (French: *Mer bleue*)
ROBERT KALAN

Brown Rabbit's Shape Book
ALAN BAKER

How Big Is a Pig?
CLARE BEATON

My Very First Book of Shapes
ERIC CARLE

Shapes
COLIN PETTY

Shapes, Shapes, Shapes
TANA HOBAN

Shapes: Slide 'n' Seek
CHUCK MURPHY

Spot Looks at Shapes
ERIC HILL

Tall
JEZ ALBOROUGH

Titch
PAT HUTCHINS

Word Bird's Shapes
JANE BELK MONCURE

Rhythms, Rhymes, and Fingerplays

Where Is Thumbkin?

Where is Thumbkin? *(hands behind back)*
Where is Thumbkin?
Here I am! *(right thumb extended in front)*
Here I am! *(left thumb extended)*
How are you this morning? *(wiggle right thumb)*
Very well, I thank you. *(wiggle left thumb)*
Run and play. *(right hand behind back)*
Run and play. *(left hand behind back)*

[Repeat with]

   Pointer *(index finger)*
   Tall-one *(middle finger)*
   Ring-one *(ring finger)*
   Baby *(little finger)*
   Everyone *(all fingers)*

Do You Know Shapes?   (tune: "Muffin Man")

Do you know a circle shape? *(hands draw
   large circles in air)*
A circle shape? A circle shape?
Round and round and round it goes,
To make a circle shape.

Do you know a triangle? *(hand draws a
   triangle in the air)*
A triangle? A triangle?
Three corners and three straight sides
Make a triangle.

Do you know a rectangle? *(hand draws a
   rectangle in the air)*
A rectangle? A rectangle?
Two long sides and two short sides
Make a rectangle.

Sometimes I Am Tall

Sometimes I am tall. *(stretch up on toes)*
Sometimes I am small. *(crouch down low)*
Sometimes I am very, very tall. *(stretch
   and reach up hands)*
Sometimes I am very, very small.
   (crouch low to floor)
Sometimes tall . . . *(stretch up)*
Sometimes small . . . *(crouch low)*
See how I am now. *(stand normally)*

Parents' Follow-Up Ideas

On a trip to a department or grocery store, look for items that have different shapes. Some shapes (such as rectangles) are easier to find than others (triangles), but it can be done. Help your children look for shapes on product labels and see how they are arranged on the shelves.

Use size-related words often when reading to your children, looking at magazines, watching TV, or taking a walk. Reinforce common words such as tall, short, big, and small with less common words that describe size: fat, skinny, huge, tiny, wide, narrow. Remember, when comparing the sizes of two objects, look at them from your children's point of view. Objects look different when seen from a different perspective.

Go on a rock-collecting walk, taking along an empty milk bottle to help carry rocks back home. Encourage your children to look for rocks that are different sizes and shapes. Can they find rocks that are round or flat? When finding a new rock, compare it with others already gathered. Have your children arrange the rocks by size to see where the new rock will fit in line. Keep the rocks in an egg carton when you get home, and when the egg carton gets full, find a good place to create a rock garden outside or on a windowsill.

Craft

Flannelboard

You will need: a piece of flat, heavy cardboard

a piece of flannel or felt, 1″ larger than the dimensions of the cardboard piece

scrap pieces of materials with naps (felt, flannel, velvet, corduroy) or sandpaper

glue

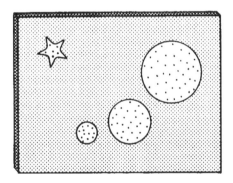 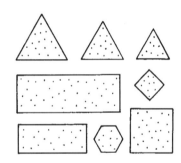

Wipe the cardboard with a clean cloth to remove dust. Spread glue over all the surface on one side of the cardboard. Put the flannel over the glue and smooth it flat. Let it dry thoroughly. Overlap the edges of the flannel over the cardboard and glue it to the other side. Weight or pin edges so they will dry flat. Let it dry thoroughly.

Cut out the shapes from the material scraps. Make basic shapes (circles, triangles, and so forth), animal shapes, people shapes, or crazy shapes. Use pictures from magazines or coloring books for patterns or glue these pictures to the material for ready-made flannel pieces. Vary the shapes in size: small, medium, and large. Pictures glued onto the smooth side of sandpaper will also stick to a flannelboard (and cutting sandpaper sharpens scissors!).

Show your child how the pieces will stick to the flannelboard; then let the child play with them alone or arrange the pieces together to tell a story, make a picture, or talk about sizes.

Program Notes

Sign Language

LITTLE   With index fingers extended, move your hands toward each other.

BIG   With hands open and palms facing, move your hands
away from each other.

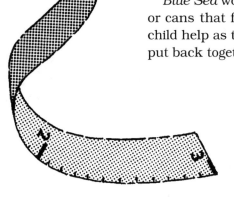

Introduce the theme with the clown-shape puzzle emphasizing the different sizes (stars are smaller than the large circle or rectangle) and the shapes themselves.

Blue Sea works well on a flannelboard. Follow it with nesting dolls or cans that fit inside each other to further explore sizes. Let each child help as the dolls are taken apart, lined up to be compared, and put back together again.

Giveaways are measuring strips made from 36″ paper or fabric by marking inches and feet with a yardstick. The strip can be attached to a child's bedroom door to measure height.

Fingertaster "tastes" flat foods, such as bread, pancakes, toast, pita bread, etc.

Children exit the story space drawing circles in the air with their fingers.

──────────────────── **Notes** ────────────────────

Sounds

Books

Bark, George
JULES FEIFFER

"Buzz" Said the Bee
WENDY CHEYETTE LEWISON

Clifford's Animal Sounds
   (Spanish: *Clifford y los
   sonidos de los animales*)
NORMAN BRIDWELL

Do Monkeys Tweet?
MELANIE WALSH

Does a Cow Say Boo?
JUDY HINDLEY

Moo, Baa, La La La!
   (Spanish: *Muu. Beee.
   ¡Así fue!*)
SANDRA BOYNTON

*Mr. Brown Can Moo!
Can You?*
DR. SEUSS

Noisy Nora
ROSEMARY WELLS

*Polar Bear, Polar Bear,
What Do You Hear?*
   (Spanish: *Oso polar, oso
   polar, ¿que es ese ruido?*)
BILL MARTIN JR.

Q Is for Duck
MARY ELTING AND
MICHAEL FOLSOM

Quiet Loud
LESLIE PATRICELLI

What Can Rabbit Hear?
   (Spanish: *¿Qué puede oir
   Blas?*)
LUCY COUSINS

What Does the Rabbit Say?
JACQUE HALL

The Wheels on the Race Car
ALEXANDER ZANE

Who Hoots?
KATIE DAVIS

Who Says Woof?
JOHN BUTLER

Rhythms, Rhymes, and Fingerplays

Boom! Bang!

Boom, bang, boom, bang! *(beat one fist in other palm)*
Rumpety, lumpety, bump! *(slap hands on knees)*
Zoom, zam, zoom, zam! *(shoot hands across front of body)*
Clippety, clappety, clump! *(nod head from side to side)*
Rustles and bustles *(hug hands to shoulders)*
And swishes and zings, *(lean side to side)*
What wonderful noises *(throw hands over head)*
A thunderstorm brings!! *(clap hands together)*

Plink, Plank, Plunk   (tune: "Three Blind Mice")

Plink, plank, plunk. *(pretend to play banjo)*
Plink, plank, plunk.
Strum, tickle-tickle, strum.
Strum, tickle-tickle, strum.

I make music
On my banjo.
I play fast,
And I play slow.
Fingers running to and fro,
Plink, plank, plunk.

Pound Goes the Hammer

Pound, pound, pound-pound-pound
    (pound one fist into other palm)
Goes the hammer.
Pound-pound-pound.

Bzz, bzz, bzz-bzz-bzz, *(hand open,*
    thumb up, make sawing motion)
Goes the saw.
Bzz-bzz-bzz.

Chop, chop, chop-chop-chop, *(hand*
    open, chop into other palm)
Goes the ax.
Chop-chop-chop.

Parents' Follow-Up Ideas

Talk to your toddler about sounds you hear. Ask some of these questions:

1. Close your eyes and listen. What sounds do you hear? Cars? Horns? Running water? Radio or television? What else?
2. Lightly put your fingers on your throat when singing or talking. Do you feel your throat tingle?
3. While talking, gently pat your chest or your mouth to make the sound change. Can you do that while singing?
4. (Put different-sized items in small covered containers and shake.) Does macaroni sound different from raisins? cereal?
5. Practice talking in a loud voice . . . now a normal voice . . . now a whisper. Can you be perfectly still? Can you hear more sounds when you are still?

Craft

Paper Plate Banjo

You will need: 2 paper plates   glue
                    scissors   4 rubber bands
                    a paint stirrer

Cut a hole in the middle of one plate. Glue the rims of the plates together with the insides facing. Let dry. Glue the paint stirrer to the plate with the hole (but not covering the hole). After the glue dries, stretch the rubber bands, two on each side of the stirrer, over the hole in the plate. Tape the rubber bands to prevent them from sliding off plate. Strum gently to make music!

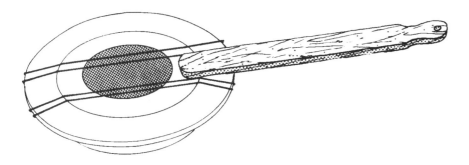

Program Notes

Sign Language

LISTEN   Cup your right hand to the ear, as if trying to hear.

Introduce the theme with different sound makers: whistle, toy piano, crumpling paper, clapping hands. Ask the children to close their eyes while you make the sound and see if they can guess the source. Always name the source of the sound and describe the sound itself (loud, soft, shrill). Encourage children to mimic the sounds in all the stories you share.

Use different noisemakers to make the sounds in the stories you share. *Polar Bear, Polar Bear, What Do You Hear?* makes a good flannelboard story.

Giveaways are pie-tin tambourines made by punching three evenly spaced holes in a small aluminum pie tin and tying a small bell into each one. Monitor children with small objects.

Fingertaster "tastes" foods that make noise, such as Rice Krispies, celery, potato chips, popcorn, etc.

Children exit the story space making quiet noises (humming, whispering, shhhh-ing).

———————— Notes ————————

Spring (Spring Holidays)

Books

The Easter Chicks
JACKIE HARLAND

Happy Easter, Biscuit!
ALYSSA SATIN CAPUCILLI

Happy Easter, Maisy!
LUCY COUSINS

Max's Chocolate Chicken
ROSEMARY WELLS

Minerva Louise and the Colorful Eggs
JANET MORGAN STOEKE

My Spring Robin
ANNE ROCKWELL

Planting a Rainbow
   (Spanish: *Cómo plantar un arco iris*)
LOIS EHLERT

Sammy Spider's First Passover
SYLVIA A. ROUSS

Spot's First Easter
ERIC HILL

Spring
   (Spanish: *La primavera*)
MARÍA RIUS

Spring Is Here
   (Spanish: *Llegó la primavera*)
TARO GOMI

Spring Is Here: A Barnyard Counting Book
PAMELA JANE

Wake Me in Spring
JAMES PRELLER

Wake Up, It's Spring!
LISA CAMPBELL ERNST

Who's Hatching?
CHARLES REASONER

Word Bird's Spring Words
JANE BELK MONCURE

Rhythms, Rhymes, and Fingerplays

Eggs   (chant)

Eggs in the treetops.
Eggs on the ground.
Eggs in the water.
Eggs all around!

[Chorus]

   Eggs. Eggs. Lots of eggs.
   "Who's inside?" the little one begs.

This one hatches, and
I see a smile.
It's a toothy crocodile.

Here's an egg
Way in back,
Out comes a baby duck,
Quack, quack, quack.

Inside this egg,
Who does dwell?
A tiny turtle in its shell.

Eggs in the water.
Make a wish.
When they pop open, there'll be fish.

Of all the eggs,
I like best
The robin's eggs in her nest.

Easter Bunnies

Five Easter bunnies *(five fingers)*
Sleeping on the floor.
One hopped away, *(hopping motion)*
And then there were four. *(four fingers)*

[Repeat with]

> Four . . . hiding near a tree . . . three.
> Three . . . sniffing at my shoe . . . two.
> Two . . . sitting in the sun . . . one.
> One . . . doesn't know what to do.
>   Back hops another . . . two.
> Two . . . what do you think they see?
>   . . . three.
> Three . . . by the garden door . . . four.
> Four . . . glad to be alive. Here comes the
>   last one . . . five.

Little Flower   (tune: "I'm a Little Teapot")

I'm a little flower, *(cupped hands held close
   to the body)*
In the ground.
When the sun shines *(wiggle shoulders
   and body)*
I wiggle all around.
This way and that way *(hands move left and right,
   raising slowly)*
I push to the top. *(hands come to rest near chin)*
I reach out my green leaves, *(extend fingers)*
And then I POP! *(fingers spring outward like
   flower petals)*

Parents' Follow-Up Ideas

Gather plastic eggs of different sizes. Cut holes of varying sizes in the
lid of a box, making certain the eggs can pass through. Talk with your
children about the differences in sizes and have them drop the eggs

one at a time into the box. Can they anticipate which eggs will fit into which holes? Collect small objects and pieces of clothing (socks, handkerchiefs) to see which fit inside which eggs.

Other plastic-egg activities include: sorting the eggs by color or size, counting them, and filling them with small snacks (raisins, carrot rounds) and hiding them for an egg-hunting picnic. To store plastic eggs, nest them (open) inside an egg carton.

Spring is an excellent time to look and listen for birds because they are more visible then, gathering nesting materials on the ground and perching in trees with bare branches. Talk about how birds fly, eat, carry things, and move on the ground (walking or hopping). Discuss how baby birds hatch from eggs. Find pictures in magazines and advertising flyers of different sizes and colors of birds. Listen for bird sounds. Can your toddlers hear a difference? Borrow a bird book from the library and help your children learn the names of birds seen most often around your home.

Eat a "flower" for lunch. Make individual pizzas, using one-half of a toasted English muffin. Evenly spread pizza sauce on top and sprinkle with mozzarella cheese. Arrange toppings into a flower shape with some ingredients becoming petals and some the center: pepperoni slices, chopped green pepper, olive slices, mushroom chunks. Bake at 425° for 10 minutes. For a no-cook flower, use a rice cake, peanut butter, raisins, banana slices, pineapple pieces, or coconut.

Craft

Chinese Lantern Tree

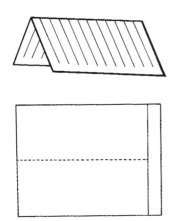

You will need: a coffee can filled with sand (or a tall flower
        vase with marbles in it)

a bare branch with several smaller twigs

rectangular pieces of construction paper

scissors

tape

colorful ribbons or yarn (optional)

Insert the base of the tree branch securely into the coffee can or vase so that the smaller twigs become the branches of a little tree. Start with a full-sized piece of construction paper to make a large lantern, since it is easier to follow directions on a larger project. For future lanterns, cut construction paper in half (or into smaller rectangles) making lanterns the appropriate size for your tree.

Cut a strip from the paper to make a handle for the lantern. Fold the remaining construction paper in half lengthwise. With the folded edge facing you, make several cuts in the paper, being careful not to cut completely across it. Unfold the paper and bring the short ends together, rolling it into a cylinder and taping the edges. Gently push the ends of the cylinder together to cause the lantern cuts to open outward, and tape the handle strip to the top. The large lantern will probably be too big for your lantern tree, so hang it from a ceiling fixture. Fill the branches of your tree with colorful small lanterns, and add bows of ribbons or yarn. The lantern tree can be made in honor of Teng Chieh, the Chinese Lantern Festival, celebrated in the spring of each year.

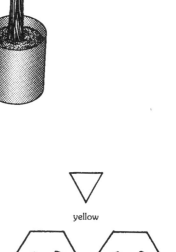

Program Notes

Sign Language

SPRING   Your left hand cups your right hand, which has the fingertips together and pointing upward. Slowly move the right hand upward, opening the fingers at the same time, like a flower emerging from the ground and blooming.

Introduce the theme with a pompom chick hidden in a plastic egg or the storytime puppet dressed as a bunny or a spring flower.

Use the "Easter Bunnies" rhyme as a flannelboard presentation or change it to "Little Bunnies." Use the "Eggs" rhyme with a flannelboard or with plastic eggs in a nest (basket) with the animals (pictures or toys) inside. Hide plastic eggs around the story space and encourage each child to find *one*, calling on each by name to search (adult can help) while the others watch.

Giveaways are pompom chicks made by gluing two small pompoms together and adding a felt beak, feet, and a comb and tiny wiggly eyes. Let children "find" them in the egg hunt.

Fingertaster "tastes" springtime foods, such as strawberries, lettuce, etc., or Easter treats (chocolate bunnies, jelly beans, etc.).

Children exit the story space "peeping" like baby chicks.

yellow

red

———————————— **Notes** ————————————

———— Summer ————

Books

At the Beach
ANNE AND HARLOW ROCKWELL

Beep, Beep, Let's Go
ELEANOR TAYLOR

Joe's Pool
CLAIRE HENLEY

Joshua by the Sea
ANGELA JOHNSON

Just Grandma and Me
MERCER MAYER

Maisy's Pool
LUCY COUSINS

Moonbear's Shadow
FRANK ASCH

Sea, Sand, Me!
PATRICIA HUBBELL

Splash, Joshua, Splash!
MALACHY DOYLE

Spot Goes to the Beach
   (Spanish: *Spot va a la playa*)
ERIC HILL

Summer
CHRIS L. DEMAREST

Summer
   (Spanish: *El verano*)
MARÍA RIUS

Summertime Waltz
NINA PAYNE

Swim!
EVE RICE

Swimsuit
KIT ALLEN

Word Bird's Summer Words
JANE BELK MONCURE

Rhythms, Rhymes, and Fingerplays

Digging in the Sand   (tune: "Farmer in the Dell")

We're digging in the sand,
   (follow the actions)
We're digging in the sand,
Hi-ho-the derrio.
We're digging in the sand.

[Repeat with]
   filling up the pail
   pouring out the sand
   making roads in sand

Inchy Pinchy Crab   (tune: "Eency Weency Spider")

Inchy pinchy crab *(wiggle fingers, moving
   hands sideways)*
Scurrying down the beach
Up comes a big wave *(sweep arms right to left)*
And carries him out to sea. *(sweep them back again)*

Swimming and swimming, *(swimming motion)*
He gets back to shore.
And inchy pinchy crab *(wiggle fingers, moving*
    hands sideways)
Goes up the beach once more.

By the Sea   (tune: "By the Beautiful Sea")

By the sea, by the sea, *(sway gently,*
    side to side)
By the beautiful sea.
You and me, you and me, *(point to*
    children and then to self)
Oh, how happy we'll be.

Splashing water and digging sand
    (mimic actions)
Watching seagulls, catching balls, and
Having fun, having fun, *(sway)*
By the beautiful sea.
You and me, you and me, *(point to*
    children and then to self)
By the sea!

Parents' Follow-Up Ideas

For ice-cream cones with less mess, here are a couple of suggestions
to make them more sturdy and absorb some of the drips. For pointed
cones, tuck a wedge of marshmallow inside the cone before adding
the ice cream. For flat-bottom cones, put a small vanilla cookie in the
bottom of the cone. These tips make getting to the bottom of the treat
even more fun.

Outside summer fun can include art projects:

1. Sidewalk chalk can decorate walks, driveways, and fences and
   will wash away with rain or a garden hose.
2. Let your child "paint" with water on fences, sidewalks, or drives.
   A bucket of water and a small paintbrush or roller can create
   wet pictures (the water darkens the surface) that then evapo-
   rate completely.
3. Put children in old bathing suits and let them paint each other
   with body paints made from no-tears shampoo and a little food
   coloring. When the works of art are finished, simply rinse them
   off with a hose or a bucket of warm water. (Food coloring may
   stain some fabrics, so you will want to test the "paint" on an inside seam first.)

Traveling with small children on vacation can be a challenge. Pack
a busy bag with several favorite tapes, books, nesting containers, and

a coffee can filled with toy animals and magnets. Sing favorite songs together and play with nursery rhyme chants. Look out the windows for different kinds of vehicles, colors, shapes, or unusual objects. Point out familiar signs: traffic signs; billboards; hospital or library signs; gas stations; and restaurant, discount, and grocery store chains. Even the youngest toddlers can recognize symbols and understand that they have meaning. This is the first step of reading preparation. Plan to stop often so all can stretch their legs and enjoy the scenery.

Craft

Water Lens

You will need: a clear, plastic, two-liter soda bottle

craft knife or scissors

cloth or duct tape (water resistant)

A water lens will allow your child to look at objects underwater in a wading pool, bathtub, or at the beach. Cut the top from a plastic soda bottle. Carefully remove the black bottom, leaving a clear, curved container. (One-piece, clear soda bottles have molded bottoms that can distort the view of objects.) Cover the rim with tape and cut two small slits, opposite each other, near the top, making handles. Tape the edges of hand slits.

Show your child how to put the curved end of the lens into the water (not so deep that water spills inside) and how to look inside to see objects, fish, plants, and toys beneath the waves or below bath bubbles.

Safety tip: Never leave your child unattended near water, no matter how shallow. Also, do not allow your child to put his or her face completely inside the water lens.

The container can also be used to carry small loads of beach toys to and from the pool or shore.

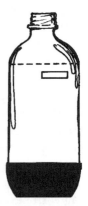

Program Notes

Sign Language

SUMMER   Drag the side of the right index finger across the forehead, curling the finger into your fist at the other side as though you were wiping sweat from your brow.

The storytime puppet introduces the theme wearing sunglasses and a summer hat.

Joe's Pool is a good flannelboard story. Between stories encourage children to mimic summer activities, like swimming, sandbox play, or playing with a beach ball.

Giveaways are visors made with poster board and yarn, letting the children decorate them at home.

Fingertaster "tastes" summer treats, such as watermelon, ice-cream cones, frozen juice, etc.

Children exit the story space pretending to walk barefooted in tickly grass (tiptoeing).

Notes

———— Trains and Planes ————

Books

Airport
BYRON BARTON

Chugga-Chugga Choo-Choo
KEVIN LEWIS

Down by the Station
JESS STOCKHAM

Freight Train
    (Spanish: *Tren de carga*)
DONALD CREWS

Go, Go, Planes!
SIMON HART

I'm Taking a Trip on My Train
SHIRLEY NEITZEL

Inside Freight Train
DONALD CREWS

Jiggle Joggle Jee!
LAURA E. RICHARDS

The Little Engine That Could
    (Spanish: *La pequeña
    locomotora que sí pudo*)
WATTY PIPER

Maisy's Train
    (Spanish: *El tren de Maisy*)
LUCY COUSINS

Planes
ANNE ROCKWELL

Planes at the Airport
PETER MANDEL

Subway
ANASTASIA SUEN

Train Song
HARRIET ZIEFERT

Trains
ANNE ROCKWELL

Two Little Trains
MARGARET WISE BROWN

Rhythms, Rhymes, and Fingerplays

Flying, Flying   (tune: "Sailing, Sailing")

Flying, flying, *(soaring with arms outstretched,
    lean side to side)*
Up in the sky so high.
In my plane I zip and zoom *(duck head on
    "zip" and "zoom")*
As I go flying by.

Fly high, fly low, *(arms up, then down)*
And loop-di-loop the sky. *(arms create circles)*
In my plane I'm like a bird *(return to soaring)*
As I go flying by.

Here Comes the Choo-Choo Train

Here comes the choo-choo train *(elbows slide along
    sides, arms make forward circles)*
Puffing down the track.

Now it's going forward . . .
Now it's going back. *(reverse circles)*
Hear the bell a-ringing. *(one hand above head,
    make bell-ringing motion)*
Ding . . . Ding . . . Ding . . . Ding
Hear the whistle blow. *(cup hands around mouth)*
Whooooo-Whoooooo!
Chug, chug, chug, chug *(make side circles slowly,
    then pick up speed)*
ch . . . ch . . . ch . . . ch . . . ch . . . ch . . . ch . . .
Shhhhhh . . . *(fold hands in lap)*
Everywhere it goes.

Parents' Follow-Up Ideas

Sounds of all kinds fascinate small children, and they love to imitate them. Make up a guessing game involving sounds of living things (cats, dogs, cows) and familiar nonliving things (cars, trains, clocks, sirens). You make the sound and let your children guess. Then let your children try to stump you.

Make a pull-toy train for your children by tying several small boxes together with shoestrings or twine. Shoe boxes without the lids are perfect for small toys or stuffed animals to ride inside. Talk about the different cars on a train and where they are in the line: first, middle, last. When stopped at a train crossing, sing a train song ("Down by the Station" or "I've Been Working on the Railroad") and try to guess what the cargo might be in different cars (people, foodstuffs, and animals—real and make believe).

Visit an airport so your children can watch the activity as airplanes land and take off. Go inside the airport to watch as planes taxi to the gate, unload and load passengers and luggage, and taxi away again. Let your toddlers imitate the actions of the workers on the ground. Watch luggage on a carousel and try to guess what's inside the bags.

Safety tip: Be very careful around the luggage carousel. Children view it as a flat merry-go-round and want to climb on it or put their hands on the moving belt, both of which are dangerous. Also, large crowds of people sweep through airports in waves. Keep an eye on your children so you do not become separated.

Craft

Train Stick Puppets

You will need: construction paper, cut in 3″ × 5″ rectangles

black construction paper (for engine and wheels)

scissors

crayons or washable markers

glue and tape

craft sticks

Make various train cars in the following manner:

Engine: 3″ × 5″ black construction paper

1″ square black paper (smokestack)

2″ square black paper, with window (cab)

triangle of black paper (scoop)

2 wheels

1 craft stick

Train cars: 3″ × 5″ construction paper (various colors for each car)

2 wheels for each car

1 craft stick

(Decorate the train cars with doors, slats, and windows.)

Attach pieces of each train car together with glue, laminate, and tape the car to a craft stick. Stand the train up along the back of a sofa with the sticks between the cushions or have a train parade when friends visit. This is also a good opportunity to talk about colors, shapes, first-middle-last, and other kinds of vehicles with your child.

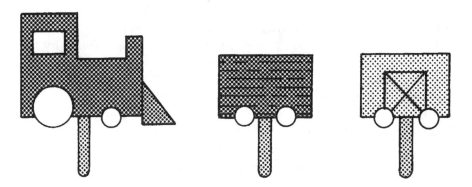

Program Notes

Sign Language

TRAIN   Extend your index and middle fingers of both hands, palms down. The fingers of the right hand lay across the fingers of the left hand and move back and forth over the backs of the left fingers, showing the cross-ties on a railroad track.

Introduce the theme as you enter the story space by making "chugging" noises like a train.

Freight Train works well both on the flannelboard and as an activity using stick puppets. Give each child a train stick puppet (keeping the engine for yourself), and ask them to follow you around the story space: chug-chugging, ringing bells, blowing whistles, and waving at still-seated adults. Vary the "speed" at which the train moves: fast, slow, stop, etc. Move in straight and winding lines. Have them "park" their train cars at the station to get the stick puppets back from them, and put the puppets out of sight.

Giveaways are train bookmarks made by photocopying this page for the pattern.

Fingertaster "tastes" foods that go together, peanut butter and jelly, ham and eggs, etc.

Children exit the story space chugging like a train.

———————————— Notes ————————————

Trucks, Cars, and Buses

Books

Away We Go!
REBECCA KAI DOTLICH

Big Wheels
ANNE ROCKWELL

The Bridge Is Up!
BABS BELL

*Bumper to Bumper:
A Traffic Jam*
JAKKI WOOD

Five Trucks
BRIAN FLOCA

Joshua James Likes Trucks
CATHERINE PETRIE

Just Us Women
JEANNETTE CAINES

Machines at Work
BYRON BARTON

Maisy Drives the Bus
   (Spanish: *El autobus
   de Maisy*)
LUCY COUSINS

Max Drives Away
ROSEMARY WELLS

*Minerva Louise and
the Red Truck*
JANET MORGAN STOEKE

My Truck Is Stuck!
KEVIN LEWIS AND DANIEL KIRK

Red Light, Green Light
ANASTASIA SUEN

School Bus
   (Spanish: *El autobus escolar*)
DONALD CREWS

Trucks Trucks Trucks
PETER SIS

Wheels on the Bus
RAFFI

Rhythms, Rhymes, and Fingerplays

Wheels on the Bus   (song)

The wheels on the bus go round and round,
   (roll hands over each other)
Round and round, round and round.
The wheels on the bus go round and round,
As it goes down the street.

[Additional verses]

The people on the bus bounce up
   and down *(bounce in place)*

The doors on the bus go open/shut *(move
   hands away from each other and back)*

The babies on the bus go "Wah! Wah!
   Wah!" *(make crying motions)*

The mommies on the bus go "Shhh!
   Shhh! Shhh!" *(make shhhh-ing motion)*
The driver on the bus says "Move on
   back!" *(motion behind over the shoulder)*

Auto, Auto

Auto, auto, may I have a ride? *(point to self)*
Yes, yes, yes, yes. Step inside. *(nod head,
   motion toward you)*
Pour in the water, *(pouring motion with right hand)*
Pump in the gas. *(pouring motion with left hand)*
Chug-away, chug-away, but not too fast!
   (steering motion)

If I Were . . .

If I were an airplane *(spread arms wide like wings)*
I would fly up in the sky. *(arms still out, lean left and right)*
If I were a tricycle *(pump legs as if peddling)*
I would wave as I went by. *(wave)*
If I were a dump truck *(elbow bent, hand on shoulder)*
I would dump my heavy load. *(let hand fall)*
But if I were a car or bus
I'd roll on down the road. *(roll hands over each other)*
If I were a choo-choo train *(hands close to sides)*
Along the tracks I'd chug. *(push-pull alternately with arms)*
And if I were a steam shovel *(hands near knees, palms up)*
I would have a big hole dug. *(scooping motion with hands)*
If I were a helicopter *(whirl hands over head)*
I'd sing a whirly tune. *(make whirrrring noise)*
But if I were a rocket ship *(palms together close to chest)*
I'd blast off to the moon! *(shoot hands upward)*

Parents' Follow-Up Ideas

Toddlers enjoy learning the names of different kinds of vehicles.
Name them for your children.

   trucks: semitrailer, tow, dump, and pickups

   cars: vans, convertibles, limousines, SUVs

   tractors

   buses

   trains

   trolleys

   airplanes

   boats

Get a book from the library and see how many types of vehicles there are. Play matching or counting games, saying "I see a pickup truck. Can you see one, too?" Do the same with colors.

When traveling with small children, take along a busy box. Fill a small box with objects that your children can play with alone: blocks and foam balls, covered containers with snap-off lids, large magnets and a small cookie sheet, a piece of cardboard covered with aluminum foil (a mirror), and a mesh bag from the produce department and yarn with tape around one end for weaving. Include a CD or tape player and stories and music. Keep the busy box just for trips, to make sure it remains a special treat. Let your children add one or two favorite toys to take along each time.

Create an easy car-bingo game for your children by drawing nine squares on a piece of cardboard. Put one picture in each square, using things that are plentiful on your journey so your toddlers will have several opportunities to see them. Draw simple pictures or cut them from magazines and glue them in the squares. Make bingo games with colors (red things), shapes (circles, triangles), familiar places (McDonalds, playgrounds, gas stations), vehicles (big trucks, school bus, trains), nature (clouds, trees, animals), etc. Each time your children find something on the bingo cards, give them a sticker to put on those squares. Make several different cards for long trips and cover them with clear contact paper to make them reusable.

Safety tip: Never leave children alone in a car.

Craft

Pretend Steering Wheel

You will need: cardboard

an oatmeal box

a brass fastener

a narrow cardboard tube
    (from pants hanger)

scissors

hole punch

Cut a 9″ circle from cardboard and cut spaces in it to create a steering wheel. Punch a hole in the side of the oatmeal box near the top, and attach the steering wheel with the brass fastener.

Poke a hole to the right of the steering wheel and push the cardboard tube into it creating a gear shift lever. The tube should fit loosely enough to be moved up and down. Place the cereal box between your child's knees, leaving hands free to "steer and change gears."

Program Notes

Sign Language

CAR   Make the motion of holding a steering wheel, moving hands slightly (in opposition to each other), as if driving a car.

Introduce the theme by "driving" into the story space, inviting children to "park" themselves on a rug spot. Use the traffic light from the colors theme. Invite the children to drive with you: go fast, go slow, stop, turning this way and that, waving at the seated adults, and finally parking their cars back in their rug-spot "garages" and putting the keys in their pockets.

Giveaways are paper-plate steering wheels made by folding the plate into quarters and cutting four wedges from it.

Fingertaster "tastes" foods from drive-in restaurants, such as hamburgers, French fries, Tater Tots, etc.

Children exit the story space "driving" their cars.

——————————————— Notes ———————————————

Walking

Books

Ben's Counting Walk
    (Spanish: *Benito pasea
    y cuenta*)
GILL MATTHEWS AND
BELINDA WORSLEY

*Big Dog and Little Dog
Going for a Walk*
DAV PILKEY

Bye-Bye, Daddy!
HARRIET ZIEFERT AND
LISA CAMPBELL ERNST

Don't Get Lost
PAT HUTCHINS

A Good Night Walk
ELISHA COOPER

*Has Anyone Here
Seen William?*
BOB GRAHAM

I Went Walking
    (Spanish: *Sali de paseo*)
SUE WILLIAMS

Let's Go Home, Little Bear
MARTIN WADDELL

*Let's Take a Walk / Vamos a
caminar* (English/Spanish)
ALAN BENJAMIN

The Listening Walk
PAUL SHOWERS

Off We Go!
JANE YOLEN

Sheep Take a Hike
NANCY SHAW

Spot's First Walk
    (French: *La première
    promenade de Spot* and
    Spanish: *El primer paseo
    de Spot*)
ERIC HILL

Taking a Walk / Caminando
(English/Spanish)
REBECCA EMBERLEY

The Trek
    (Spanish: *El trayecto*)
ANN JONAS

Walking through the Jungle
JULIE LANCOME

Rhythms, Rhymes, and Fingerplays

As I Was Walking   (tune: "Rig-a-Jig-Jig")

As I was walking down the street, *(march in place)*
Down the street, down the street,
As I was walking down the street,
Hi, ho! Hi, ho! Hi, ho! *(clap hands and march)*

Max and his mom I chanced to meet.
    (wave at child and adult)
Chanced to meet, chanced to meet.
Max and his mom I chanced to meet.
Hi, ho! Hi, ho! Hi, ho! *(clap hands)*

A rig-a-jig-jig and away we go, *(clapping
    hands, walk in a small circle)*
Away we go, away we go.

A rig-a-jig-jig and away we go. *(return
   back to your starting place)*
Hi, ho! Hi, ho! Hi, ho!

[Repeat, greeting other children and adults.]

Walking

One foot, *(raise one leg)*
Now the other, *(raise other leg)*
We walk down the street. *(march in place)*
Walking fast . . . *(march fast)*
Walking slow . . . *(march slow)*
We walk on two feet. *(march in place)*

[Continue with]

> Dogs walk down the street. *(add arms
>   to marching motion)* . . . four feet
> Spiders . . . *(add wiggling fingers)* . . .
>   eight feet

Here We Go   (tune: "Looby Loo")

Here we go walking slow, *(march in place, slowly)*
Here we go walking fast, *(march quickly)*
Here we go walking round and round, *(march in circle)*
Round the block and back. *(back to original position)*

[Additional verses]

> We hold hands walking slow . . . *(swing hands)*
> We climb steps so slow . . . *(climbing stairs motion)*
> We watch for cars going slow . . . *(look left and right)*

[Repeat first verse.]

Parents' Follow-Up Ideas

Take a discovery walk of your neighborhood or a favorite park. Children love to bring home souvenirs to remind them of the things they've seen, but be selective about the types of remembrances you choose. Remind children not to pick living plants without permission; it's better to look and smell but leave plants intact. Explain that bird feathers can have small insects living in them. *Safety tip:* Watch that your children do not put their hands in their mouths after handling "found" objects.

To bring souvenirs home, put a loop of masking tape around the child's wrist, sticky side out. Small treasures can be safely attached for the return walk. Once home, examine the treasures and recall where or how they were found. Put a sticker on your walk map (see the "Craft" section) to mark the treasure, and then keep the souvenir in a "discovery" box . . . use it to make a mobile or art collage or return it to the outdoors.

Keep walks with your children short so they do not get overly tired. Taking walks together is good exercise, but wearing your children out leaves a cranky, unhappy memory of the activity. Introduce them to new or potentially frightening experiences gently. Young children can become overwhelmed by the presence of many people or by excited pets. Be a buffer when your children need it, but let them explore with you close by when they want.

Be sensitive to the world from your children's point of view. Many things adults find interesting are blocked from toddlers' vision by low bushes, bodies, or cars. Try to get close enough that they can see interesting things without being lifted to your height. Squat down to examine things from their perspective. You may discover the world in a brand-new way, and you will send a message to your children that being small is okay—they don't have to be tall to see the "good stuff."

Craft

Walk Map

You will need: 2 pieces of cardboard the same size

pencil

clear packing tape

cloth tape

washable markers, paints, or crayons

pictures cut from magazines or photographs

clear contact paper (optional)

Create a fold-up map of your neighborhood or a park where you walk most often with your toddler. Start by taking a short walk together

along your most common walking route. Draw a quick sketch of the route, noting the landmarks and objects that interest your child. To make the map, tape together two pieces of cardboard on the back side. Lay out a *very* simple map of your route that starts and ends at your house, including only a few of your child's landmarks. Paint or color the map simply, green for grass, blue for water, etc. Draw landmarks with markers or glue to the map photographs or pictures from magazines to mark points of interest. When the paint and glue are dry, tape the fold on the front of the map with clear tape so that it will not tear. Cover the edges with cloth tape. (Optional: To further protect the surface, laminate or cover on both sides with clear contact paper.)

Take the map with you on your next walk, pointing to landmarks and showing how to use the map to get home. Let your child use the map to plan a walk before you take it, deciding which direction you will walk and what you will see. Encourage your child to play with the map, building houses with boxes and blocks or driving cars down the streets. The map can be folded for storage, and stickers can be added when new landmarks become important or as reminders of special memories. Make other simple maps of favorite places like the zoo, the park, the playground, grandma's yard, etc.

Program Notes

Sign Language

WALK   Have your hands in front, palms down, with fingers pointed away from the body. Alternately swing hands down in a motion like the legs walking.

The storyteller introduces the theme by inviting children to "go for a walk" as they enter the story space. Walk around the rug spots, pointing out things of interest at toddlers' eye levels: a picture on the wall, drinking fountain, elevator button, etc.

Storytime puppet leads the song, "As I Was Walking," waving and greeting each child or shaking hands, if they will. If you have a group that works well independently, let the first child and adult become the greeters as everyone sings, claps, and marches in place: "As Max and his mom walked down the street . . . Keisha and her dad they chanced to meet," and so on.

Giveaways can be simple, hand-drawn maps of the library or the library grounds, with three or four "landmarks" of interest to toddlers. Encourage the adults to point them out as they leave.

Fingertaster "tastes" foods from other places, such as tacos, spaghetti, fried rice, pineapple, etc.

Children exit the story space as explorers, looking for something specific (red or a smiling face or a bird).

———————————— Notes ————————————

Wind

Books

Away Went the Farmer's Hat
JANE BELK MONCURE

Bear and Kite
CLIFF WRIGHT

Boo and Baa in Windy Weather
OLOF AND LENA LANDSTRÖM

Bright and Breezy
   (Spanish: *Sol y lluvia*)
ALAN ROGERS

Gilberto and the Wind
   (Spanish: *Gilberto y el viento*)
MARIE HALL ETS

Kipper's Kite: Touch and Feel
MICK INKPEN

Kite Flying
GRACE LIN

Kite in the Park
LUCY COUSINS

Like a Windy Day
FRANK AND DEVIN ASCH

One Windy Wednesday
PHYLLIS ROOT

Please, Wind?
CAROL GREENE

*Spot's Windy Day and
Other Stories*
ERIC HILL

When the Wind Stops
CHARLOTTE ZOLOTOW

While You Were Chasing a Hat
LILIAN MOORE

The Wind Blew
PAT HUTCHINS

A Windy Day
LAURA PEGRAM

Rhythms, Rhymes, and Fingerplays

Five Bright Kites   (tune: "Three Blind Mice")

Five bright kites. *(show five fingers)*
Five bright kites.
See how they fly *(sway arms over head)*
Up in the sky.
One dives low *(arms swing down)*
And one swoops high. *(arms swing high)*
Two get tangled *(arms cross)*
And the last floats by. *(move one hand slowly)*
I love to watch my kites in the sky. *(shade eyes
   and peer upward)*
Five bright kites. *(show five fingers)*

Wind Tricks

The wind is full of tricks today; *(shake index finger)*
It blew my daddy's hat away. *(hand on head)*
It chased our paper down the street *(reach down
   to one side)*

And almost blew us off our feet. *(jump up and down)*
It makes the trees and bushes dance. *(wave arms)*
Just listen to it howl and prance. *(cup hand to ear)*
Whooooooooo-ooooooooo.

Five Winds

(point to fingers one at a time with each line)
This little wind blows rain.
This little wind drifts snow.
This little wind whistles a tune. *(whistle)*
This little wind whispers low. *(whisper)*
And this little wind rocks baby birds
To and fro, to and fro, to and fro.
(hands together, rock back and forth)

Parents' Follow-Up Ideas

Make a paper fan by pleating a piece of paper and folding it in half. Show your children how to make "wind" by moving the fan. See if your children can make enough wind to blow a piece of paper off a table. How about a feather? Or a button? Talk about the differences in weight and how the wind can move some things but not others.

Observe the weather each day and talk with your toddlers about the changes. "Yesterday was sunny, but today is raining." Mark on the calendar with stickers or crayons the days that are sunny, snowy, rainy, cloudy, or windy.

To help your children understand that air is all around us, point out things moving in the wind, such as flags, leaves, or stray pieces of paper. Help your toddlers notice birds flying and air blowing from heating or cooling vents in the house. Walk against the wind, blow bubbles, or drop confetti from your hand into an air current. Give your children a light scarf or several crepe paper streamers to dance outside with the wind or with air currents inside the house.

Craft

A Shape Kite

You will need: construction paper in bright colors

scissors

tape

string

a small stick or unsharpened pencil

Cut a circle, a triangle, a rectangle, a star, and a crescent shape from the construction paper, keeping them all about the same size. Lay the shapes in a line on a flat surface leaving 1″ between them.

Tie one end of the string to the stick and lay the stick down in front of the line of shapes, leaving 1″ between the stick and the first shape. Stretch the string across the shapes and tape it securely to the back of each one.

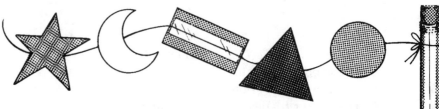

When you take the shape kite outside, the wind will blow the shapes. If there is no wind, hold the stick up high and walk with it. The shape kite will float behind you like a banner.

By cutting shapes out of plastic container lids and painting them, you can create another version of a shape kite to attach outside. Punch holes on opposite edges of each shape and assemble them in a line by tying them together with string. Attach this to a tree or pole that is visible from a window, and your child can tell you if the wind is blowing outside without leaving the house.

Program Notes

Sign Language

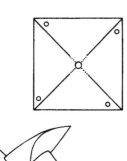

WIND   With the fingers of both hands extended and spread wide, palms facing each other, move hands simultaneously to the right and then left, as if they were blowing in the wind.

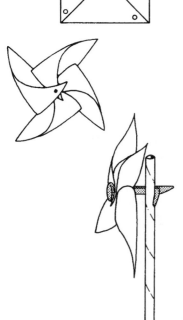

Introduce the theme using a pinwheel and letting each child blow to make it turn. If a child cannot blow hard enough, the storyteller should help.

Away Went the Farmer's Hat can be shared with a real straw hat to show the various positions of the hat in the story and to help children understand why the animals thought it was something else. *The Wind Blew* makes a good flannelboard story, shortening the number of items if necessary. Also use a flannelboard with the rhyme "Five Bright Kites."

Giveaways are pinwheels made from a square of paper clipped on the diagonals with corners folded to the center. Attach it to the end of a straw with a brass fastener.

Fingertaster "tastes" foods that are light enough to blow in the wind, such as marshmallows, coconut, bread, corn chips, etc.

Children exit the story space flying like kites or making their pinwheels spin.

───────────────────────── Notes ─────────────────────────

Winter

Books

Bob's Vacation
DANA MEACHEN RAU

Duck Skates
LYNNE BERRY

The First Snowfall
ANNE AND HARLOW ROCKWELL

Frozen Noses
JAN CARR

In the Snow
SHARON PHILLIPS DENSLOW

In the Snow
HUY VOUN LEE

The Lonesome Polar Bear
JANE CABRERA

The Mitten
ALVIN TRESSELT

Mouse's First Snow
LAUREN THOMPSON

No! No! Word Bird
JANE BELK MONCURE

Oh!
KEVIN HENKES

Snowballs
LOIS EHLERT

The Snowy Day
   (Spanish: *Un día de nieve*)
EZRA JACK KEATS

There Was a Cold Lady Who Swallowed Some Snow
LUCILLE COLANDRO

Tiny the Snow Dog
CARI MEISTER

Winter
   (Spanish: *El invierno*)
MARÍA RIUS

Rhythms, Rhymes, and Fingerplays

It's Snowing   (tune: "A Tisket, a Tasket")

It's snowing! It's snowing!
The winter wind is blowing
Snowflakes swirling round and round
And covering the ground.
The ground, the ground.
Snowflakes all around,
Snow is falling from the sky
And covering the ground.

Snowman

Here's a jolly snowman *(form chubby tummy
   with hands)*
He has a carrot nose *(touch nose)*
Along came a bunny *(hop)*
Looking for some lunch *(look around)*
He ate that snowman's carrot nose *(touch nose)*
Nibble *(hop)*, Nibble *(hop)*, Crunch! *(sit down)*

Five Little Snowmen

Five little snowmen all in a row *(hold up five fingers)*
Each with a hat *(pat top of head)*
And a big red bow. *(pull at neck like fixing a bow tie)*
Out came the sun *(arms form big circle over head)*
And it stayed all day. *(lean to the left)*
And one of those snowmen melted away! *(make melting motion with arms and body)*

[Repeat with]

    Four
    Three
    Two
    One

Parents' Follow-Up Ideas

During quiet time look through a photo album and let your toddler identify the people he or she knows. Children like seeing pictures of themselves and acknowledging how much they are growing.

Children love to see things go in one end of a cardboard tube and come out the other end. The longer the tube the better! Talk about what will fit in the tube and what is too big for it. Put two things in and see which comes out first.

Trace your toddler's hands onto a paper sack for a mitten pattern. Cut two mittens from several kinds of materials (paper, cloth, sandpaper, cardboard). Put one of each kind on a table and the others in a paper sack. Have your child pull one mitten from the sack and match it with its mate. This matching game will work with socks, towels, shoes, or any paired items in the home.

Craft

Five Little Snowmen

You will need: white, black, and red felt
                 scissors
                 glue
                 pen or washable marker
                 a flannelboard

Draw five snowmen (three circles on top of each other) on the white felt. Make them all different sizes and shapes. Draw five different-sized hats on the black and bows on the red felt. Cut them out. Turn the pencil marks to the back and assemble each snowman by gluing the hat and bow in place. Draw a face on each one.

Line the snowmen up on the flannelboard or a sofa cushion and recite the "Five Little Snowmen" rhyme. Remove one snowman as each melts. Your child will soon take over the task of "melting" the snowmen. Use the snowmen to talk about size and placement in line: "Let's melt the big one," or "The one in the middle is going to melt next."

Program Notes

Sign Language

SNOW   Hold hands high with palms facing down. Wiggle your fingers gently and slowly move them down like snow gently falling.

Introduce the theme with the storytime puppet bundled up for cold weather with a scarf and hat.

After using *The Snowy Day*, invite the children to pretend to dress warm enough to go out in the snow. Let them pretend to scoot their feet, knock snow from a tree branch with it landing on their heads, build a snowman, make a snow angel, and put a snowball in their pockets. Flannelboard presentations for this program can include the rhyme "Five Little Snowmen" and *The Mitten* (use only the first five animals and the cricket for the story and make the mitten in two pieces so the animals can get inside).

Giveaways are paper snowflakes cut from paper lace doilies with their edges shaped like snowflakes.

Fingertaster "tastes" cold foods, such as ice cream, frozen juice, snow cones, etc.

Children exit the story space "walking fat" like snowmen.

———————————— Notes ————————————

Zoos

Books

At the Zoo / Vamos al zoo
(English/Spanish)
MANDY STANLEY

Bruno Munari's Zoo
BRUNO MUNARI

Can You Cuddle Like a Koala?
JOHN BUTLER

*Curious George's First Words
at the Zoo*
MARGRET AND H. A. REY

Dear Zoo
ROD CAMPBELL

Feed the Animals
H. A. REY

Fun at the Zoo
  (Spanish: *Me divierto en el zoo*)
LARA JONES

Miffy at the Zoo
  (Spanish: *Miffy en el zoo*)
DICK BRUNA

My Beak, Your Beak
MELANIE WALSH

1, 2, 3 to the Zoo
ERIC CARLE

Peek-a-Zoo!
MARIE TORRES CIMARUSTI

Sam Who Never Forgets
EVE RICE

We've All Got Bellybuttons!
DAVID MARTIN

Whose Feet?
JEANETTE ROWE

Zoo
GAIL GIBBONS

Zoo Parade!
HARRIET ZIEFERT AND SIMMS TABACK

Rhythms, Rhymes, and Fingerplays

Zoo Animals   (tune: "If You're Happy")

If you want to be a monkey, jump up high. *(jump)*
If you want to be a monkey, jump up high.
If you want to be a monkey, if you want to be a monkey,
If you want to be a monkey, jump up high.

[Repeat with]

> eagle . . . flap your wings
> elephant . . . swing your trunk
> crab . . . walk like this *(sideways)*
> lion . . . roar out loud
> giraffe . . . stand up tall
> snake . . . slither slow

Horse in Striped Pajamas   (chanting rhyme)

Look, Daddy, look! *(clap hands with*
   the rhythm of the chant)
Do you see?
There's a horse
In striped pajamas.

No, no, no!
That's not what it is.
That's an animal
People call a zebra.

[Repeat with]

   cat with polka dots on . . .
      leopard
   bird in its tuxedo . . .
      penguin

At the Zoo

At the zoo, we saw a bear *(shade eyes, then*
   look surprised)
With great big paws and shaggy hair.
   (raise hands like claws, then touch hair)
At the zoo, a zebra we found *(shade eyes, then*
   look surprised)
With black and white stripes all around.
   (hands crisscross in front of body)
At the zoo, a giraffe so tall *(reach arms overhead)*
It could look right over the top of the wall.
   (hands at eye level, lower them under chin
   as though peeking over a wall)
At the zoo, the monkeys run *(run in place)*
And jump and swing having lots of fun.
   (jump, swing arms)

Parents' Follow-Up Ideas

Much has changed in zoos. Where once animals paced in small, barred cages, modern zoos have exhibits that present the natural habitat of animals as much as possible. There's a lot of glass and very few bars. Make opportunities to visit a zoo often with your children. Exploring all the exhibits may take several trips. Talk about the different kinds of animals and how they are related to each other (cats, bears, birds). Encourage your toddlers to compare and contrast animals (which is taller? fatter?) or to put them into categories by color, size, number of legs, where they live (water, trees, rocks), and if they have feathers or fur. Help your children learn the animals' names and collect pictures from magazines and zoo brochures to make a zoo book of favorites. Stop by the zoo gift shop and look for inexpensive toy animals to play with at home, now that your children have seen them, heard them, and watched them move. Explore "adopt-an-animal" programs at your local zoo. After the zoo visit, help your children remember which were the biggest, smallest, tallest, or loudest animals you saw that day.

Most zoos have a petting zoo where younger children can touch, pet, and feed domestic animals. Stay close to your child in petting areas, since eager animals can frighten young children, especially when being fed by visitors. Help your children learn the names of different kinds of animals and see the similarities and differences between them. If your zoo has opportunities to meet exotic animals firsthand, find out how old children need to be to participate. For many children this is the only opportunity they will have to touch animals most people see only in books or on television.

Craft

Zoo Animals

You will need: animal pictures cut from
                 magazines or brochures
            index cards
            scissors
            glue
            craft sticks

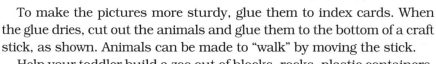

To make the pictures more sturdy, glue them to index cards. When the glue dries, cut out the animals and glue them to the bottom of a craft stick, as shown. Animals can be made to "walk" by moving the stick.

Help your toddler build a zoo out of blocks, rocks, plastic containers, etc. He or she can act out stories or re-create zoo exhibits with these stick puppets. They can also be used in matching games (find another bird, an animal with stripes, or another of the same color) or can be sorted by where they live (water, trees) or how they move (crawl, slither, fly, run).

Program Notes

Sign Language

ZOO Extend the fingers of your left hand pointing up and
fold your thumb into the palm, palm outward. Your
right index finger makes a Z starting at the left index
finger and ending along the top of the thumb.

The storytime puppet introduces the zoo theme with toy animals or
brings books to the storyteller.

The storyteller and puppet chant "Horse in Striped Pajamas" using
toy animals or flannelboard pictures. Change "Daddy" in the chant to
the storyteller's name, and the puppet takes the child's part. *Sam
Who Never Forgets* works well as a flannelboard story using animal
pictures glued to felt to create a flannelboard zoo. Let children imitate
the actions (swinging elephant's trunk, galloping zebras) or the
sounds (roaring lions, hissing snakes) of the animals in the zoo.

Giveaways can be brochures from the local zoo or animal posters
gathered from children's magazines or publishers.

Fingertaster "tastes" silly zoo foods, such as kangaroo bread, monkey pudding, zebra Jello, etc.

Children exit the story space walking like a zoo animal.

 Notes

APPENDIX A

Construction of Storytime Materials

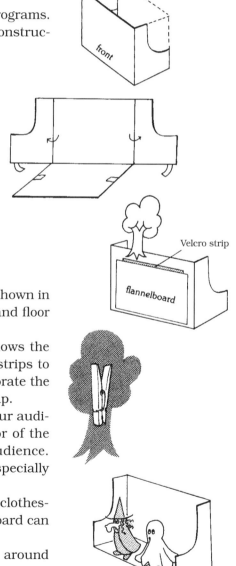

There are several items that are used in many, if not all, programs. The following instructions will assist the storyteller in the construction of these materials.

Lap Stage

Used with puppets and lap-board presentations

You will need: a cardboard box (at least 10″ × 13″ × 16″)

contact paper, burlap, or paint

box cutter or craft knife

glue

Velcro strips

spring clothespins (optional)

Cut the top and back off the box and cut the two sides as shown in the illustration. The remaining whole sides will be the front and floor of the stage.

Separate the sides and the stage floor as shown. This allows the stage to fold flat for storage or transportation. Glue Velcro strips to the sides and floor to stabilize the lap stage during use. Decorate the stage by painting it or covering it with contact paper or burlap.

To use the stage, set it on your lap with the front facing your audience. Puppets, props, or a script can lie inside on the floor of the stage, easily accessible to you but out of sight of your audience. Finger puppets, rod puppets, or small hand puppets are especially suitable for use with a lap stage.

Scenery can be attached to the stage by gluing it to spring clothespins that are clipped to the top of the stage. A small flannelboard can be attached to the front of the stage with Velcro strips.

The stage can also be used as a lap board (simply turn it around with the floor facing your audience). Stand-up figures, toys, or props can be manipulated across the stage floor as a story is told.

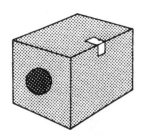

Touch Box

Used for touch-box activities and storage during programs

You will need: a cardboard box (all sides intact and
a lid that opens)

box cutter or craft knife

contact paper, material, or paint

ribbed top from a sock

glue

straight pins

Velcro strips

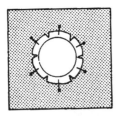

Cut a circular hole in one side of the box, large enough for your hand to easily pass through. Cover the box with contact paper, material, or paint.

Insert one end of the sock top into the hole and glue it on the *inside* of the box. Stretch and clip the sock edges to make it fit. Pin the sock in place until the glue dries thoroughly. Remove the pins. Glue the Velcro strips to the lid of the box so that it closes securely.

To use, put an object inside the box and close the lid. Demonstrate to the children how your hand can go into the box through the sock. Instruct them to feel what is inside the box (but *not* to pull it out through the sock). Encourage them to talk about what they feel: "Is it soft or hard? little or big? warm or cold? Do you know what it is?"

When each child has had a turn, remove the object through the lid of the box. Give them time to see and touch it a second time if they want. Describe the object (color, texture, size, and so on) as they examine it; always name the object (balloon, ball, banana, and so on).

By using the touch box to keep storytime props, giveaway items, and puppets out of view until they are needed in the program, you make it a familiar part of your storytime. Children will participate more fully in touch-box activities when they see the box often. They like to put things into containers and will readily return storytime props (musical instruments, rod puppets, and so on) to the touch box when you finish with them.

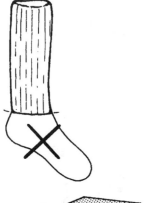

Generic Glove Puppet

Used with fingerplays and glove-puppet stories

You will need: a plain cotton gardening glove

Velcro tabs

needle and thread

pompoms or felt figures

Sew Velcro tabs to the front and back of each fingertip of the glove. Sew a strip of Velcro to the palm of the glove for scenery or props.

Make figures to use with the glove from pompoms or felt as shown. Sew a tab of Velcro to the figures so they will adhere to the tabs on the glove.

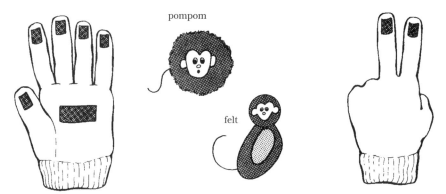

Scenery or props set the stage for a glove-puppet story. They can be made from felt or cardboard and attached to the palm of the glove with Velcro strips.

For counting rhymes, use the Velcro tabs on the back of the glove fingers. Objects can appear or disappear completely as fingers are folded into the fist.

Sock Puppet Fingertaster

Used for tasting fingers and saying good-bye

You will need: a kneesock

needle and thread

notions for facial features
    (buttons, pompoms, yarn)

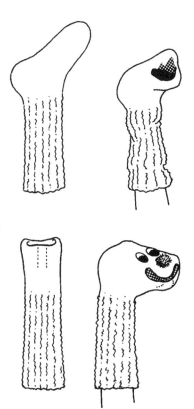

Place your hand inside the sock with the tips of your fingers near the toe and the heel across your knuckles as shown.

Open your hand wide inside the sock and tuck the toe into the palm of your hand to form the mouth. Sew a slot through both thicknesses of fabric into the bottom of the mouth for your thumb to slide into. This secures the mouth.

Sew on eyes (buttons), keeping them close to the mouth. This makes the puppet less threatening to young children. Add a nose (pompom), hair (yarn) . . . whatever other features or clothing you want to make the puppet special. No teeth, please. Avoid using materials that cannot be washed (like felt)—this puppet gets a lot of "loving."

Sock puppets are very flexible and they "make faces" easily. Practice moving your fingers inside the puppet to make it smile, frown, or turn into a silly face.

Practice "talking" by using the puppet in front of a mirror.

To taste fingers, the puppet asks the children if they want their fingers tasted. If so, the puppet sucks or licks the offered finger with a slurping sound. The puppet then tells each child what his or her finger tasted like. Use flavors with which children are familiar: fruit, soft drinks, dinner items. If children return for additional "tasting," the puppet can oblige but does not need to remember what flavor individuals were. Often the child simply wants to be touched again.

Clown-Shape Puzzle

Used in opening routine

You will need: brightly colored felt in the following shapes:

    1 1″ × 4″ rectangle

    1 triangle (base 3″; height $4\frac{1}{2}$″)

    2 circles (1 large, 1 small)

    2 small stars

    1 crescent (for a smile)

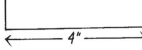
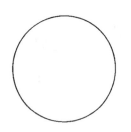

Use bright colors of felt that contrast with each other in basic hues: yellow, orange or pink, red, purple, blue, green. Toddlers can easily distinguish these colors from each other.

Trace around objects such as water glasses or salt shakers to obtain patterns for the circles, keeping them in the proportions as shown.

Cut the shapes from felt and place them at random on the flannelboard. As they are rearranged into a clown, name each shape and its relationship to the others. For instance: "This is a triangle. I will put it on top of the big circle . . . put the little circle at the top of the triangle."

As your group becomes familiar with the shapes and their place in the puzzle, put a piece in the wrong place (rectangle at the top of the triangle) and ask them if it looks right. The children will enjoy the surprise and helping you to "get it right."

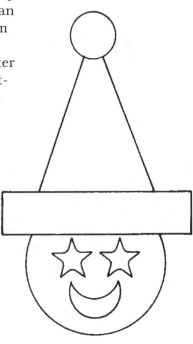

Clown Name Tag

Used to identify children by name

You will need: construction paper in basic colors
(pink, green, blue, yellow, orange,
red, tan, purple)

scissors

glue

gummed stars

clear contact paper

yarn

hole punch

safety pins (optional)

Cut the shapes shown from various colors of construction paper
and assemble them into the clown's face. Cut twice as many rectangles and crescents as you need. Glue the shapes together, adding the
gummed stars as eyes. Glue a second rectangle and second face to
the back of each name tag in the same position as the first. Print each
child's name on *both* sides of the name tag. Laminate or cover each
name tag with clear contact paper.

Punch a hole in the circle pompom and thread it with yarn. Use
enough yarn to slip the name tag over each child's head or cut it shorter
and attach a small safety pin to be pinned to the child's clothing.

Parents' name tags are squares or rectangles of construction paper
with both their first and last names printed on them. Punch a hole in
the top and add yarn and a safety pin to attach to the parents' clothing. Keep the name tags of child and parent paper-clipped together
between programs.

I Know an Old Lady Sack Puppet

Used during the song in Mealtimes and for presentation of shapes
and colors

You will need: 2 grocery sacks

scissors

stapler

tape

$8\frac{1}{2}'' \times 11''$ piece of clear acetate
(book report cover)

cardboard face, hands, and feet

material scraps

glue

poster board

Cut a window (7″ × 10″) in one sack as shown. Cut a slot under the flap of the sack and another slot along the side fold.

Tape the edges of the window and the slots to reinforce them. Glue the clear acetate on the inside of the sack so that it covers the window.

Insert the second sack into the one with the holes, making all corners and edges fit exactly. Staple both sacks across the front just under the window. This keeps the figures from sliding down too far to be seen in the window.

Cover the sack with material, leaving open the slots and window. Glue material securely. Glue on face, hands, and feet.

Insert your hand inside the sack so that the fingers make the flap move up and down. When the Old Lady "swallows" something, the flap moves upward and objects are dropped into the slot under it. They then appear in the window. They can be removed through the slot in the sack's side.

Make the objects to be swallowed from felt or heavy poster board. If felt is used, it must be weighted with fishing or drapery weights so that they drop into the window. Poster board slides down easily.

Create the animals in the song (fly, spider, and so on) and as the song is sung, drop each animal into the window where it can be seen by the children. Also use this puppet to introduce colors, shapes, and alphabet letters. There is no end to the things the Old Lady can eat.

Caterpillar and Butterfly Sock Puppets

Used with *The Very Hungry Caterpillar* in Bugs and Caterpillars

You will need: brightly colored or striped sock

white sock, same size as colored sock

a finger from an old glove

felt in the same colors as the sock puppet

glue

buttons and craft eyes

For the caterpillar, insert the white sock into the colored one. Construct the mouth as described for the sock puppet, sewing through both socks to secure the mouth. Add buttons near the mouth for the puppet's eyes.

For the butterfly, make and decorate felt wings. Glue craft eyes to the finger from the old glove to make the butterfly's body. Glue the wings to the body.

To use the puppets, fold the butterfly's wings over its body and flatten. Slide the butterfly between the white and colored socks. The caterpillar sock puppet stays on the hand for most of the story. To spin a cocoon, turn both socks inside out as you pull the puppet off your hand. The butterfly then emerges from its hidden pocket.

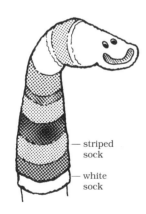

— striped sock

— white sock

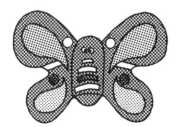

detail of finger puppet

socks inside out

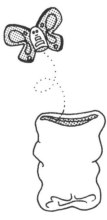

cocoon

Clip Art

This clip art figure can be copied and enlarged for a coloring page giveaway, or it can be used as a logo for toddler storytime programs in library handouts and publicity. It can also become a T-shirt transfer using fabric crayons.

Professional Bibliography

Program Planning and Program Resources

Association for Library Services to Children. *Programming for Very Young Children: Birth through Age Five*. ALA, 1996.

Baby Names, Toddler Games, and Parent Strain: Public Library Services to Young Families, recorded at the Public Library Association National Conference held March 20–23, 1991, in San Diego, California. Audiocassette.

Bauer, Caroline Feller. *Leading Kids to Books through Crafts*. ALA, 2000.

———. *Leading Kids to Books through Magic*. ALA, 2000.

———. *Leading Kids to Books through Puppets*. ALA, 1997.

———. *The New Handbook for Storytellers*. 2nd edition. ALA, 1995.

Briggs, Diane. *52 Programs for Preschoolers: The Librarian's Year-Round Planner*. ALA, 1997.

———. *Toddler Storytime Programs*. Scarecrow Press, 1993.

Carlson, Ann. *Flannelboard Stories for Infants and Toddlers, Bilingual Edition*. (Spanish/English) ALA, 2005.

Davis, Robin Works. *Toddle on Over: Developing Infant and Toddler Literature Programs*. Alleyside Press, 1998.

DeSalvo, Nancy N. *Beginning with Books, Library Programming for Infants, Toddlers, and Preschoolers*. Library Professional Publications, 1997.

Ghoting, Saroj Nadkarni, and Pamela Martin-Diaz. *Early Literacy Storytimes @ your library: Partnering with Caregivers for Success*. ALA, 2005.

Greene, Ellin. *Books, Babies, and Libraries: Serving Infants, Toddlers, Their Parents and Caregivers*. ALA, 1991.

Jeffrey, Debby Ann. *Literate Beginnings: Programs for Babies and Toddlers*. ALA, 1995.

Lima, Carolyn W., and John Lima. *A to Zoo: Subject Access to Children's Picture Books*. 7th edition. Libraries Unlimited, 2005.

Miller, Anne Meeker. *Baby Sing and Sign: A Play-Filled Language Development Program for Hearing Infants and Toddlers*. Love Language Publications, 2005.

Richey, Virginia H., and Katharyn E. Puckett. *Wordless/Almost Wordless Picture Books: A Guide*. Libraries Unlimited, 1992.

Schiller, Pam. *The Complete Resource Book for Toddlers and Twos: Over 2000 Experiences and Ideas*. Gryphon House, 2003.

Sierra, Judy. *The Flannelboard Storytelling Book: 50 Stories, Poems, and Songs, and Over 300 Patterns*. 2nd edition. H. W. Wilson, 1997.

———. *Mother Goose's Playhouse: Toddler Tales and Nursery Rhymes with Patterns for Puppets and Feltboards*. Bob Kaminski Media Arts, 1994.

———. *Multicultural Folktales for the Feltboard and Readers' Theater*. Oryx Press, 1996.

Sierra, Judy, and Robert Kaminski. *Multicultural Folktales: Stories to Tell Young Children*. Oryx Press, 1991.

Totline Staff, comp. *1001 Teaching Props: Simple Props to Make for Working with Young Children*. Illus. by Gary Mohrmann. Totline Publications, 1992.

Trostle, Susan Louise. *Storytelling in Emergent Literacy: Fostering Multiple Intelligence.* Thomson Delmar Learning, 2000.

Wilmes, Liz, and Dick Wilmes. *Felt Board Stories.* Illus. by Janet McDonnell. Building Blocks, 2001.

——. *2's Experience Dramatic Play.* Illus. by Janet McDonnell. Building Blocks, 1997.

——. *2's Experience Stories.* Illus. by Janet McDonnell. Building Blocks, 1999.

——— Activities and Crafts ———

Brennan, Jan. *Treasured Time with Your Toddler: A Monthly Guide to Activities.* Revised edition. August House, 1993.

Chernoff, Goldie Taub. *Easy Costumes You Don't Have to Sew.* Simon & Schuster, 1984.

Cole, Ann, Carolyn Buhai Haas, Faith Bushnell, and Betty Weinberger. *I Saw a Purple Cow and 100 Other Recipes for Learning.* Illus. by True Kelley. Little, Brown, 1997.

Ellison, Sheila. *365 Games Toddlers Play: Creative Time to Imagine, Grow and Learn.* Sourcebooks, 2003.

Haas, Carolyn Buhai. *Look at Me: Creative Learning Activities for Babies and Toddlers.* Chicago Review Press, 1987.

Herr, Judy, and Terri Swim. *Rhyming Books, Marble Painting, and Many Other Activities for Toddlers: 25 to 36 Months.* Thomson Delmar Learning, 2002.

——. *Shapes, Show Me, and Many Other Activities for Toddlers: 13 to 24 Months.* Thomson Delmar Learning, 2002.

Hodges, Susan. *Toddler Art.* Totline Publications, 1998.

Honig, Alice S. *Playtime Learning Games for Young Children.* Syracuse University Press, 1982.

Kohl, MaryAnn F., Renee F. Ramsey, Dana Bowman, and Katheryn Davis. *First Art: Art Experiences for Toddlers and Twos.* Gryphon House, 2002.

Kuffner, Trish. *The Toddlers Busy Book: 365 Creative Games and Activities to Keep Your 1½- to 3-Year-Old Busy.* Meadowbrook, 1999.

Martin, Elaine. *Baby Games: The Joyful Guide to Child's Play from Birth to Three Years.* Revised and updated. Running Press, 1988.

McKinnon, Elizabeth, and Gayle Bittinger. *Busy Bees Spring: Fun for Two's and Three's.* Illus. by Barb Tourtillotte. Totline Publications, 1995. (Also: *Busy Bees Fall, Busy Bees Summer,* and *Busy Bees Winter.*)

Miller, Karen. *More Things to Do with Toddlers and Twos.* Telshare Publications, 1990.

Raines, Shirley, Karen Miller, and Leah Curry-Rood. *Story S-T-R-E-T-C-H-E-R-S for Infants, Toddlers: Experiences, Activities, and Games for Popular Children's Books.* Gryphon House, 2002.

Reitzes, Fretta, Beth Teitelman, and Lois Alter Mark. *Wonderplay: Interactive and Developmental Games, Crafts, and Creative Activities for Infants, Toddlers, and Preschoolers.* Running Press Books, 1995.

Renfro, Nancy. *Bags Are Big! Paper Bag Craft Book.* Nancy Renfro Studios, 1986.

Ross, Kathy. *Storytime Craft Book.* Millbrook Press, 2003.

Sattler, Helen Roney. *Recipes for Art and Craft Materials.* Illus. by Marti Shohet. HarperTrophy, 1994.

Schiller, Pam, and Jackie Silberg. *The Complete Book of Activities, Games, Stories, Props, Recipes, and Dances for Preschoolers.* Gryphon House, 2003.

Silberg, Jackie. *Games to Play with Toddlers.* Revised edition. Gryphon House, 2002.

——. *More Games to Play with Toddlers.* Illus. by Cheryl Kirk Noll. Gryphon House, 1996.

Totten, Kathryn. *Seasonal Storytime Crafts.* Upstart Books, 2002.

——. *Storytime Crafts.* Upstart Books, 1998.

Wilmes, Liz, and Dick Wilmes. *2's Experience Art.* Illus. by Janet McDonnell. Building Blocks, 1995.

——. *2's Experience Sensory Play.* Illus. by Janet McDonnell. Building Blocks, 1997.

Fingerplays, ——— Puppets, and Music ———

Ada, Alma Flor, and F. Isabel Campoy. *Mama Goose: A Latino Nursery Treasury.* Illus. by Maribel Suarez. Hyperion Books, 2005.

——. *Pio Peep! Traditional Spanish Nursery Rhymes.* (English/Spanish) Illus. by Vivi Escriva. Rayo, 2003.

Baker, Georgette. *Cantemos Chiquitos: Songs and Fingerplays from Spanish Speaking Countries.* Cantemos, 2000. (Book and CD)

Brown, Margaret Wise. *Give Yourself to the Rain: Poems for the Very Young.* Illus. by Teri L. Weidner. McElderry Books, 2002.

Calmenson, Stephanie. *Good for You! Toddler Rhymes for Toddler Storytimes.* HarperCollins, 2001.

Cole, Joanna, Stephanie Calmenson, and Alan Tiegreen. *Eentsy, Weentsy Spider: Fingerplays and Action Rhymes.* Morrow, 1991.

Collins, S. Harold. *Songs in Sign.* Illus. by Kathy Kifer. Garlic Press, 1995.

Connors, Abigail Flesch. *101 Rhythm Activities for Young Children.* Illus. by Deborah Wright. Gryphon House, 2004.

Defty, Jeff. *Creative Fingerplays and Action Rhymes: An Index and Guide to Their Use.* Illus. by Ellen Kate Hester. Oryx Press, 1992.

Dowell, Ruth I. *Move Over, Mother Goose! Finger Plays, Action Verses, and Funny Rhymes.* Illus. by Concetta C. Scott. Gryphon House, 1994.

Hunt, Tamara, and Nancy Renfro. *Puppetry in Early Childhood Education.* Nancy Renfro Studios, 1982.

Kleiner, Lynn. *Toddlers Make Music! Ones and Twos! For Parents and Their Toddlers.* Alfred Publications, 2000.

Roberts, Lynda. *Mitt Magic: Fingerplays for Finger Puppets.* Illus. by James Morris. Gryphon House, 1985.

Rottman, Fran. *Easy to Make Puppets and How to Use Them.* Regal Books, 1995.

Signed English Dictionary for Preschool and Elementary Levels. Edited by Harry Bornstein and others. Gallaudet College Press, 1975.

Silberg, Jackie, and Pam Schiller. *The Complete Book of Rhymes, Songs, Poems, Fingerplays, and Chants.* Illus. by Debbie Wright. Gryphon House, 2006. (Book and CD)

Smrke, Connie. *Poems and Rhymes and Things to Do Now That I'm a Toddler, Too.* Incentive Publications, 1992.

Stetson, Emily, and Vicky Congdon. *Little Hands Fingerplays and Action Songs: Seasonal Activities and Creative Play for 2- to 6-Year-Olds.* Illus. by Betsy Day. Williamson, 2001.

Totline Staff, comp. *Totline 1001 Rhymes and Fingerplays.* Illus. by Gary Mohrmann. Warren, 1994.

Wilmes, Liz, and Dick Wilmes. *2's Experience Fingerplays.* Illus. by Janet McDonnell. Building Blocks, 1994.

Wirth, Marian. *Musical Games, Fingerplays, and Rhythmic Activities for Early Childhood.* Parker, 1983.

Wiseman, Ann. *Making Musical Things.* Scribner, 1979.

Toddler Characteristics and Parenting Books

Anderson, Rita, and Linda Neumann. *Partners in Play: Creative Homemade Toys for Toddlers.* Holt, 1995.

Anthony, Michelle, and Reyna Lindert. *Signing Smart with Babies and Toddlers: A Parent's Strategy and Activity Guide.* St. Martin's Griffin, 2005.

Barnes, Bridget A., and Steven M. York. *Common Sense Parenting of Toddlers and Preschoolers.* Boys Town Press, 2001.

Brown, Laurene Krasny. *Toddler Time: A Book to Share with Your Toddler.* Little, Brown, 1990.

Butler, Dorothy. *Babies Need Books.* Heinemann, 1998.

Devine, Monica. *Baby Talk: The Art of Communicating with Infants and Toddlers.* Plenum, 1991.

Dexter, Sandi. *Joyful Play with Toddlers: Recipes for Fun with Odds and Ends.* Illus. by Karen Pew. Parenting Press, 1995.

Goldberg, Sally. *Make Your Own Preschool Games: A Personalized Play and Learn Program.* Perseus Publishing, 2002.

Jones, Claudia. *Parents Are Teachers, Too: Enriching Your Child's First Six Years.* Williamson, 1988.

Karp, Harvey. *The Happiest Toddler on the Block: The New Way to Stop the Daily Battle of Wills and Raise a Secure and Well-Behaved One- to Four-Year-Old.* Bantam, 2005.

Kuhn, Brett, and Joe Borgenicht. *The Toddler Owner's Manual: Operating Instructions, Troubleshooting Tips, and Advice on System Maintenance.* Quirk Books, 2005.

Lindsay, Jean Warren. *Teens Parenting—Discipline from Birth to Three: How to Prevent and Deal with Discipline Problems with Babies and Toddlers.* Morning Glory Press, 1991.

Maddigan, Beth, Roberta Thompson, and Stefanie Drennan. *The Big Book of Stories, Songs, and Sing-Alongs: Programs for Babies, Toddlers, and Families.* Libraries Unlimited, 2003.

Miller, Lynn G., and Mary Jo Gibbs. *Making Toys for Infants and Toddlers: Using Ordinary Stuff for Extraordinary Play.* Gryphon House, 2002.

Odean, Kathleen. *Great Books for Babies and Toddlers: More than 500 Recommended Books for Your Child's First Three Years.* Ballantine Books, 2003.

Silberg, Jackie. *125 Brain Games for Toddlers and Twos: Simple Games to Promote Early Brain Development.* Gryphon House, 2000.

Spencer, Paula. *Parenting Guide to Your Toddler.* Ballantine Books, 2000.

Straub, Judy, and K. J. Dell-Antonia. *Reading with Babies, Toddlers and Twos: A Guide to Choosing, Reading and Loving Books Together.* Sourcebooks, 2006.

Varni, James W., and Donna G. Corwin. *Time-Out for Toddlers: Positive Solutions to Typical Problems in Children.* Berkley, 1991.

Wardley, Bridget L., and Judy More. *The Big Book of Recipes for Babies, Toddlers, and Children: 365*

Quick, Easy, and Healthy Dishes. Duncan Baird Publishers, 2005.

Watson, Susan, and Loretta Trezzo. *Sugar-Free Toddlers: Over 100 Recipes plus Sugar Ratings for Store-Bought Foods.* Williamson Publishing, 1991.

Whitford, Rebecca. *Little Yoga: A Toddler's First Book of Yoga.* Henry Holt, 2005.

Wilkoff, William. *How to Say No to Your Toddler: Creating a Safe, Rational, and Effective Discipline Program for Your 9-Month-Old to 3-Year-Old.* Broadway, 2003.

Early Childhood
—— Educators Resources ——

Catlin, Cynthia. *More Toddlers Together: The Complete Planning Guide for a Toddler Curriculum Volume II.* Gryphon House, 1996.

———. *Toddlers Together: The Complete Planning Guide for a Toddler Curriculum.* Illus. by Karen Theusen. Gryphon House, 1994.

Davidson, Jane Ilene. *Emergent Literacy and Dramatic Play in Early Education.* Thomson Delmar Learning, 1995.

Dombro, Amy Laura, Laura J. Colker, and Diane Trister Dodge. *Creative Curriculum for Infants and Toddlers.* Revised edition. Thomson Delmar Learning, 1997.

Ezell, Helen K. *Shared Storybook Reading: Building Young Children's Language and Emergent Literacy Skills.* Brookes Publishing, 2005.

Gonzalez-Mena, Janet, and Dianne Widmeyer Eyer. *Infants, Toddlers, and Caregivers: A Curriculum of Respectful, Responsive Care and Education.* 6th edition. McGraw-Hill, 2003.

Greenman, Jim, and Anne Stonehouse. *Prime Times: A Handbook for Excellence in Infant and Toddler Programs.* Redleaf Press, 1996.

Hamilton, Darlene Softley, and Bonnie Mack Fleming. *Resources for Creative Teaching in Early Childhood Education.* 2nd edition. Songs and parodies by JoAnne Deal Hicks. Singular, 1990.

Hodge, Mary A., Gayle Bittinger, Jenny C. Rose, and Kathleen Cubley. *Small Motor Play (101 Tips for Toddler Teachers).* Totline Publications, 1997.

———. *Terrific Tips for Toddler Teachers.* Totline Publications, 1998.

Kinnell, Gretchen. *No Biting: Policy and Practice for Toddler Programs.* Redleaf Press, 2002.

Knoll, Michelle, and Marion O'Brien. *Quick Quality Check for Infant and Toddler Programs.* Redleaf Press, 2001.

Mayesky, Mary. *Creative Activities for Young Children.* 7th edition. Thomson Delmar Learning, 2001.

Raikes, Helen, and Jane McCall Whitmer. *Beautiful Beginnings: A Developmental Curriculum for Infants and Toddlers.* Brookes Publishing, 2005.

Strickland, Dorothy S. *Emerging Literacy: Young Children Learn to Read and Write.* International Reading Association, 1989.

Striker, Susan. *Young at Art: Teaching Toddlers Self-Expression, Problem-Solving Skills, and an Appreciation for Art.* Owl Books, 2001.

Warren, Jean. *Nursery Rhyme Theme-a-Saurus: The Great Big Book of Nursery Rhyme Teaching Themes.* Illus. by Barb Tourtillotte. Totline Publications, 1993.

———. *Toddler Theme-a-Saurus: The Great Big Book of Toddler Teaching Themes.* Illus. by Judy Shimono. Totline Publications, 1990.

Wittmer, Donna, and Sandy Petersen. *Infant and Toddler Development and Responsive Program Planning: A Relationship-Based Approach.* Prentice Hall, 2005.

—————— Periodicals ——————

Babybug. Carus Publishing, Cricket Magazine Group, 315 Fifth St., Peru, IL 61354. http://www.cricketmag.com. Published monthly.

Kidstuff: A Treasury of Early Childhood Enrichment Materials. Guidelines Press, 1307 S. Killian Dr., Lake Park, FL 33403. Published monthly.

Ladybug. Carus Publishing, Cricket Magazine Group, 315 Fifth St., Peru, IL 61354. http://www.cricketmag.com. Published monthly.

Magazines for Children: A Guide for Parents, Teachers, and Librarians. By Selma K. Richardson. 2nd edition. ALA, 1991.

Parent and Preschooler Newsletter. (English/Spanish) Linden Early Childhood Training Institute, 4800 Old Westbury Rd., Roslyn, NY 11577-2215. Published 11 issues/year.

Parenting Magazine. Time Publishing, 1325 Avenue of the Americas, 27th Floor, New York, NY 10019. http://www.parenting.com/parenting. Published 11 issues/year.

Parents Magazine. Gruner & Jahr, 375 Lexington Ave., New York, NY 10017. http://www.parents.com. Published monthly. Regular monthly column: "As They Grow/Two-Year-Olds."

Preschool Playroom Magazine. Redan, Inc., Canon Ct. E., Abbey Lawn, Shrewsbury SY2 5DE UK. http://www.redan.co.uk. Published bimonthly.

Sesame Street Magazine. Sesame Workshop, 1 Lincoln Plaza, New York, NY 10023. http://www.sesameworkshop.org. Published monthly.

Totline Newsletter. Totline Press, P.O. Box 2255, Everett, WA 98203. Published monthly.

Turtle Magazine. Children's Better Health Institute, 1100 Waterway Blvd., P.O. Box 567, Indianapolis, IN 46206. http://www.cbhi.org/magazines/turtle. Published bimonthly.

Your Big Backyard. National Wildlife Federation, 11100 Wildlife Center Dr., Reston, VA 20190-5362. http://www.nwf.org/yourbigbackyard. Published monthly.

Zootles Magazine. Zoobooks, 12233 Thacker Ct., Poway, CA 92064. Published bimonthly.

Websites

Dialogic Reading: http://www.ala.org/ala/pla/plaissues/earlylit/researchandeval/dialogicreading.htm

Emergent Literacy: http://www.ala.org/ala/pla/plaissues/earlylit/earlyliteracy.htm

Bibliography of Titles
Used in the Programs

Adams, Pam. *Mrs. Honey's Hat.* Child's Play International, 1999. Hats

Agassi, Martine. *Hands Are Not for Hitting.* Illus. by Marieka Heinlen. Free Spirit Publishing, 2002. (Board book) My Body

Agell, Charlotte. *Up the Mountain.* DK, 2000. Rain

Ahlberg, Allan. *Treasure Hunt.* Illus. by Gillian Tyler. Candlewick Press, 2002. Peek, Peek

Alborough, Jez. *Hide and Seek: A Flip-the-Flap Book.* Candlewick Press, 1999. Peek, Peek

———. *Hug.* Candlewick Press, 2001. Monkeys

———. *Tall.* Candlewick Press, 2005. Sizes and Shapes

———. *Whose Socks Are Those? A Flip-the-Flap Book.* Candlewick Press, 1999. Getting Dressed

Aliki. *All by Myself.* HarperCollins, 2000. Growing Up Safe

———. *One Little Spoonful.* HarperFestival, 2001. My Body

Allen, Jonathan. *Who's at the Door?* Orchard Books, 1993. Peek, Peek

Allen, Kit. *Swimsuit.* Houghton Mifflin, 2003. (Board book) Summer

Allen, Pamela. *Who Sank the Boat?* Putnam, 1996. Boats

Anderson, Peggy Perry. *To the Tub.* Houghton Mifflin, 2001. Frogs and Turtles

Andrews, Sylvia. *Dancing in My Bones.* Illus. by Ellen Mueller. HarperFestival, 2001. Dancing

Anholt, Catherine, and Laurence Anholt. *What Makes Me Happy?* Candlewick Press, 1996. Feelings

Appelt, Kathi. *Bubbles, Bubbles.* Illus. by Fumi Kosaka. HarperFestival, 2001. Bath Time

Arno, Iris Hiskey. *I Like a Snack on an Iceberg.* Illus. by John Sandford. HarperFestival, 1999. Mealtimes

Arnold, Tedd. *No More Water in the Tub!* Dial Books, 1995. Bath Time

Arnosky, Jim. *Rabbits and Raindrops.* Putnam, 2001. Rabbits

Asch, Frank. *Goodbye House.* Simon & Schuster, 1989. Homes

———. *Just Like Daddy.* Simon & Schuster, 1984. Family

———. *Moonbear's Bargain.* Sagebrush, 1999. Friends

———. *Moonbear's Pet.* Simon & Schuster, 1997. Frogs and Turtles

———. *Moonbear's Shadow.* Aladdin, 2000. Summer

———. *Moonbear's Skyfire.* Aladdin, 2000. Rain

———. *Moongame.* Simon & Schuster, 1984. Also in big book format (Scholastic, 1992). Peek, Peek

Asch, Frank, and Devin Asch. *Like a Windy Day.* Gulliver Books, 2002. Wind

Ashman, Linda. *Can You Make a Piggy Giggle?* Illus. by Henry Cole. Dutton, 2002. Playing

Axworthy, Anni. *Guess What I Am: A Peephole Book.* Candlewick Press, 1998. Peek, Peek

———. *Guess What I'll Be: A Peephole Book.* Candlewick Press, 1998. Growing Up Safe

Baer, Gene. *Thump, Thump, Rat-a-Tat-Tat.* Illus. by Lois Ehlert. HarperCollins, 1989. Parades

Bajaj, Varsha. *How Many Kisses Do You Want Tonight?* Illus. by Ivan Bates. Little, Brown, 2004. Bedtime

Baker, Alan. *Brown Rabbit's Shape Book.* Kingfisher, 1994. (Board book) Sizes and Shapes

———. *Little Rabbits' First Word Book.* Kingfisher, 1996. (Board book) Rabbits

———. *White Rabbit's Color Book.* Kingfisher, 1995. (Board book) Colors

Balan, Bruce. *Cows Going Past.* Illus. by Scott Nash. Dial Books, 2005. Colors

Balian, Lorna. *Humbug Witch.* Star Bright Books, 2003. Autumn

Ballard, Robin. *I Used to Be the Baby.* Greenwillow Books, 2002. Growing Up Safe

Bang, Molly. *One Fall Day.* Greenwillow Books, 1994. Autumn

———. *Ten, Nine, Eight.* Greenwillow Books, 1983. Also in Spanish: *Diez, nueve, ocho* (Rayo, 1997). Bedtime

Barner, Bob. *Bugs! Bugs! Bugs!* Chronicle Books, 1999. Bugs and Caterpillars

Barton, Byron. *Airport.* HarperTrophy, 1987. Trains and Planes

———. *Boats.* HarperCollins, 1986. Boats

———. *Building a House.* HarperTrophy, 1990. Also in big book format (Hampton-Brown Books, 1992). Homes

———. *Buzz! Buzz! Buzz!* Simon & Schuster, 1995. Bugs and Caterpillars

———. *The Little Red Hen.* HarperFestival, 1997. (Board book) Also in Spanish: *La gallinita roja* (Barcelona Publications, 2004). Read to Me!

———. *Machines at Work.* HarperFestival, 1997. (Board book) Trucks, Cars, and Buses

———. *Three Bears.* HarperCollins, 1999. Also in big book format (HarperCollins, 1994). Read to Me!

———. *Where's Al?* Clarion, 1989. Dogs

Bates, Ivan. *Five Little Ducks.* Orchard Books, 2006. Birds

Bauer, Marion Dane. *Toes, Ears, and Nose! A Lift-the-Flap Book.* Illus. by Karen Katz. Little Simon, 2003. (Board book) My Body

Beaton, Clare. *How Big Is a Pig?* Illus. by Stella Blackstone. Barefoot Books, 2000. Sizes and Shapes

———. *There's a Cow in the Cabbage Patch.* Illus. by Stella Blackstone. Barefoot Books, 2001. Also in Spanish: *Hay una vaca entre las coles* (Barefoot Books, 2003). Homes

Beaumont, Karen. *Baby Danced the Polka.* Illus. by Jennifer Plecas. Dial Books, 2004. Dancing

Beck, Scott. *Little House, Little Town.* Harry Abrams, 2004. Homes

Bell, Babs. *The Bridge Is Up!* Illus. by Rob Hefferan. HarperCollins, 2004. Trucks, Cars, and Buses

Benjamin, Alan. *Let's Eat / Vamos a comer.* (English/Spanish) Illus. by Hideo Shirotani. Libros para Niños, 1992. (Board book) Mealtimes

———. *Let's Play / Vamos a jugar.* (English/Spanish) Illus. by Hideo Shirotani. Libros para Niños, 1992. (Board book) Playing

———. *Let's Take a Walk / Vamos a caminar.* (English/Spanish) Illus. by Hideo Shirotani. Libros para Niños, 1992. (Board book) Walking

———. *What Color? / ¿Que color?* (English/Spanish) Illus. by Hideo Shirotani. Libros para Niños, 1992. (Board book) Colors

Bentley, Dawn. *Good Night, Sweet Butterflies: A Color Dreamland.* Illus. by Heather Cahoon. Little Simon, 2003. (Warning: contains small parts) Bugs and Caterpillars

———. *Icky Sticky Frog.* Illus. by Salina Yoon. Piggy Toes Press, 1999. Frogs and Turtles

Berends, Polly Berrien. *I Heard Said the Bird.* Illus. by Brad Sneed. Puffin, 1998. Babies

Berenstain, Stan, and Jan Berenstain. *Old Hat, New Hat.* Random House, 1970. Hats

Berry, Holly. *Old MacDonald Had a Farm.* North-South Books, 1997. Farms

Berry, Lynne. *Duck Skates.* Illus. by Hiroe Nakata. Holt, 2005. Winter

Big Enough for a Bike: A Sesame Street Book. Random House, 2002. (Board book) Growing Up Safe

Bilgrami, Shaheen. *Whose Clothes Are Those?* Illus. by Sally Chambers. Barron's, 2001. (Lift-the-flap board book) Getting Dressed

Black, Sonia. *Animal Homes.* Cartwheel Press, 2002. (Board book) Homes

Blackstone, Stella. *Bear in a Square.* Illus. by Debbie Harter. Barefoot Books, 2000. (Board book) Sizes and Shapes

———. *Bear's Busy Family.* Illus. by Debbie Harter. Barefoot Books, 1999. Also in Spanish: *La familia activa de oso* (Barefoot Books, 2003). Bears

———. *Ship Shapes.* Illus. by Siobhan Bell. Barefoot Books, 2006. Boats

Bloom, Suzanne. *A Splendid Friend, Indeed.* Boyds Mills Press, 2005. Friends

Bogdanowicz, Basia. *Yellow Hat, Red Hat.* Millbrook Press, 1998. Hats

Bornstein, Ruth. *Little Gorilla.* Clarion Books, 1979. Also in Spanish: *Gorilita* (Clarion, 2004). (Board book) Monkeys

Bowie, C. W. *Busy Toes.* Illus. by Fred Willingham. Whispering Coyote Press, 1998. My Body

Boxall, Ed. *Scoot on Top of the World.* Candlewick Press, 2004. Dogs

Boyd, Lizi. *I Love Daddy.* Candlewick Press, 2004. (Board book) Frogs and Turtles

Boynton, Sandra. *A Is for Angry: An Animal and Adjective Alphabet.* Workman, 1987. Feelings

———. *Barnyard Dance!* Workman, 1993. (Board book) Dancing

———. *Belly Button Book.* Workman, 2005. My Body

———. *Birthday Monsters!* Workman, 1993. (Board book) Birthdays

———. *Blue Hat, Green Hat.* Little Simon, 1995. Also in Spanish: *Azul el sombrero, verde el sombrero* (Libros para Niños, 2003). (Board book) Hats

———. *Doggies: A Counting and Barking Book.* Simon & Schuster, 2001. Also in Spanish: *Perritos: Un libro para contar y ladrar* (Libros para Niños, 2004). (Board book) Dogs

———. *The Going to Bed Book.* Little Simon, 2004. Also in Spanish: *Buenas noches a todos* (Libros para Niños, 2004). (Board book) Bedtime

———. *Hey! Wake Up!* Workman, 2000. (Board book) Morning

———. *Moo, Baa, La La La!* Gardner Books, 2004. Also in Spanish: *Muu. Beee. ¡Así fue!* (Libros para Niños, 2003). Sounds

———. *My Piggy Book.* Little Simon, 2006. (Rag book) Farms

———. *One, Two, Three!* Workman, 1993. (Board book) Counting

———. *Snuggle Puppy! (A Love Song).* Workman, 2003. (Board book) Love

———. *Yay, You! Moving Out, Moving Up, Moving On.* Little Simon, 2001. Playing

———. *Your Personal Penguin.* Workman, 2006. Birds

Brannon, Tom. *Monster Faces.* Random House, 1996. (Board book) Feelings

Braun, Sebastian. *I Love My Daddy.* HarperCollins, 2004. Bears

Braun, Trudi. *My Goose Betsy.* Illus. by John Bendall-Brunello. Candlewick Press, 1998. Birds

Bridwell, Norman. *Clifford and the Big Parade.* Cartwheel Press, 1998. Parades

———. *Clifford at the Circus.* Scholastic, 1985. Circus

———. *Clifford the Firehouse Dog.* Cartwheel Books, 2005. Also in Spanish: *Clifford el perro bombero* (Scholastic en Español, 1999). Firefighters

———. *Clifford's Animal Sounds.* Cartwheel Books, 1991. Also in Spanish: *Clifford y los sonidos de los animales* (Scholastic en Español, 2003). Sounds

———. *Clifford's Good Deeds.* Cartwheel Books, 2005. Also in Spanish: *Las buenas acciones de Clifford* (Scholastic en Español, 1989). Helping

Brown, Janet Allison. *Hurray for Elephant!* Illus. by Paula Knight. Tiger Tales, 2003. (Board book) Helping

Brown, Margaret Wise. *Big Red Barn.* Illus. by Felicia Bond. HarperCollins, 1989. Also in big book format (HarperTrophy, 1991); and in Spanish: *El gran granero rojo* (Rayo, 2003). Farms

———. *Goodnight Moon.* Illus. by Clement Hurd. HarperCollins, 1947. Also in pop-up book format: *Goodnight Moon Room: A Pop-Up Book* (Harper-

Festival, 1985); and in Spanish: *Buenas noches, Luna* (Rayo, 1995). Bedtime

———. *The Runaway Bunny.* Illus. by Clement Hurd. HarperCollins, 2005. Also in Spanish: *El conejito andarín* (Rayo, 2002). Rabbits

———. *Two Little Trains.* Illus. by Leo and Diane Dillon. HarperCollins, 2001. Trains and Planes

Brown, Rick. *Old MacDonald Had a Cow.* Sterling, 2005. (Texture book) Farms

Brown, Ruth. *A Dark, Dark Tale.* Puffin, 1992. Autumn

———. *Ladybug, Ladybug.* Puffin, 1992. Bugs and Caterpillars

———. *Ten Seeds.* Knopf, 2001. Gardens

Bruna, Dick. *Miffy at the Zoo.* Big Tent Entertainment, 2004. Also in Spanish: *Miffy en el zoo* (Destino Ediciones, 2002). (Board book) Zoos

Bunting, Eve. *Flower Garden.* Illus. by Kathryn Hewitt. Harcourt, 1994. Gardens

———. *My Big Boy Bed.* Illus. by Maggie Smith. Clarion, 2003. Growing Up Safe

Burningham, John. *Mr. Gumpy's Outing.* Holt, 1971. Also in big book format (Holt, 1995). Boats

Butler, Dorothy. *My Brown Bear Barney.* Illus. by Elizabeth Fuller. Morrow, 2006. Bears

Butler, John. *Can You Cuddle Like a Koala?* Peachtree Publishers, 2003. Zoos

———. *Who Says Woof?* Viking, 2003. Sounds

———. *Whose Baby Am I?* Viking, 2001. (Board book) Babies

Butterfield, Moira. *Peek-a-Who? A Lift-the-Flap Book.* Illus. by Rachael O'Neil. Scholastic, 2004. Peek, Peek

Butterworth, Nick. *When We Play Together.* Collins, 1994. (Board book) Playing

Cabrera, Jane. *Bear's Good Night.* Candlewick Press, 2002. (Board book) Bears

———. *Cat's Colors.* Puffin Books, 2000. Colors

———. *Dog's Day.* Scholastic, 2000. Dogs

———. *If You're Happy and You Know It: A Sing-Along Action Book.* Holiday House, 2005. Feelings

———. *The Lonesome Polar Bear.* Random House, 2003. Winter

———. *Monkey's Play Time.* Candlewick Press, 2002. (Board book) Monkeys

———. *Old Mother Hubbard.* Illus. by Sarah Catherine Martin. Holiday House, 2001. Read to Me!

Caines, Jeannette. *Just Us Women.* Illus. by Pat Cummings. HarperTrophy, 1984. Trucks, Cars, and Buses

Campbell, Rod. *Dear Zoo: A Lift-the-Flap Book.* Little Simon, 1999. Zoos

———. *Little Bird.* Campbell Books, 2000. Birds

Capucilli, Alyssa Satin. *Biscuit.* Illus. by Pat Schories. HarperTrophy, 1997. Dogs

———. *Biscuit Finds a Friend.* Illus. by Pat Schories. HarperTrophy, 1998. Friends

———. *Happy Easter, Biscuit!* Illus. by Pat Schories. HarperFestival, 2000. (Lift-the-flap book) Spring

Carle, Eric. *Do You Want to Be My Friend?* Philomel, 1988. Friends

———. *Have You Seen My Cat?* Aladdin, 1997. Cats

———. *My Apron.* Philomel, 1995. Helping

———. *My Very First Book of Colors.* Philomel, 2005. (Board book) Colors

———. *My Very First Book of Shapes.* Philomel Press, 2005. (Board book) Sizes and Shapes

———. *1, 2, 3 to the Zoo: A Counting Book.* Philomel, 1996. (Board book) Zoos

———. *The Secret Birthday Message.* HarperCollins, 1972. Birthdays

———. *The Very Hungry Caterpillar.* Philomel, 1994. Also in big board book format (Philomel, 2001); in French: *La chenille qui fait des trous* (French & European Publications, 2005); in Spanish: *La oruga muy hambrienta* (Philomel Books, 1994); and in Vietnamese: *Chu sau rom qua doi* (Black Butterfly Books, 1994). Bugs and Caterpillars

———. *The Very Quiet Cricket.* Philomel, 1990. Bugs and Caterpillars

Carlstrom, Nancy White. *Jesse Bear's Tra-La Tub.* Illus. by Bruce Degen. Little Simon, 1994. (Board book) Bath Time

———. *The Way to Wyatt's House.* Illus. by Mary Morgan-Vanroyen. Walker & Company, 2000. Friends

———. *Where Is Christmas, Jesse Bear?* Illus. by Bruce Degen. Simon & Schuster, 2000. December

Carr, Jan. *Frozen Noses.* Illus. by Dorothy Donohue. Holiday House, 1999. Winter

Carter, David A. *Who's Under That Hat?* Text by Sarah Weeks. Red Wagon Books, 2005. (Lift-the-flap board book) Hats

Carter, Noelle. *Where's My Christmas Stocking? A Lift-and-Touch Book.* Scholastic, 1995. (Texture book) December

Cartwright, Stephen. *Find the Teddy.* Educational Development Corporation, 1984. Peek, Peek

Castañeda, Omar S. *Abuela's Weave.* Illus. by Enrique O. Sanchez. Lee & Low, 1993. Also in Spanish: *El tapiz de Abuela* (Lee & Low, 1994). Family

Chaconas, Dori. *On a Wintry Morning.* Illus. by Stephen T. Johnson. Viking, 2000. Morning

Chambers, Sally. *Tarquin's Shell.* Barron's, 1998. (Book and puppet) Frogs and Turtles

Chitwood, Suzanne Tanner. *Wake Up, Big Barn!* Cartwheel, 2002. Morning

Chocolate, Debbi. *Kente Colors.* Illus. by John Ward. Walker Books, 1997. December

Chodos-Irvine, Margaret. *Best Best Friends.* Harcourt, 2006. Birthdays

———. *Ella Sarah Gets Dressed.* Harcourt, 2003. Getting Dressed

Christelow, Eileen. *Five Little Monkeys Bake a Birthday Cake.* Clarion, 2005. Also available: *Five Little Monkeys Finger Puppets* (MerryMakers, 2004). Birthdays

———. *Five Little Monkeys Jumping on the Bed.* Clarion, 1989. Also in Spanish: *Cinco monitos brincando en la cama* (Clarion, 2005). (Board book) Playing

———. *Five Little Monkeys Play Hide-and-Seek.* Clarion, 2004. Peek, Peek

———. *Five Little Monkeys Sitting in a Tree.* Clarion, 1991. Also in Spanish: *En un árbol están los cinco monitos* (Clarion, 2007). Monkeys

———. *Five Little Monkeys Wash the Car.* Clarion, 2000. Helping

Christian, Cheryl. *Where's the Kitten? Kote ti chat la ye?* (English/Haitian Creole) Photos by Laura Dwight. Star Bright Books, 2005. (Board book) Cats

Churchill, Vicki, and Charles Fuge. *Sometimes I Like to Curl Up in a Ball.* Sterling, 2001. Dancing

Cimarusti, Marie Torres. *Peek-a-Zoo!* Illus. by Stephanie Peterson. Dutton, 2003. Zoos

Circus Opposites with Disappearing Animals: A Wacky Flaps Book. Illus. by Martin Lemelman. Innovative Kids, 2000. Circus

Colandro, Lucille. *There Was a Cold Lady Who Swallowed Some Snow.* Illus. by Jared Lee. Scholastic, 2003. Winter

Cole, Joanna, and Stephanie Calmenson, comps. *Pat-a-Cake and Other Play Rhymes.* Illus. by Alan Tiegreen. HarperTrophy, 1992. Read to Me!

Cooper, Elisha. *A Good Night Walk.* Orchard Books, 2005. Walking

Corey, Dorothy. *Will It Ever Be My Birthday?* Illus. by Eileen Christelow. Albert Whitman, 1986. Birthdays

Cousins, Lucy. *Bedtime, Maisy!* Candlewick Press, 2001. Also in Spanish: *Maisy se va a la cama* (Serres, 1997). Bedtime

———. *Doctor Maisy.* Candlewick Press, 2001. Also in Spanish: *La doctora Maisy* (Lectorum, 2005). Growing Up Safe

———. *Garden Animals.* Candlewick Press, 2004. (Board book) Gardens

———. *Happy Easter, Maisy!* Candlewick Press, 2007. (Board book) Spring

———. *Hen on the Farm.* Candlewick Press, 1992. (Rag book) Birds

———. *Katy Cat and Beaky Boo.* Walker Books, 2001. Also in Spanish: *La Gata Katy y Piquito de Oro juegan* (Serres, 2000). Cats

———. *Kite in the Park.* Candlewick Press, 1992. (Rag book) Wind

———. *Maisy at the Fair.* Candlewick Press, 2001. Circus

———. *Maisy at the Farm.* Candlewick Press, 1998. Also in Spanish: *Maisy en la granja* (Serres, 1999). (Lift-the-flap book) Farms

———. *Maisy Cleans Up.* Candlewick Press, 2002. Helping

———. *Maisy Dresses Up.* Candlewick Press, 1999. Also in Spanish: *Maisy se disfraza* (Lectorum, 2005). Getting Dressed

———. *Maisy Drives the Bus.* Candlewick Press, 2000. Also in Spanish: *El autobus de Maisy* (Serres, 2001). Trucks, Cars, and Buses

———. *Maisy Goes Camping.* Candlewick Press, 2004. Picnics

———. *Maisy Goes to the Library.* Candlewick Press, 2005. Read to Me!

———. *Maisy Goes to the Playground.* Candlewick Press, 1992. (Lift-the-flap book) Picnics

———. *Maisy Likes Dancing.* Candlewick Press, 2003. (Board book) Dancing

———. *Maisy Likes Music.* Candlewick Press, 2002. (Board book) Parades

———. *Maisy Makes Gingerbread.* Candlewick Press, 1999. Mealtimes

———. *Maisy Takes a Bath.* Candlewick Press, 2000. Also in Spanish: *Maisy se bana* (Lectorum, 2002). Bath Time

———. *Maisy's Big Flap Book.* Candlewick Press, 2001. Also in Spanish: *Diviertete y aprende con Maisy* (Serres, 2001). (Board book) Playing

———. *Maisy's Fire Engine.* Candlewick Press, 2002. Also in Spanish: *El coche de bomberos de Maisy* (Serres, 2004). (Board book) Firefighters

———. *Maisy's Halloween.* Gardners Books, 2004. Autumn

———. *Maisy's Morning on the Farm.* Candlewick Press, 2001. Morning

———. *Maisy's Pool.* Candlewick Press, 1999. Summer

———. *Maisy's Snowy Christmas Eve.* Candlewick Press, 2003. December

———. *Maisy's Train.* Candlewick Press, 2002. Also in Spanish: *El tren de Maisy* (Serres, 2004). (Board book) Trains and Planes

———. *Noah's Ark.* Candlewick Press, 1995. Also in Spanish: *El arca de Noé* (Serres, 1998). Boats

———. *1 2 3, Maisy.* Candlewick Press, 2005. Counting

———. *What Can Rabbit Hear?* Gardners Books, 2005. Also in Spanish: *¿Qué puede oir Blas?* (Serres, 2000). Sounds

———. *What Can Rabbit See?* Gardners Books, 2005. Also in Spanish: *¿Qué puede ver Blas?* (Serres, 2000). (Board book) Rabbits

———. *Where Does Maisy Live?* Walker Books, 2000. Also in Spanish: *¿Donde vive Maisy?* (Distribooks, 2000). (Board book) Homes

———. *Where Is Maisy?* Walker Books, 1999. Also in Spanish: *¿Donde se esconde Maisy?* (Lectorum, 1999). (Board book) Peek, Peek

Cowell, Cressida. *What Shall We Do with the Boo-Hoo Baby?* Illus. by Ingrid Godon. Scholastic, 2000. Babies

Cowen-Fletcher, Jane. *Mama Zooms.* Scholastic, 1996. Family

Cowley, Joy. *Mrs. Wishy-Washy Makes a Splash.* Illus. by Elizabeth Fuller. Philomel Books, 2003. (Board book) Bath Time

———. *Mrs. Wishy-Washy's Farm.* Illus. by Elizabeth Fuller. Philomel Books, 2003. (Board book) Farms

Crews, Donald. *Carousel.* Greenwillow Books, 1982. Circus

———. *Freight Train.* Greenwillow Books, 1978. Also in big book format (HarperTrophy, 1993); in board book format (Greenwillow Books, 1996); and in Spanish: *Tren de carga* (Rayo, 2003). Trains and Planes

———. *Inside Freight Train.* HarperFestival, 2001. (Board book) Trains and Planes

———. *Night at the Fair.* Greenwillow Books, 1998. Circus

———. *Parade.* HarperTrophy, 1986. Parades

———. *School Bus.* HarperFestival, 2002. (Board book) Also in Spanish: *El autobus escolar* (Scholastic, 1991). Trucks, Cars, and Buses

———. *Ten Black Dots.* Greenwillow Books, 1986. Also in Spanish: *Diez puntos negros* (Scholastic en Español, 1986). Counting

Cronin, Doreen. *Wiggle.* Illus. by Scott Menchin. Atheneum, 2005. Dancing

Cummings, Pat. *Purrrrr.* HarperFestival, 1999. (Board book) Cats

Cusimano, Maryann K. *You Are My I Love You.* Illus. by Satomi Ichikawa. Philomel, 2001. Bears

Dabcovich, Lydia. *Sleepy Bear.* Puffin, 1993. Bears

Dann, Penny. *Row, Row, Row Your Boat.* Little Barron's, 2000. Boats

Davis, Katie. *Who Hoots?* Voyager Books, 2000. Sounds

de Paola, Tomie. *Tomie's Baa, Baa, Black Sheep and Other Rhymes.* Putnam, 2004. (Board book) Read to Me!

———. *Too Many Bunnies.* Troll, 2000. Rabbits

Demarest, Chris L. *Summer.* Red Wagon Books, 1997. (Board book) Summer

Denslow, Sharon Phillips. *In the Snow.* Illus. by Nancy Tafuri. Greenwillow Books, 2005. Winter

Dewan, Ted. *Bing: Go Picnic.* David Fickling Books, 2005. Picnics

———. *Bing: Make Music.* David Fickling Books, 2005. Parades

———. *Bing: Something for Daddy.* David Fickling Books, 2003. Rabbits

Dijs, Carla. *Hurry Home, Hungry Frog.* Little Simon, 1995. (Pop-up book) Frogs and Turtles

Dillon, Diane, and Leo Dillon. *Rap a Tap Tap: Here's Bojangles—Think of That!* Blue Sky Press, 2002. Dancing

DiPucchio, Kelly. *What's the Magic Word?* Illus. by Marsha Winborn. HarperCollins, 2004. Helping

Dodd, Emma. *Dog's Colorful Day: A Messy Story about Colors and Counting.* Dutton Books, 2001. Colors

Donohue, Dorothy. *Big and Little on the Farm.* Golden Books, 1999. Sizes and Shapes

Dorman, Helen, and Clive Dorman. *Okomi Enjoys His Outings.* Illus. by Tony Hutchings. Dawn Publications, 2004. Monkeys

Dorros, Arthur. *This Is My House.* Scholastic, 1992. Also in big book format (Scholastic, 1998); and in Spanish: *Ésta es mi casa* (Scholastic en Español, 1995). Homes

Dotlich, Rebecca Kai. *Away We Go!* Illus. by Dan Yaccarino. HarperFestival, 2000. Trucks, Cars, and Buses

Doyle, Malachy. *Splash, Joshua, Splash!* Illus. by Ken Wilson-Max. Bloomsbury Books, 2004. Summer

Dubarle-Bossy, Philippe. *Flora the Frog: Playful Puppet Books.* Illus. by Luana Rinaldo. Barron's, 2005. (Rag book used as a puppet) Frogs and Turtles

Duncan, Alice Faye. *Honey Baby Sugar Child.* Illus. by Susan Keeter. Simon & Schuster, 2005. Love

Dunn, Opal. *Little Boat: A Track-Me-Back Book.* Illus. by Bettina Paterson. Holt, 2000. (Board book) Boats

Dunrea, Oliver. *Gossie and Gertie.* Houghton Mifflin, 2002. Parades

Eastman, P. D. *Big Dog . . . Little Dog.* Illus. by Tony Eastman. Random House, 2003. Also in Spanish: *Perro grande, perro pequeño* (Random House, 1982). Sizes and Shapes

Edwards, Pamela Duncan. *The Grumpy Morning.* Illus. by Darcia Labrosse. Hyperion Books, 1998. Morning

Ehlert, Lois. *Fish Eyes: A Book You Can Count On.* Harcourt, 1990. Also in board book format (Red Wagon Books, 2001). Counting

———. *Growing Vegetable Soup.* Red Wagon Books, 2004. (Board book) Also in Spanish: *A sembrar sopa de verduras* (Libros Viajeros, 1996). Gardens

———. *Planting a Rainbow.* Harcourt, 1988. Also in big book format (Harcourt, 1992); and in Spanish: *Cómo plantar un arco iris* (Libros Viajeros, 2006). (Board book) Spring

———. *Red Leaf, Yellow Leaf.* Harcourt, 1991. Autumn

———. *Snowballs.* Harcourt, 1995. Winter

Elgar, Rebecca. *Jack—Happy Birthday.* Kingfisher, 1998. (Board book) Birthdays

Ellis, Libby. *Buenos Dias Baby!* Chronicle Books, 2004. Babies

Elting, Mary, and Michael Folsom. *Q Is for Duck: An Alphabet Guessing Game.* Illus. by Jack Kent. Clarion Books, 2005. Sounds

Emberley, Ed, and Anne Miranda. *Glad Monster, Sad Monster.* Little, Brown, 1997. (Foldout book) Feelings

Emberley, Rebecca. *My Animals / Mis animales.* (English/Spanish) Little, Brown, 2002. (Board book) Farms

———. *My Clothes / Mi ropa.* (English/Spanish) Little, Brown, 2002. (Board book) Getting Dressed

———. *My Day / Mi día.* (English/Spanish) Little, Brown, 2000. Morning

———. *My Food / Mi comida.* (English/Spanish) Little, Brown, 2002. (Board book) Mealtimes

———. *My Garden / Mi jardín.* (English/Spanish) Little, Brown, 2005. (Board book) Gardens

———. *My House / Mi casa.* (English/Spanish) Little, Brown, 1993. Homes

———. *My Toys / Mis juguetes.* (English/Spanish) Little, Brown, 2002. (Board book) Playing

———. *Piñata!* (English/Spanish) Little, Brown, 2004. Birthdays

———. *Taking a Walk / Caminando.* (English/Spanish) Little, Brown, 1994. Walking

Ernst, Lisa Campbell. *Wake Up, It's Spring!* HarperCollins, 2004. Spring

Ets, Marie Hall. *Gilberto and the Wind.* Puffin, 1978. Also in Spanish: *Gilberto y el viento* (Live Oak Media, 2005). (Book with CD) Wind

———. *Play with Me.* Puffin, 1976. Playing

Evans, Katie. *Hunky Dory Ate It.* Illus. by Janet Morgan Stoeke. Puffin, 1996. Mealtimes

———. *Hunky Dory Found It.* Illus. by Janet Morgan Stoeke. Dutton, 1994. Dogs

Evans, Lezlie. *Can You Count Ten Toes? Count to Ten in Ten Different Languages.* Illus. by Denis Roche. Houghton Mifflin, 1999. Counting

Falwell, Cathryn. *We Have a Baby.* Clarion Books, 1993. Babies

Faulkner, Keith. *The Wide-Mouthed Frog: A Pop-Up Book.* Illus. by Jonathan Lambert. Dial Books, 1996. Frogs and Turtles

Feelings, Muriel. *Jambo Means Hello: Swahili Alphabet Book.* Illus. by Tom Feelings. Puffin, 1992. Friends

Feiffer, Jules. *Bark, George.* HarperCollins, 1999. Sounds

Ferreri, Della Ross. *How Will I Ever Sleep in This Bed?* Illus. by Capucine Mazille. Sterling, 2005. Bedtime

Flack, Marjorie. *Ask Mr. Bear.* Simon & Schuster, 1968. Also in big book format (Macmillan, 1990). Love

Fleming, Candace. *Smile, Lily!* Illus. by Yumi Heo. Atheneum, 2004. Feelings

Fleming, Denise. *Lunch.* Holt, 1992. Also in board book format (Holt, 1998). Mealtimes

Floca, Brian. *Five Trucks.* DK, 1999. Trucks, Cars, and Buses

Flynn, Kitson. *Carrot in My Pocket.* Illus. by Denise Ortakales. Moon Mountain Publishing, 2001. Farms

Ford, Juwanda G. *K Is for Kwanzaa: A Kwanzaa Alphabet Book.* Illus. by Ken Wilson-Max. Cartwheel Press, 2003. December

Fox, Diane, and Christyan Fox. *Bathtime Piggy-Wiggy: A Pull-the-Page Book.* Handprint, 2001. Bath Time

Freeman, Don. *Bearymore.* Puffin, 1979. Circus

———. *Corduroy.* Viking, 1968. Also in board book format (Viking, 2002); and in Spanish (Live Oak Media, 1990). (Book with cassette) Love

———. *Dandelion.* Puffin, 1977. Birthdays

———. *A Pocket for Corduroy.* Viking, 1978. Also in Spanish: *Un bolsillo para Corduroy* (Puffin, 1995). Getting Dressed

———. *Rainbow of My Own.* Puffin, 1978. Rain

Freeman, Lydia. *Corduroy's Day.* Illus. by Lisa McCue. Viking, 2005. (Board book) Counting

Fuge, Charles. *Swim, Little Wombat, Swim!* Sterling, 2005. Friends

———. *Yip! Snap! Yap!* Tricycle Press, 2003. (Board book) Dogs

Gackenbach, Dick. *Claude the Dog: A Christmas Story.* Clarion Books, 1984. December

Galdone, Paul. *The Little Red Hen.* Clarion Books, 1979. Helping

———. *Three Little Kittens.* Clarion Books, 1986. Cats

Gave, Marc. *Monkey See, Monkey Do.* Illus. by Jacqueline Rogers. Cartwheel Books, 1993. Monkeys

Gay, Marie-Louise. *Good Morning, Sam.* Groundwood Books, 2003. Morning

Gershator, Phillis, and David Gershator. *Greetings, Sun.* Illus. by Synthia Saint James. DK, 1998. Morning

Gerth, Melanie. *Five Little Ladybugs.* Illus. by Laura Huliska-Beith. Piggy Toes Press, 2003. Bugs and Caterpillars

Gibbons, Gail. *Zoo.* HarperTrophy, 1991. Zoos

Gikow, Louise. *Red Hat! Green Hat!* Illus. by Joe Mathieu. Golden Books, 2000. Hats

Ginsburg, Mirra. *The Chick and the Duckling.* Illus. by Jose Aruego and Ariane Dewey. Aladdin, 1988. Birds

———. *Good Morning, Chick.* Illus. by Byron Barton. Greenwillow Books, 1980. Morning

———. *Mushroom in the Rain.* Illus. by Jose Aruego and Ariane Dewey. Simon & Schuster, 1987. Rain

Gliori, Debi. *Mr. Bear's Picnic.* Orchard Books, 1995. Picnics

Golding, Kim. *Counting Kids.* DK, 2000. Counting

Gomi, Taro. *Spring Is Here.* Simon & Schuster, 1996. Also in Spanish: *Llegó la primavera* (Chronicle Books, 2006). Spring

Got, Yves. *Sweet Dreams, Sam.* Chronicle Books, 2000. Rabbits

Graham, Bob. *Has Anyone Here Seen William?* Candlewick Press, 2001. Walking

———. *Oscar's Half Birthday.* Candlewick Press, 2005. Birthdays

Gray, Rita. *Nonna's Porch.* Illus. by Terry Widener. Hyperion Books, 2004. Homes

Greene, Carol. *Hi, Clouds.* Illus. by Gene Sharp. Children's Press, 1983. Rain

———. *Please, Wind?* Illus. by Gene Sharp. Children's Press, 1982. Wind

Greene, Rhonda Gowler. *Firebears: The Rescue Team.* Illus. by Dan Andreasen. Holt, 2005. Firefighters

Greenfield, Eloise. *I Make Music.* Illus. by Jan Spivey Gilchrist. Writers and Readers, 1991. (Board book) Parades

———. *Water, Water.* Illus. by Jan Spivy Gilchrist. HarperFestival, 1999. Rain

Greenstein, Elaine. *One Little Seed.* Viking, 2004. Gardens

Gunzi, Christiane. *My Very First Look at Clothes.* Two-Can, 2003. Getting Dressed

———. *My Very First Look at My Home.* Two-Can, 2003. Homes

Gutman, Anne. *Daddy Cuddles.* Illus. by Georg Hallensleben. Chronicle Books, 2005. (Board book) Family

Guy, Ginger Foglesong. *¡Fiesta!* (English/Spanish) Illus. by René King Moreno. Rayo, 2003. (Board book) Birthdays

———. *Siesta.* (English/Spanish) Illus. by René King Moreno. Rayo, 2005. Bedtime

Hall, Jacque. *What Does the Rabbit Say?* Illus. by Reg Cartwright. Doubleday, 2000. Sounds

Hall, Kirsten. *At the Carnival.* Illus. by Laura Rader. Scholastic, 1996. Circus

Hall, Zoe. *It's Pumpkin Time!* Illus. by Shari Halpern. Scholastic, 1994. Also in Spanish: *¡Tiempo de calabazas!* (Scholastic en Español, 2002). Autumn

Halpern, Shari. *Moving from One to Ten.* Simon & Schuster, 1993. Homes

Hamsa, Bobbie. *Dirty Larry.* Illus. by Donna Catanese. Children's Press, 2003. Bath Time

Harland, Jackie. *The Easter Chicks: A Lift-the-Flap Storybook.* Little, Brown, 1996. Spring

Harper, Piers. *If You Love a Bear.* Candlewick Press, 1998. Bears

Harrison, David L. *Wake Up, Sun!* Illus. by Hans Wilhelm. Random House, 1986. Morning

Hart, Simon. *Go, Go, Boats!* Price Stern Sloan, 2004. (Board book) Boats

———. *Go, Go, Planes!* Price Stern Sloan, 2004. (Board book) Trains and Planes

Haskamp, Steve. *Eight Silly Monkeys.* Intervisual Books, 2003. Also in Spanish: *Ocho monitos* (Piggy Toes Press, 2004). (Warning: contains small parts) Monkeys

Haugen, Brenda. *Birthdays.* Illus. by Todd Ouren. Picture Window Books, 2004. Birthdays

Havill, Juanita. *Jamaica and Brianna.* Illus. by Anne Sibley O'Brien. Houghton Mifflin, 1993. Getting Dressed

Hawkins, Colin, and Jacqui Hawkins. *I Know an Old Lady Who Swallowed a Fly.* Putnam, 1987. Also in lift-the-flap format (Egmont Books, 2004). Mealtimes

Hayes, Sarah. *This Is the Bear.* Illus. by Helen Craig. Gardners Books, 2003. Also in Spanish: *Yo soy el oso* (Anayaeditores, 1988). Bears

———. *This Is the Bear and the Picnic Lunch.* Illus. by Helen Craig. Walker Books, 1998. Picnics

Helldorfer, M. C. *Got to Dance.* Illus. by Hiroe Nakata. Doubleday, 2004. Dancing

Heller, Lora. *I'm Feeling . . . Teaching Your Baby to Sign (Baby Fingers).* Sterling, 2006. (Board book) Feelings

Henkes, Kevin. *Bailey Goes Camping.* HarperTrophy, 1997. Picnics

———. *Oh!* Illus. by Laura Dronzek. Greenwillow Books, 1999. Winter

———. *So Happy!* Illus. by Anita Lobel. Greenwillow Books, 2005. Gardens

Henley, Claire. *Joe's Pool.* Hyperion Books, 1994. Summer

Hennessy, B. G. *Corduroy Goes to the Fire Station: A Lift-the-Flap Book.* Illus. by Lisa McCue. Viking, 2003. Firefighters

———. *Corduroy's Halloween: A Lift-the-Flap Book.* Illus. by Lisa McCue. Viking, 1995. Autumn

Herman, Gail. *What a Hungry Puppy!* Illus. by Norman Gorbaty. Grosset & Dunlap, 1993. Dogs

Hest, Amy. *In the Rain with Baby Duck.* Illus. by Jill Barton. Candlewick Press, 1995. Rain

Hill, Eric. *Night-Night, Spot.* Grosset & Dunlap, 2005. Also in Spanish: *Buenas noches, Spot* (Sudamericana, 2001). (Lift-the-flap book) Bedtime

———. *Spot and His Grandparents Go to the Carnival.* Puffin, 1999. (Lift-the-flap book) Circus

———. *Spot at Home.* Putnam, 2004. Also in Spanish: *Spot en casa* (Sudamericana, 2004). (Lift-the-flap book) Rain

———. *Spot Counts from 1 to 10.* Putnam, 2003. (Board book) Counting

———. *Spot Goes Splash!* Putnam, 2003. (Bath book) Bath Time

———. *Spot Goes to the Beach.* Putnam, 2005. Also in big board book format: *Spot at the Beach* (Putnam, 2005); and in Spanish: *Spot va a la playa* (Putnam, 1985). Summer

———. *Spot Goes to the Circus.* Puffin, 2006. Circus

———. *Spot Goes to the Farm.* Putnam, 1987. Also in Spanish: *Spot va a la granja* (Sudamericana, 2002). Farms

———. *Spot Goes to the Park.* Putnam, 2005. Also in Spanish: *Spot va al parque* (Putnam, 1993). Picnics

———. *Spot Helps Out.* Putnam, 1999. (Board book) Helping

———. *Spot Looks at Colors.* Putnam, 2003. (Board book) Colors

———. *Spot Looks at Shapes.* Putnam, 2003. (Board book) Sizes and Shapes

———. *Spot Loves His Daddy.* Putnam, 2005. (Board book) Feelings

———. *Spot Sleeps Over.* Puffin, 2004. (Lift-the-flap book) Growing Up Safe

———. *Spot Visits His Grandparents.* Putnam, 1996. Also in French: *Spot chez papi et mamie* (Nathan Jeunesse, 1996). Family

———. *Spot's Baby Sister.* Puffin, 2004. Babies

———. *Spot's Birthday Party.* Gardners Books, 2005. Also in French: *L'anniversaire de Spot* (Nathan Jeunesse, 1991); and in Spanish: *El cumpleaños de Spot* (Sudamericana, 2002). Birthdays

———. *Spot's First Christmas.* Puffin, 2004. Also in Spanish: *La primera Navidad de Spot* (Sudamericana, 2002). December

———. *Spot's First Easter.* Puffin, 2004. Spring

———. *Spot's First Picnic and Other Stories.* Grosset & Dunlap, 2001. Picnics

———. *Spot's First Walk.* Puffin, 2004. Also in French: *La première promenade de Spot* (Nathan Jeunesse, 1991); and in Spanish: *El primer paseo de Spot* (Putnam, 1983). (Lift-the-flap book) Walking

———. *Spot's Halloween.* Putnam, 2003. (Board book) Autumn

———. *Spot's Little Book of Fun in the Garden.* Putnam, 2003. (Touch-and-feel book) Gardens

———. *Spot's Marching Band.* Gardners Books, 2004. (Board book with sounds) Parades

———. *Spot's Thanksgiving.* Putnam, 2003. (Board book) Mealtimes

———. *Spot's Toy Box.* Putnam, 1991. Also in Spanish: *Los juguetes de Spot* (Sudamericana, 2001). Playing

———. *Spot's Treasure Hunt.* Putnam, 2002. Peek, Peek

———. *Spot's Windy Day and Other Stories.* Grosset & Dunlap, 2000. (Lift-the-flap book) Wind

———. *Where's Spot?* Putnam, 1980. Also in French: *Où est Spot, mon petit chien?* (Nathan Jeunesse, 1991); and in Spanish: *¿Dónde está Spot?* (Puffin, 1996). Dogs

Hindley, Judy. *Does a Cow Say Boo?* Illus. by Brita Granström. Candlewick Press, 2002. Sounds

———. *Eyes, Nose, Fingers, and Toes: A First Book All about You.* Illus. by Brita Granström. Candlewick Press, 2002. My Body

Hines, Anna Grossnickle. *Big Help.* Clarion Books, 1995. Helping

———. *Big Like Me.* Greenwillow Books, 1989. Growing Up Safe

———. *Curious George and the Firefighters.* Houghton Mifflin, 2004. Firefighters

Ho, Minfong. *Hush! A Thai Lullaby.* Illus. by Holly Meade. Scholastic, 2000. Bedtime

———. *Peek! A Thai Hide-and-Seek.* Illus. by Holly Meade. Candlewick Press, 2004. Peek, Peek

Hoban, Tana. *Red, Blue, Yellow Shoe.* Greenwillow Books, 1986. (Board book) Getting Dressed

———. *Shapes, Shapes, Shapes.* Greenwillow Books, 1986. Sizes and Shapes

Hodge, Marie. *Are You Sleepy Yet, Petey?* Illus. by Renée Graef. Sterling, 2005. Bedtime

Holm, Sharon Lane. *Zoe's Hats: A Book of Colors and Patterns.* Boyds Mills Press, 2003. Hats

Holub, Joan. *Kwanzaa Kids.* Illus. by Ken Wilson-Max. Puffin, 2002. (Lift-the-flap book) December

Horwood, Annie. *Cats Go . . .* Grosset & Dunlap, 2001. (Board book) Cats

———. *Dogs Go . . .* Grosset & Dunlap, 2001. (Board book) Dogs

How Do I Feel? / ¿Cómo me siento? (English/Spanish) Illus. by Pamela Zagarenski. Houghton Mifflin, 2001. (Board book) Feelings

Hubbell, Patricia. *Sea, Sand, Me!* Illus. by Lisa Campbell Ernst. HarperCollins, 2001. Summer

Hudson, Cheryl Willis. *Good Morning, Baby.* Illus. by George Ford. Cartwheel Books, 1997. (Board book) Morning

———. *Good Night, Baby.* Illus. by George Ford. Cartwheel Books, 1997. (Board book) Babies

———. *Hands Can.* Photos by John-Francis Bourke. Candlewick Press, 2003. My Body

Hudson, Cheryl Willis, and Bernette G. Ford. *Bright Eyes, Brown Skin.* Illus. by George Ford. Just Us Books, 1990. My Body

Hutchins, Pat. *Don't Get Lost.* Greenwillow Books, 2004. Walking

———. *The Doorbell Rang.* Greenwillow Books, 1986. Also in big book format (HarperTrophy, 1994); and in Spanish: *Llaman a la puerta* (Rayo, 1994). Friends

———. *Good-Night, Owl!* Simon & Schuster, 1972. Birds

———. *Happy Birthday, Sam.* HarperTrophy, 1991. Birthdays

———. *Rosie's Walk.* Simon & Schuster, 1968. Also in board book format (Little Simon, 1998); in big book format (Scholastic, 1992); and in Spanish: *El paseo de Rosie* (Aladdin, 1997). Birds

———. *Ten Red Apples.* Greenwillow Books, 2000. Counting

———. *Tidy Titch.* Greenwillow Books, 1991. Helping

———. *Titch.* Aladdin, 1993. Sizes and Shapes

———. *We're Going on a Picnic.* Greenwillow Books, 2002. Picnics

―――. *The Wind Blew.* Aladdin, 1993. Wind

―――. *You'll Soon Grow into Them, Titch.* Harper-Trophy, 1992. Getting Dressed

Inkpen, Mick. *Kipper's Kite: Touch and Feel.* Red Wagon Books, 2002. (Board book) Wind

Ives, Penny. *Rabbit Pie.* Viking, 2006. Rabbits

Jane, Pamela. *Spring Is Here: A Barnyard Counting Book.* Illus. by Melissa Sweet. Little Simon, 2004. (Board book) Spring

Janovitz, Marilyn. *Look Out, Bird!* North-South Books, 1997. Also in Spanish: *¡Cuidado pajarito!* (North-South Books, 1997). Birds

Johnson, Angela. *Joshua by the Sea.* Illus. by Rhonda Mitchell. Scholastic, 1994. Summer

―――. *One of Three.* Illus. by David Soman. Orchard Books, 1995. Family

―――. *Rain Feet.* Illus. by Rhonda Mitchell. Scholastic, 1994. (Board book) Rain

Johnson, Audean. *Soft as a Kitten.* Random House, 1982. (Texture book) Cats

Johnston, Tony. *Sticky People.* Illus. by Cyd Moore. HarperCollins, 2006. Bath Time

Jonas, Ann. *Splash!* Greenwillow Books, 1995. Counting

―――. *The Trek.* Greenwillow Books, 1985. Also in Spanish: *El trayecto* (Lectorum, 1991). Walking

Jones, Lara. *Fun at the Park.* Barron's, 2003. (Board book) Picnics

―――. *Fun at the Zoo.* Macmillan, 2002. Also in Spanish: *Me divierto en el zoo* (Combel, 2003). (Board book) Zoos

Jones, Sally Lloyd. *Farmyard Boogie!* Illus. by Simone Abel. Silver Dolphin, 2001. (Board book) Dancing

―――. *Jungle Jive!* Illus. by Simone Abel. Silver Dolphin, 2001. (Board book) Dancing

Kalan, Robert. *Blue Sea.* Illus. by Donald Crews. Greenwillow Books, 1979. Also in French: *Mer bleue* (Kaleidoscope, 1998). Sizes and Shapes

―――. *Jump, Frog, Jump!* Illus. by Byron Barton. Greenwillow Books, 1995. Also in big book format (HarperTrophy, 1989); in board book format (HarperFestival, 2003); and in Spanish: *¡Salta, ranita, salta!* (Rayo, 1994). Frogs and Turtles

―――. *Moving Day.* Illus. by Yossie Abolafia. Greenwillow Books, 1996. Homes

―――. *Rain.* Illus. by Donald Crews. HarperTrophy, 1991. Rain

Kasza, Keiko. *A Mother for Choco.* Putnam, 1992. Also in board book format (Putnam, 2003). Family

Katz, Karen. *Best-Ever Big Sister.* Grosset & Dunlap, 2006. (Board book) Family

―――. *Counting Kisses.* McElderry Books, 2001. Love

―――. *Over the Moon: An Adoption Tale.* Holt, 2001. Babies

―――. *Ten Tiny Tickles.* McElderry Books, 2005. Playing

―――. *What Does Baby Say?* Little Simon, 2004. (Lift-the-flap board book) Babies

―――. *Where Is Baby's Belly Button?* Little Simon, 2000. (Lift-the-flap board book) My Body

―――. *Wiggle Your Toes.* Little Simon, 2006. (Board book) My Body

Keats, Ezra Jack. *Jennie's Hat.* Puffin, 2003. Hats

―――. *Kitten for a Day.* Viking, 2002. Cats

―――. *Peter's Chair.* Viking, 1998. Also in big book format (HarperCollins, 1993); in board book format (Viking, 2006); and in Spanish: *La silla de Pedro* (HarperCollins, 1996). Babies

―――. *The Snowy Day.* Viking, 1962. Also in big book format (Scholastic, 1993); in board book format (Viking, 1996); and in Spanish: *Un día de nieve* (Live Oak Media, 2005). (Book with CD) Winter

Keller, Holly. *Sophie's Window.* Greenwillow Books, 2005. Helping

Kent, Jack. *The Caterpillar and the Polliwog.* Aladdin, 1985. Frogs and Turtles

Kimble, Warren. *The Cat's Meow.* Walker Books, 2006. Cats

Knudsen, Michelle. *Autumn Is for Apples.* Illus. by Denise and Fernando. Random House, 2001. Autumn

Koller, Jackie French. *One Monkey Too Many.* Illus. by Lynn Munsinger. Harcourt, 1999. Monkeys

Kopper, Lisa. *Good Dog, Daisy!* Dutton, 2001. Dogs

Kowalczyk, Carolyn. *Purple Is Part of a Rainbow.* Illus. by Gene Sharp. Children's Press, 1985. Also in Spanish: *El morado es parte del arco iris* (Children's Press, 1989). Colors

Kraus, Robert. *Milton the Early Riser.* Illus. by Jose Aruego and Ariane Dewey. Simon & Schuster, 1987. Morning

Krauss, Ruth. *The Carrot Seed.* Illus. by Crockett Johnson. HarperCollins, 2004. Also in board book format (HarperFestival, 1993); and in Spanish: *La semilla de zanahoria* (Scholastic en Español, 1996). Gardens

―――. *Goodnight, Goodnight Sleepyhead.* Illus. by Jane Dyer. HarperCollins, 2004. Bedtime

―――. *You're Just What I Need.* Illus. by Julia Noonan. HarperCollins, 1998. Peek, Peek

Kress, Camille. *Let There Be Lights!* Urj, 1997. (Board book) December

Kroll, Virginia. *Jaha and Jamil Went Down the Hill: An African Mother Goose.* Illus. by Katherine Roundtree. Charlesbridge, 1995. Read to Me!

Kubler, Annie. *Over in the Meadow.* Illus. by Michael Evans. Child's Play International, 2003. (Board book) Counting

Kunhardt, Dorothy. *Pat the Bunny.* Golden Books, 2001. (Texture book) Rabbits

Kunhardt, Edith. *Pat the Cat.* Golden Books, 1998. (Texture book) Cats

———. *Pat the Pony.* Golden Books, 2000. (Spiral-bound texture book) Farms

———. *Pat the Puppy.* Golden Books, 2001. (Texture book) Dogs

Kutner, Merrily. *Down on the Farm.* Illus. by Will Hillenbrand. Holiday House, 2004. Farms

Lacome, Julie. *Walking through the Jungle.* Candlewick Press, 1993. Also in big book format (Candlewick Press, 2004). Walking

Laden, Nina. *Grow Up!* Chronicle Books, 2003. (Board book) Growing Up Safe

———. *Ready, Set, Go!* Chronicle Books, 2000. (Board book) Peek, Peek

Landström, Olof, and Lena Landström. *Boo and Baa in Windy Weather.* R & S Books, 1996. Wind

Lawrence, John. *This Little Chick.* Candlewick Press, 2002. Birds

Lawston, Lisa. *Can You Hop?* Illus. by Ed Vere. Scholastic, 1999. (Board book) Frogs and Turtles

Le Jars, David. *Uno, dos, hola y adiós.* Two-Can, 2001. Friends

Lee, Huy Voun. *In the Snow.* Holt, 2000. Winter

Lee, Spike, and Tonya Lewis Lee. *Please, Baby, Please.* Illus. by Kadir Nelson. Simon & Schuster, 2002. Playing

Leslie, Amanda. *Jumping Frog.* Tiger Tales, 2001. (Board book) Frogs and Turtles

Lewin, Hugh. *Jafta.* Illus. by Lisa Kopper. Carolrhoda Books, 1989. Also in French (L'École des Loisirs, 1995). Feelings

———. *Jafta: The Homecoming.* Illus. by Lisa Kopper. Puffin, 1996. Family

Lewis, Edwina. *Who Eats?* Illus. by Ant Parker. Chrysalis Books, 2004. (Pop-up book) Mealtimes

Lewis, Kevin. *Chugga-Chugga Choo-Choo.* Illus. by Daniel Kirk. Hyperion Books, 1999. Trains and Planes

Lewis, Kevin, and Daniel Kirk. *My Truck Is Stuck!* Hyperion, 2002. Trucks, Cars, and Buses

Lewis, Rose A. *I Love You Like Crazy Cakes.* Illus. by Jane Dyer. Little, Brown, 2000. Love

Lewison, Wendy Cheyette. *"Buzz," Said the Bee.* Illus. by Hans Wilhelm. Cartwheel Books, 1992. Sounds

———. *Don't Wake the Baby!* Illus. by Jerry Smath. Grosset & Dunlap, 1996. Babies

Lin, Grace. *Kite Flying.* Dragonfly Books, 2004. Wind

Lindgren, Barbro. *Sam's Ball.* Illus. by Eva Eriksson. HarperFestival, 1983. Playing

———. *Sam's Cookie.* Illus. by Eva Eriksson. HarperFestival, 1982. Mealtimes

———. *Sam's Potty.* Illus. by Eva Eriksson. HarperFestival, 1986. Growing Up Safe

Lionni, Leo. *Inch by Inch.* HarperTrophy, 1995. Bugs and Caterpillars

Little Bee: Finger Puppet Book. Chronicle Books, 2006. (Board book with puppet) Bugs and Caterpillars

Little Duck: Finger Puppet Book. Chronicle Books, 2005. (Board book with puppet) Birds

Little Ladybug: Finger Puppet Book. Chronicle Books, 2005. (Board book with puppet) Bugs and Caterpillars

Loesser, Frank, and Rosemary Wells. *I Love You! A Bushel and a Peck.* HarperCollins, 2005. Love

London, Jonathan. *Crunch Munch.* Illus. by Michael Rex. Red Wagon Books, 2002. (Board book) Mealtimes

MacAulay, Craig. *Ten Men on a Ladder.* Illus. by Hélène Desputeaux. Annick Press, 1993. Firefighters

Maccarone, Grace. *Pizza Party!* Illus. by Emily Arnold McCully. Cartwheel Press, 1994. Helping

Mack, Stanley. *Ten Bears in My Bed: A Goodnight Countdown.* Random House, 1974. Bears

MacKinnon, Debbie. *Daniel's Duck.* Photographs by Anthea Sieveking. Dial Books, 1997. (Lift-the-flap book) Bath Time

———. *Eye Spy Colors.* Illus. by Anthea Sieveking. Charlesbridge, 1998. (Peephole book) Colors

MacLean, Christine Kole. *Even Firefighters Hug Their Moms.* Illus. by Mike Reed. Puffin, 2002. Firefighters

Maitland, Barbara. *Moo in the Morning.* Illus. by Andrew Kulman. Farrar, Straus, and Giroux, 2000. Morning

Mallat, Kathy. *Brave Bear.* Walker, 1999. Helping

Mallett, David. *Inch by Inch: The Garden Song.* Illus. by Ora Eitan. HarperTrophy, 1997. Gardens

Mandel, Peter. *Boats on the River.* Illus. by Edward Miller. Cartwheel Press, 2004. (Board book) Boats

———. *Planes at the Airport.* Illus. by Edward Miller. Cartwheel Press, 2004. (Board book) Trains and Planes

Marshall, James. *Hey Diddle Diddle.* Farrar, Straus, and Giroux, 2003. (Board book) Read to Me!

Martin, Bill, Jr. *Brown Bear, Brown Bear, What Do You See?* Illus. by Eric Carle. Holt, 1992. Also in big book format (Harcourt, 1989); in board book format (Holt, 1996); and in Spanish: *Oso pardo, oso pardo, ¿qué ves ahí?* (Holt, 1998). Colors

———. *Polar Bear, Polar Bear, What Do You Hear?* Illus. by Eric Carle. Holt, 1991. Also in big book format (Holt, 1992); and in Spanish: *Oso polar, oso polar, ¿qué es ese ruido?* (Holt, 2000). Sounds

Martin, Bill, Jr., and John Archambault. *Up and Down on the Merry-Go-Round.* Illus. by Ted Rand. Holt, 1991. Circus

Martin, David. *We've All Got Bellybuttons!* Illus. by Randy Cecil. Candlewick Press, 2005. Zoos

Marzollo, Jean. *I Am Water.* Illus. by Judith Moffatt. Cartwheel Books, 1996. Also in Spanish: *Soy el agua* (Scholastic en Español, 1999). Bath Time

Masurel, Claire. *Ten Dogs in the Window.* Illus. by Pamela Paparone. North-South Books, 2000. Dogs

Masurel, Claire, and Marie H. Henry. *Good Night!* Chronicle Books, 1995. Bedtime

Masurel, Claire, and Bob Kolar. *A Cat and a Dog.* North-South Books, 2003. Friends

Matthews, Gill, and Belinda Worsley. *Ben's Counting Walk.* Gingham Dog Press, 2006. Also in Spanish: *Benito pasea y cuenta* (Gingham Dog Press, 2006). Walking

Mayer, Mercer. *All by Myself.* Golden Books, 2001. Also in Spanish: *Yo solito* (Golden Books, 1997). Growing Up Safe

———. *Just a Rainy Day.* Golden Books, 1999. Rain

———. *Just Grandma and Me.* Sagebrush, 2001. Summer

———. *The New Baby.* Golden Books, 2001. Also in Spanish: *El nuevo bebé* (Golden Books, 1997). Babies

Mayo, Margaret. *Emergency!* Illus. by Alex Ayliffe. Carolrhoda, 2002. Firefighters

McBratney, Sam. *Guess How Much I Love You.* Illus. by Anita Jeram. Walker Books, 2003. Also in big book format (Candlewick Press, 2003); in board book format with stuffed toy (Candlewick Press, 2002); and in Spanish: *Adivina cuanto te quiero* (Lectorum, 1995). Love

———. *I Love It When You Smile.* Illus. by Charles Fuge. HarperCollins, 2006. Feelings

McCloskey, Robert. *Blueberries for Sal.* Viking, 1948. Bears

McCue, Lisa. *Corduroy Goes to the Doctor.* Viking, 2001. Also in board book format (Viking, 2005). Growing Up Safe

McDonnell, Flora. *I Love Boats.* Walker Books, 1995. Boats

McKissack, Patricia. *Who Is Coming?* Illus. by Clovis Martin. Children's Press, 1986. Monkeys

McKissack, Patricia, and Fredrick McKissack. *Messy Bessey's Holidays.* Illus. by Dana Regan. Children's Press, 1999. December

McMenemy, Sarah. *Jack's New Boat.* Candlewick Press, 2005. Boats

McMullan, Kate, and Jim McMullan. *No No, Jo!* HarperFestival, 1998. (Lift-the-flap book) Cats

Meister, Cari. *Tiny Goes Camping.* Illus. by Rich Davis. Puffin Books, 2006. Picnics

———. *Tiny Goes to the Library.* Illus. by Rich Davis. Puffin Books, 2000. Read to Me!

———. *Tiny the Snow Dog.* Illus. by Rich Davis. Puffin Books, 2001. Winter

———. *Tiny's Bath.* Illus. by Rich Davis. Puffin Books, 1999. Bath Time

Melmed, Laura Krauss. *I Love You as Much . . .* Illus. by Henri Sorensen. HarperCollins, 1993. Also in board book format (HarperFestival, 1998). Love

Milbourne, Anna, and Sarah Gill. *The Rainy Day.* Usborne Books, 2005. Also in Spanish: *Un dia de lluvia* (Usborne Books, 2005). Rain

Milios, Rita. *Bears, Bears, Everywhere.* Illus. by Tom Dunnington. Children's Press, 1988. Also in Spanish: *Osos, osos, aqui y alli* (Children's Press, 1989). Bears

Miller, Margaret. *Big and Little.* Greenwillow Books, 1998. Sizes and Shapes

———. *Where Does It Go?* HarperTrophy, 1998. Getting Dressed

Miller, Virginia. *I Love You Just the Way You Are.* Candlewick Press, 1998. Bears

———. *In a Minute!* Candlewick Press, 2001. Picnics

———. *Ten Red Apples: A Bartholomew Bear Counting Book.* Candlewick Press, 2002. Counting

Moncure, Jane Belk. *Away Went the Farmer's Hat.* Illus. by Terri Super. Children's Press, 1988. Wind

———. *Here Comes the Big Parade.* Illus. by Linda Hohag. Child's World, 1997. Parades

———. *No! No! Word Bird.* Illus. by Chris McEwan. Child's World, 2002. Winter

———. *What Do You Say When a Monkey Acts This Way?* Illus. by Terri Super. Children's Press, 1988. Monkeys

———. *Word Bird's Christmas Words.* Illus. by Vera Kennedy Gohman. Children's Press, 1987. December

———. *Word Bird's Halloween Words.* Illus. by Chris McEwan. Child's World, 2001. Autumn

———. *Word Bird's Rainy-Day Dance.* Illus. by Linda Hohag. Child's World, 1990. Dancing

———. *Word Bird's Shapes.* Illus. by Chris McEwan. Child's World, 2002. Sizes and Shapes

———. *Word Bird's Spring Words.* Illus. by Chris McEwan. Child's World, 2001. Spring

———. *Word Bird's Summer Words.* Illus. by Chris McEwan. Child's World, 2001. Summer

———. *Word Bird's Valentine's Day Words.* Illus. by Chris McEwan. Child's World, 2001. Love

Moore, Lilian. *While You Were Chasing a Hat.* Illus. by Rosanne Litzinger. HarperFestival, 2001. Wind

Morris, Ann. *Hats, Hats, Hats.* Photos by Ken Heyman. HarperTrophy, 1993. Hats

———. *Houses and Homes.* Photos by Ken Heyman. HarperCollins, 1992. Homes

Moss, Lloyd. *Our Marching Band.* Illus. by Diana Cain Bluthenthal. Putnam, 2001. Parades

Munari, Bruno. *Bruno Munari's Zoo.* Chronicle Books, 2005. Zoos

Murphy, Chuck. *Shapes: Slide 'n' Seek.* Little Simon, 2001. (Board book) Sizes and Shapes

Murphy, Mary. *How Kind!* Candlewick Press, 2004. (Board book) Helping

———. *I Like It When . . .* Red Wagon Books, 2005. (Board book) Feelings

Murphy, Stuart J. *The Best Bug Parade.* Illus. by Holly Keller. HarperTrophy, 1996. Parades

My First Body Board Book / Mi primer libro del cuerpo. (English/Spanish) DK, 2005. My Body

My First Look at Colors. DK, 2001. Colors

Neasi, Barbara J. *Just Like Me.* Illus. by Johanna Hantel. Children's Press, 2003. Family

Neitzel, Shirley. *I'm Taking a Trip on My Train.* Illus. by Nancy Winslow Parker. Greenwillow Books, 1999. Trains and Planes

Nicholas, Christopher. *Follow That Fire Truck.* Illus. by Joseph Ewers. Random House, 2002. (Lift-the-flap book) Firefighters

Nodset, Joan L. *Who Took the Farmer's Hat?* Illus. by Fritz Siebel. HarperTrophy, 1988. Hats

Numeroff, Laura. *If You Give a Mouse a Cookie.* Illus. by Felicia Bond. Laura Geringer, 1985. Also in big book format (HarperTrophy, 1996); and in Spanish: *Si le das una galletita a un ratón* (Rayo, 1995). Friends

———. *If You Give a Pig a Party.* Illus. by Felicia Bond. Laura Geringer, 2005. Also in Spanish: *Si le haces una fiesta a una cerdita* (Rayo, 2006). Birthdays

———. *What Aunts Do Best / What Uncles Do Best.* Illus. by Lynn Munsinger. Simon & Schuster, 2004. (Flip-over book) Family

Numeroff, Laura, and Felicia Bond. *The Best Mouse Cookie.* HarperFestival, 1999. (Board book) Mealtimes

O'Hair, Margaret. *Twin to Twin.* Illus. by Thierry Courtin. McElderry Books, 2003. Family

Opie, Iona, ed. *Here Comes Mother Goose.* Illus. by Rosemary Wells. Candlewick Press, 1999. Read to Me!

Ormerod, Jan. *Peekaboo!* Bodley Head Books, 1997. (Board book) Peek, Peek

———. *Sunshine.* Frances Lincoln, 2004. Morning

O'Rourke, Page Eastburn. *Rub-a-Dub-Dub.* Grosset & Dunlap, 1993. (Board book) Bath Time

Oxenbury, Helen. *All Fall Down.* Walker Books, 1998. (Board book) Playing

———. *Tom and Pippo Read a Story.* Aladdin, 1988. Read to Me!

———. *Tom and Pippo's Day.* Aladdin, 1989. Monkeys

Palatini, Margie. *Goldie Is Mad.* Hyperion Books, 2001. Feelings

Pan, Hui-Mei. *What's in Grandma's Grocery Bag?* Star Bright Books, 2004. Colors

Paterson, Brian. *Zigby Camps Out.* HarperCollins, 2003. Picnics

Patricelli, Leslie. *Big Little.* Candlewick Press, 2003. (Board book) Sizes and Shapes

———. *Quiet Loud.* Candlewick Press, 2003. (Board book) Sounds

———. *Yummy Yucky.* Candlewick Press, 2003. (Board book) Mealtimes

Patrick, Denise Lewis. *Red Dancing Shoes.* Illus. by James E. Ransome. HarperCollins, 1993. Dancing

Paul, Ann Whitford. *Hello Toes! Hello Feet!* Illus. by Nadine Bernard Westcott. DK, 1998. My Body

———. *Little Monkey Says Good Night.* Illus. by David Walker. Farrar, Straus, and Giroux, 2003. Circus

Payne, Nina. *Summertime Waltz.* Illus. by Gabi Swiatkowska. Farrar, Straus, and Giroux, 2005. Summer

Pedersen, Janet. *Millie in the Meadow.* Candlewick Press, 2003. Farms

———. *Millie Wants to Play!* Candlewick Press, 2004. Playing

Peek, Merle. *Mary Wore Her Red Dress and Henry Wore His Green Sneakers.* Clarion, 2006. Also in board book format (Clarion, 1998). Birthdays

Pegram, Laura. *Rainbow Is Our Face.* Illus. by Cozbi S. Cabrera. Writers and Readers, 1995. (Board book) My Body

———. *A Windy Day.* Illus. by Cozbi S. Cabrera. Writers and Readers, 1995. Wind

Perkins, Al. *Hand, Hand, Fingers, Thumb.* Illus. by Eric Gurney. Random House, 1969. My Body

Petrie, Catherine. *Joshua James Likes Trucks.* Illus. by Joel Snyder. Children's Press, 2000. Trucks, Cars, and Buses

Petty, Colin. *Shapes.* Barron's, 2006. (Slide-and-see board book) Sizes and Shapes

Pieńkowski, Jan. *Boats.* Illus. by Renée Jablow and Helen Balmer. Dutton, 1997. Boats

———. *Oh My, a Fly!* Piggy Toes Press, 2000. (Pop-up book) Bugs and Caterpillars

Pilkey, Dav. *Big Dog and Little Dog.* Red Wagon Books, 1997. (Board book) Dogs

———. *Big Dog and Little Dog Going for a Walk.* Red Wagon Books, 1997. (Board book) Walking

Pinkney, Andrea, and Brian Pinkney. *Shake Shake Shake.* Red Wagon Books, 1997. (Board book) Parades

———. *Watch Me Dance.* Red Wagon Books, 1997. (Board book) Dancing

Piper, Watty. *The Little Engine That Could.* Illus. by George and Doris Hauman. Grosset & Dunlap, 1990. Also in board book format, illus. by Cristina Ong (Grosset & Dunlap, 1991); in pop-up book format, illus. by Richard Walz and Keith Moseley (Grosset & Dunlap, 1984); and in Spanish: *La pequeña locomotora que sí pudo* (Grosset & Dunlap, 1992). Trains and Planes

Pomerantz, Charlotte. *Where's the Bear?* Illus. by Byron Barton. HarperCollins, 2003. Bears

Porter-Gaylord, Laurel. *I Love My Mommy Because . . .* Illus. by Ashley Wolff. Dutton, 1991. Family

Potter, Beatrix. *Listen! Peter Rabbit.* Warne, 2002. (Board book) Read to Me!

Powell, Richard. *Bobalong Boat.* Silver Dolphin, 2002. Boats

———. *Hoot! Hoot! A Lift-the-Flap Book.* Illus. by Ana Martin Larrañaga. Candlewick Press, 2003. Birds

Prater, John. *Number One, Tickle Your Tum.* Red Fox, 2002. Counting

Preller, James. *Wake Me in Spring.* Illus. by Jeffrey Scherer. Cartwheel Books, 1994. Spring

Raffi. *Shake My Sillies Out.* Illus. by David Allender. Crown Books, 1988. Feelings

———. *Spider on the Floor.* Illus. by True Kelley. Crown Books, 1996. Bugs and Caterpillars

———. *Wheels on the Bus.* Illus. by Sylvie Kantorowitz Wickstrom. Crown, 1998. (Board book) Trucks, Cars, and Buses

Randall, Ronne. *Don't Be Pesky, Little Monkey: Touch and Play!* Illus. by Caroline Jayne Church. Silver Dolphin, 2002. (Pop-up book) Monkeys

Rathmann, Peggy. *Good Night, Gorilla.* Putnam, 1994. Also in board book format (Putnam, 1996). Monkeys

Rau, Dana Meachen. *Bob's Vacation.* Children's Press, 1999. Winter

Reasoner, Charles. *Who's Hatching? A Sliding Surprise Book.* Price Stern Sloan, 2003. (Board book) Spring

———. *Whose House Is This? A Sliding Surprise Book.* Price Stern Sloan, 2002. (Board book) Homes

Reidy, Hannah. *All Sorts of Clothes!* Illus. by Emma Dodd. Evans Brothers, 2003. Getting Dressed

Relf, Adam. *Fox Makes Friends.* Sterling, 2005. Friends

Rex, Michael. *Firefighter.* Cartwheel Press, 2003. Firefighters

Rey, H. A. *Curious George.* Houghton Mifflin, 1973. Also in Spanish: *Jorge el curioso* (Houghton Mifflin, 1976). Monkeys

———. *Curious George and the Bunny.* Houghton Mifflin, 2004. (Board book) Rabbits

———. *Feed the Animals.* Houghton Mifflin, 1998. (Lift-the-flap book) Zoos

———. *Where's My Baby?* Houghton Mifflin, 1998. (Lift-the-flap book) Babies

Rey, Margret, and H. A. Rey. *Curious George at the Parade.* Houghton Mifflin, 1999. Parades

———. *Curious George Goes Camping.* Houghton Mifflin, 1999. Picnics

———. *Curious George's First Words at the Circus.* Illus. by Greg Paprocki. Houghton Mifflin, 2005. (Board book) Circus

———. *Curious George's First Words at the Zoo.* Illus. by Greg Paprocki. Houghton Mifflin, 2005. (Board book) Zoos

Rice, Eve. *Sam Who Never Forgets.* HarperTrophy, 1987. Zoos

———. *Swim!* Illus. by Marisabina Russo. Greenwillow Books, 1996. Summer

Richards, Laura E. *Jiggle Joggle Jee!* Illus. by Sam Williams. Greenwillow, 2001. Trains and Planes

Rius, María. *Fall.* Barron's, 1998. Also in Spanish: *El otoño* (Barron's, 1999). Autumn

———. *Spring.* Barron's, 1998. Also in Spanish: *La primavera* (Barron's, 1999). Spring

———. *Summer.* Barron's, 1998. Also in Spanish: *El verano* (Barron's, 1999). Summer

———. *Winter.* Barron's, 1998. Also in Spanish: *El invierno* (Barron's, 1999). Winter

Robinson, Fay, comp. *A Frog Inside My Hat: A First Book of Poems.* Illus. by Cyd Moore. Troll, 1997. Hats

Rockwell, Anne. *Apples and Pumpkins.* Illus. by Lizzy Rockwell. Simon & Schuster, 1989. Gardens

———. *Big Wheels.* Walker Books, 2003. Trucks, Cars, and Buses

———. *Boats.* Puffin, 1993. Boats

———. *Fire Engines.* Puffin, 1993. Firefighters

———. *My Spring Robin.* Illus. by Harlow and Lizzy Rockwell. Aladdin, 1996. Spring

———. *No! No! No!* Simon & Schuster, 1995. Feelings

———. *One Bean.* Illus. by Megan Halsey. Walker Books, 1999. Gardens

———. *Planes.* Puffin, 1993. Trains and Planes

———. *Pumpkin Day, Pumpkin Night.* Illus. by Megan Halsey. Walker Books, 1999. Autumn

———. *Trains.* Puffin, 1993. Trains and Planes

Rockwell, Anne, and Harlow Rockwell. *At the Beach.* Aladdin, 1991. Summer

———. *The First Snowfall.* Aladdin, 1992. Winter

Rockwell, Lizzy. *Hello Baby!* Dragonfly Books, 2000. Babies

Rogers, Alan. *Blue Tortoise.* World Book, 1997. Also in Spanish: *La tortuga azul* (Turtleback Books, 2000). Picnics

———. *Bright and Breezy.* World Book, 1999. Also in Spanish: *Sol y lluvia* (Sagebrush, 2001). Wind

Rogers, Paul, and Emma Rogers. *Ruby's Dinnertime.* Dutton Books, 2002. Mealtimes

Rohmann, Eric. *My Friend Rabbit.* Roaring Brook Press, 2002. Friends

Root, Phyllis. *One Windy Wednesday.* Illus. by Helen Craig. Candlewick Press, 1997. Wind

Rosen, Michael, and Helen Oxenbury. *We're Going on a Bear Hunt.* Aladdin, 2003. Bears

Rouss, Sylvia A. *Sammy Spider's First Passover.* Illus. by Katherine Janus Kahn. Kar-Ben, 1995. Spring

Rowe, Jeanette. *Whose Feet?* Little, Brown, 1999. (Lift-the-flap book) Zoos

Ruane, Joanna. *Boats, Boats, Boats.* Illus. by Patti Boyd. Children's Press, 2004. Boats

Rusackas, Francesca. *Daddy All Day Long.* Illus. by Priscilla Burris. HarperCollins, 2004. Family

———. *I Love You All Day Long.* Illus. by Priscilla Burris. HarperTrophy, 2004. Love

Russo, Marisabina. *Come Back, Hannah!* Greenwillow Books, 2001. Babies

Ryder, Joanne. *My Father's Hands.* Illus. by Mark Graham. HarperCollins, 1994. Gardens

Ryder, Joanne, and Melissa Sweet. *Won't You Be My Hugaroo?* Gulliver Books, 2006. Love

Sampson, Michael, and Mary Beth Sampson. *Star of the Circus.* Illus. by Jose Aruego and Ariane Dewey. Holt, 1997. Circus

Santoro, Christopher. *Open the Barn Door . . .* Random House, 1993. (Board book) Farms

Schaefer, Lola M. *This Is the Sunflower.* Illus. by Donald Crews. Greenwillow Books, 2000. Gardens

Schindel, John, and Luiz Claudio Marigo. *Busy Monkeys.* Tricycle Press, 2002. (Board book) Monkeys

Schindel, John, and Beverly Sparks. *Busy Doggies.* Tricycle Press, 2003. (Board book) Dogs

Scott, Ann Herbert. *On Mother's Lap.* Illus. by Glo Coalson. Clarion Books, 1992. Also in board book format (Clarion Books, 2000); and in Spanish: *En las piernas de Mamá* (Clarion Books, 2007). Love

Sendak, Maurice. *Where the Wild Things Are.* HarperCollins, 1988. Read to Me!

Serfozo, Mary. *Who Said Red?* Illus. by Keiko Narahashi. Houghton Mifflin, 1999. Colors

Seuss, Dr. *Mr. Brown Can Moo! Can You?* Random House, 1996. (Board book) Sounds

Shannon, George. *Dance Away.* Illus. by Jose Aruego and Ariane Dewey. HarperTrophy, 1991. Dancing

———. *The Surprise.* Illus. by Jose Aruego and Ariane Dewey. Greenwillow Books, 1983. Peek, Peek

Shaw, Charles G. *It Looked Like Spilt Milk.* HarperTrophy, 1988. Also in big book format (HarperTrophy, 1992); and in board book format (HarperFestival, 1993). Rain

Shaw, Nancy. *Sheep Take a Hike.* Illus. by Margot Apple. Houghton Mifflin, 1996. Walking

Shostak, Myra. *Rainbow Candles: A Hanukkah Counting Book.* Illus. by Sally Springer. Kar-Ben, 2001. (Board book) December

Showers, Paul. *The Listening Walk.* Illus. by Aliki. HarperTrophy, 1993. Also in Spanish: *Los sonidos a mi alrededor* (Rayo, 1996). Walking

Simon, Norma. *Fire Fighters.* Illus. by Pam Paparone. Aladdin, 1998. Firefighters

———. *What Do I Do?* (English/Spanish) Illus. by Joe Lasker. Albert Whitman, 1969. Helping

Sis, Peter. *Trucks Trucks Trucks.* Greenwillow Books, 1999. (Board book) Trucks, Cars, and Buses

Slater, Teddy. *All Aboard Fire Trucks.* Illus. by Tom LaPadula. Grosset & Dunlap, 1991. Firefighters

———. *The Bunny Hop.* Illus. by Larry Di Fiori. Cartwheel Books, 1992. Rabbits

Slobodkina, Esphyr. *Caps for Sale: A Tale of a Peddler, Some Monkeys, and Their Monkey Business.* HarperCollins, 1947. Also in big book format (HarperTrophy, 1996); and in Spanish: *Se venden gorras: La historia de un vendedor ambulante, unos monos y sus travesuras* (Rayo, 1995). Hats

————. *The Wonderful Feast.* Greenwillow Books, 1993. Farms

Spicer, Maggee, and Richard Thompson. *We'll All Go Sailing.* Illus. by Kim LaFave. Fitzhenry & Whiteside, 2001. Colors

Spier, Peter. *Peter Spier's Circus!* Dragonfly Books, 1995. Circus

Spinelli, Eileen. *Do You Have a Hat?* Illus. by Geraldo Valério. Simon & Schuster, 2004. Hats

Spinelli, Eileen, and Anne Mortimer. *Kittycat Lullaby.* Hyperion Books, 2001. Cats

Stanley, Mandy. *At the Zoo / Vamos al zoo.* (English/Spanish) Kingfisher, 2003. (Board book) Zoos

Stevens, Janet, and Susan Stevens Crummel. *My Big Dog.* Golden Books, 2005. Cats

Stiegemeyer, Julie. *Cheep! Cheep!* Illus. by Carol Baicker-McKee. Bloomsbury Books, 2006. (Board book) Birds

Stockham, Jess. *Down by the Station.* Child's Play, 2005. (Board book with holes) Trains and Planes

Stoeke, Janet Morgan. *Five Little Kitty Cats.* Dutton, 1998. Cats

————. *A Friend for Minerva Louise.* Dutton, 1997. Friends

————. *A Hat for Minerva Louise.* Puffin, 1997. Hats

————. *Hide and Seek.* Dutton, 1999. (Board book) Peek, Peek

————. *Minerva Louise.* Dutton, 1988. Birds

————. *Minerva Louise and the Colorful Eggs.* Dutton, 2006. Spring

————. *Minerva Louise and the Red Truck.* Dutton, 2002. Trucks, Cars, and Buses

————. *Minerva Louise at School.* Dutton, 1996. Growing Up Safe

————. *Minerva Louise at the Fair.* Dutton, 2000. Circus

————. *One Little Puppy Dog.* Dutton, 1998. Dogs

————. *Rainy Day.* Dutton, 1999. (Board book) Rain

Stojic, Manya. *Rain.* Crown, 2000. Rain

Sturges, Philemon. *Ten Flashing Fireflies.* Illus. by Anna Vojtech. North-South Books, 1995. Bugs and Caterpillars

Suen, Anastasia. *Red Light, Green Light.* Illus. by Ken Wilson-Max. Harcourt, 2005. Trucks, Cars, and Buses

————. *Subway.* Illus. by Karen Katz. Viking, 2004. Trains and Planes

Sykes, Julie. *This and That.* Illus. by Tanya Linch. Farrar, Straus, and Giroux, 1998. Cats

Tabby, Abigail. *Snap! Button! Zip!* Illus. by Christopher Moroney. (Sesame Street book) Random House, 2003. Getting Dressed

Tafuri, Nancy. *Early Morning in the Barn.* Mulberry Books, 1992. Morning

————. *Goodnight, My Duckling.* Scholastic, 2005. Birds

————. *This Is the Farmer.* Greenwillow Books, 1994. Farms

Tanner, Suzy-Jane. *The Great Hanukkah Party.* HarperFestival, 1998. (Lift-the-flap book) December

Taylor, Eleanor. *Beep, Beep, Let's Go!* Bloomsbury Books, 2005. Summer

Teddy Bear, Teddy Bear. Illus. by Michael Hague. HarperFestival, 1997. (Board book) Read to Me!

Thomas, Joyce Carol. *You Are My Perfect Baby.* Illus. by Nneka Bennett. HarperFestival, 1999. (Board book) Babies

Thompson, Lauren. *Little Quack's New Friend.* Illus. by Derek Anderson. Simon & Schuster, 2006. Frogs and Turtles

————. *Mouse's First Snow.* Illus. by Buket Erdogan. Simon & Schuster, 2005. Winter

Thong, Roseanne. *One Is a Drummer: A Book of Numbers.* Illus. by Grace Lin. Chronicle Books, 2004. Counting

Todd, Mark. *What Will You Be for Halloween?* Houghton Mifflin, 2001. Autumn

Tolstoy, Alexei. *The Great Big Enormous Turnip.* Illus. by Helen Oxenbury. Egmont Books, 1998. Gardens

Touch and Feel Fire Engine. DK, 2002. (Texture book) Firefighters

Tresselt, Alvin. *The Mitten.* Illus. by Yaroslava. Harper-Trophy, 1989. Winter

Trumbull, Peter. *Whose Hat Is That?* Illus. by Lori Reiser. School Zone, 1995. (Fisher Price book) Hats

Turner, Ann. *Let's Be Animals.* Illus. by Rick Brown. HarperFestival, 1998. Playing

Udry, Janice May. *A Tree Is Nice.* Illus. by Marc Simont. HarperTrophy, 1987. Also in Spanish: *Un árbol es hermoso* (Rayo, 2006). Picnics

Uff, Caroline. *Hello, Lulu.* Walker Books, 2004. (Board book) Friends

————. *Lulu's Busy Day.* Walker Books, 2004. (Board book) Playing

Van Fleet, Matthew. *One Yellow Lion.* Dial Books, 1992. Counting

Van Genechten, Guido. *The Cuddle Book.* Harper-Collins, 2004. Love

Van Laan, Nancy. *This Is the Hat: A Story in Rhyme.* Illus. by Holly Meade. Hyperion Books, 1995. Hats

Van Laan, Nancy, and Bernadette Pons. *Tickle Tum.* Atheneum, 2001. Rabbits

Vaughan, Marcia. *The Dancing Dragon.* Illus. by Stanley Wong Hoo Foon. Mondo, 1996. Parades

Verdick, Elizabeth. *Feet Are Not for Kicking.* Illus. by Marieka Heinlen. Free Spirit Publishing, 2004. (Board book) My Body

———. *Teeth Are Not for Biting.* Illus. by Marieka Heinlen. Free Spirit Publishing, 2003. (Board book) My Body

Waddell, Martin. *Can't You Sleep, Little Bear?* Illus. by Barbara Firth. Candlewick Press, 2002. Bears

———. *Let's Go Home, Little Bear.* Illus. by Barbara Firth. Candlewick Press, 1995. Walking

———. *You and Me, Little Bear.* Illus. by Barbara Firth. Candlewick Press, 1998. Helping

Walsh, Ellen Stoll. *Hop Jump.* Voyager Books, 1996. Frogs and Turtles

———. *Mouse Paint.* Harcourt, 1989. Also in big book format (Harcourt, 1991); and in board book format (Red Wagon Books, 1995). Colors

Walsh, Melanie. *Do Donkeys Dance?* Houghton Mifflin, 2000. Dancing

———. *Do Lions Live on Lily Pads?* Houghton Mifflin, 2006. Homes

———. *Do Monkeys Tweet?* Egmont Books, 1998. Sounds

———. *My Beak, Your Beak.* Houghton Mifflin, 2002. Zoos

Walton, Rick, and Paige Miglio. *So Many Bunnies: A Bedtime ABC and Counting Book.* HarperCollins, 1998. Also in braille (National Braille Press, 2000). Rabbits

Warnes, Tim. *Mommy Mine.* Illus. by Jane Chapman. HarperCollins, 2005. Family

Watanabe, Shigeo. *How Do I Put It On?* Illus. by Yasuo Ohtomo. Philomel Books, 1980. Getting Dressed

Watt, Fiona. *Baby's Bathtime.* Illus. by Rachel Wells. EDC, 2001. Also in Spanish: *¡Al agua patos!* (Usborne Books, 2000). Bath Time

———. *Baby's Bedtime.* Illus. by Rachel Wells. EDC, 1999. Also in Spanish: *¡Felices sueños!* (Usborne Books, 2000). Bedtime

———. *Frog.* Illus. by Rachel Wells. Usborne Books, 2003. (Rag book) Frogs and Turtles

———. *That's Not My Bunny . . . Its Tail Is Too Fluffy.* Illus. by Rachel Wells. Usborne Books, 2005. (Texture board book) Rabbits

Weare, Tim. *I'm a Little Monkey.* Michael O'Mara Books, 2004. (Board book with puppet) Monkeys

Weeks, Sarah. *Mrs. McNosh and the Great Big Squash.* Illus. by Nadine Bernard Westcott. HarperFestival, 2000. Gardens

———. *Mrs. McNosh Hangs Up Her Wash.* Illus. by Nadine Bernard Westcott. HarperFestival, 1998. Getting Dressed

Weiss, Nicki. *Where Does the Brown Bear Go?* Puffin, 1990. Bedtime

Wellington, Monica. *Apple Farmer Annie.* Puffin, 2004. Autumn

Wells, Rosemary. *Carry Me!* Hyperion Books, 2006. Rabbits

———. *Felix Feels Better.* Candlewick Press, 2000. Growing Up Safe

———. *The Itsy-Bitsy Spider.* Scholastic, 1998. (Board book) Bugs and Caterpillars

———. *Max Drives Away.* Viking, 2003. (Board book) Trucks, Cars, and Buses

———. *Max's Bath.* Dial Books, 1998. (Board book) Bath Time

———. *Max's Birthday.* Viking, 2004. (Board book) Birthdays

———. *Max's Breakfast.* Viking, 2004. (Board book) Mealtimes

———. *Max's Chocolate Chicken.* Puffin, 2000. Spring

———. *Max's Christmas.* Puffin, 2000. December

———. *Max's Dragon Shirt.* Puffin, 2000. Getting Dressed

———. *Max's Halloween.* Viking, 2004. (Board book) Autumn

———. *Max's Toys: A Counting Book.* Viking, 2004. Counting

———. *Noisy Nora.* Viking, 1999. Sounds

———. *Read to Your Bunny.* Scholastic, 1999. Read to Me!

———. *Shy Charles.* Viking, 2001. Feelings

Westcott, Nadine Bernard. *Skip to My Lou.* Megan Tingley, 2000. (Board book) Dancing

What Color Is It? / ¿Qué color es éste? (English/Spanish) Illus. by Pamela Zagarenski. Houghton Mifflin, 2001. (Board book) Colors

Wheeler, Lisa. *Te Amo, Bebé, Little One.* (Spanish/English) Illus. by Maribel Suárez. Little, Brown, 2004. Growing Up Safe

Whitman, Candace. *Now It Is Morning.* Farrar, Straus, and Giroux, 1999. Morning

Wild, Margaret, and Bridget Strevens-Marzo. *Kiss Kiss!* Simon & Schuster, 2003. Love

Williams, Garth. *The Chicken Book.* Yearling Books, 1992. Birds

Williams, Sue. *I Went Walking.* Illus. by Julie Vivas. Gulliver Books, 1990. Also in big book format (Harcourt, 1991); in lap-size board book format (Red Wagon Books, 2005); and in Spanish board book: *Sali de paseo* (Red Wagon Books, 2005). Walking

Wilson, Karma, and Jane Chapman. *Bear's New Friend.* McElderry Books, 2006. Friends

Wilson, Sarah. *A Nap in a Lap.* Illus. by Akemi Gutierrez. Holt, 2003. Bedtime

Wilson-Max, Ken. *Firefighter.* Abrams Books, 2005. (Sound effects book) Firefighters

Winter, Jeanette. *The Itsy-Bitsy Spider.* Red Wagon Books, 2000. (Board book) Bugs and Caterpillars

Wolff, Ferida, and Dolores Kozielski. *On Halloween Night.* Illus. by Dolores Avendaño. HarperTrophy, 1997. Autumn

Wong, Janet S. *Buzz.* Illus. by Margaret Chodos-Irvine. Harcourt, 2000. Bugs and Caterpillars

Wood, Audrey. *The Napping House.* Illus. by Don Wood. Harcourt, 1984. Also in board book format (Red Wagon Books, 2005); and in Spanish: *La casa adormecida* (Libros Viajeros, 1995). Bedtime

Wood, Jakki. *Animal Parade: An Alphabet Safari.* Frances Lincoln, 1996. Parades

———. *Bumper to Bumper: A Traffic Jam.* Simon & Schuster, 1996. Trucks, Cars, and Buses

Wormell, Mary. *Why Not?* Farrar, Straus, and Giroux, 2000. Cats

Wright, Cliff. *Bear and Kite.* Chronicle Books, 2005. (Board book) Wind

Wyndham, Robert. *Chinese Mother Goose Rhymes.* Illus. by Ed Young. Putnam, 1998. Read to Me!

Yashima, Taro. *Umbrella.* Puffin, 1977. Rain

Yolen, Jane. *Baby Bear's Chairs.* Illus. by Melissa Sweet. Gulliver Books, 2005. Bears

———. *Hoptoad.* Illus. by Karen Lee Schmidt. Silver Whistle, 2003. Frogs and Turtles

———. *Off We Go!* Illus. by Laurel Molk. Little, Brown, 2000. Walking

Yoon, Salina. *Fire Truck.* Price Stern Sloan, 2005. (Board book) Firefighters

Zane, Alexander. *The Wheels on the Race Car.* Illus. by James Warhola. Orchard Books, 2005. Sounds

Ziefert, Harriet. *Animal Music.* Illus. by Donald Saaf. Houghton Mifflin, 1999. Parades

———. *Brothers Are for Making Mud Pies: A Lift-the-Flap Book.* Illus. by Chris Demarest. Puffin, 2001. Family

———. *Circus Parade.* Illus. by Tanya Roitman. Blue Apple, 2005. Circus

———. *Nicky Upstairs and Down.* Illus. by Richard Brown. Puffin, 1994. Homes

———. *Sara's Potty.* Illus. by Emily Bolam. DK, 1999. (Lift-the-flap book) Growing Up Safe

———. *Train Song.* Illus. by Donald Saaf. Orchard Books, 2000. Trains and Planes

———. *What Is Hanukkah?* Illus. by Rick Brown. HarperFestival, 1994. (Lift-the-flap book) December

———. *What Is Thanksgiving?* Illus. by Claire Schumacher. HarperFestival, 1992. (Lift-the-flap book) Mealtimes

———. *What Is Valentine's Day?* Illus. by Claire Schumacher. Sterling, 2004. (Lift-the-flap book) Love

Ziefert, Harriet, and Lisa Campbell Ernst. *Bye-Bye, Daddy!* Viking, 1988. (Board book) Walking

Ziefert, Harriet, and Simms Taback. *Noisy Barn!* Blue Apple, 2003. (Board book) Farms

———. *Zoo Parade!* Blue Apple, 2003. (Board book) Zoos

Zion, Gene. *Harry the Dirty Dog.* Illus. by Margaret Bloy Graham. HarperCollins, 1956. Also in board book format (HarperFestival, 2006); and in Spanish: *Harry, el perrito sucio* (Rayo, 1996). Bath Time

Zocchi, Judith Mazzeo. *On Kwanzaa.* Illus. by Rebecca Wallis. Dingles, 2006. Also in Spanish: *La Kwanzaa* (Dingles, 2006). December

Zolotow, Charlotte. *Mr. Rabbit and the Lovely Present.* Illus. by Maurice Sendak. HarperCollins, 1962. Also in Spanish: *El señor Conejo y el hermoso regalo* (Rayo, 2006). Rabbits

———. *When the Wind Stops.* Illus. by Stefano Vitale. HarperCollins, 1995. Wind

Discography

The following are sources for tunes used in songs in the thematic units. For other sources, search Rob Reid, *Children's Jukebox: The Select Subject Guide to Children's Musical Recordings*, second edition (ALA, 2007), or search song titles on the Internet.

"A-Hunting We Will Go." Cedarmont Kids Singers. *Preschool Songs: 21 Classic Songs for Kids.* Cedarmont Music, 1995. Compact disc.

"A-tisket, A-tasket." *Toddler Trio.* Music for Little People, 2000. Compact disc.

"Baby Bumble Bee." Linda Arnold. *Sing Along Stew.* A&M Records, 1995. Compact disc.

"By the Beautiful Sea." *Coney Island Baby.* Intersound, 1991. Compact disc.

"Bye Baby Bunting." Pamela Conn Beall and Susan Hagen Nipp. *Wee Sing Nursery Rhymes and Lullabies.* Price Stern Sloan, 1985. Compact disc.

"Did You Ever See a Lassie." *Best 101 Children's Songs.* Nancy Music, 1988. Compact disc.

"Down by the Station." *Mickey's Favorites Sing Along.* Walt Disney, 1996. Audiocassette.

"Eency Weency Spider (Itsy Bitsy)." *Toddlers Sing Storytime.* Music for Little People, 2000. Compact disc.

"The Farmer in the Dell." Wonder Kids Choir. *Ultimate Kids Song Collection: Favorite Sing-a-Longs.* Madacy Entertainment, 2000. Compact disc.

"Frere Jacques (Are You Sleeping?)." Bob McGrath. *Songs and Games for Toddlers.* Bob's Kids Records, 2000. Compact disc.

"Good Morning." Nacio Herb Brown and Arthur Freed. *Singin' in the Rain: Original MGM Soundtrack.* CBS Special Products, 1990. Compact disc.

"Good Night, Ladies." *Mickey's Favorites Sing Along.* Walt Disney, 1996. Audiocassette.

"Happy Birthday to You." *Toddler Trio.* Music for Little People, 2000. Compact disc.

"Head, Shoulders, Knees, and Toes." Cedarmont Kids Singers. *Preschool Songs: 21 Classic Songs for Kids.* Cedarmont Music, 1995. Compact disc.

"How Much Is That Doggie in the Window?" Persuasions and the Lollipop Kid Chorus. *On the Good Ship Lollipop.* Music for Little People, 1999. Compact disc.

"Hush Little Baby." Bob McGrath. *Sing Along with Bob #2.* Golden, 1996. Compact disc.

"I Know an Old Lady Who Swallowed a Fly." Pete Seeger. *Birds, Beasts, Bugs, and Fishes, Little and Big.* Smithsonian Folkways, 1998. Compact disc.

"If You're Happy and You Know It." Bob McGrath. *Sing Along with Bob #2.* Golden, 1996. Compact disc.

"I'm a Little Teapot." *Mickey's Favorites Sing Along.* Walt Disney, 1996. Audiocassette.

"Little Drummer Boy." *Sounds of the Season.* BMG Music, 1993. Compact disc.

"London Bridge (Is Falling Down)." Wonder Kids Choir. *Ultimate Kids Song Collection: Favorite Sing-a-Longs.* Madacy Entertainment, 2000. Compact disc.

"Looby-Loo (Here We Go)." *Twenty-Five Fun Songs for Kids.* Madacy Entertainment, 2001. Compact disc.

"Mary Had a Little Lamb." Bob McGrath. *Sing Along with Bob #2.* Golden, 1996. Compact disc.

"Me and My Shadow." Judy Garland. *Judy.* 32 Records, 1998. Compact disc.

"Muffin Man (Do You Know the)." *Toddlers Sing Storytime.* Music for Little People, 2000. Compact disc.

"The Mulberry Bush (Here We Go Round)." *Toddler Trio.* Music for Little People, 2000. Compact disc.

"Old MacDonald Had a Farm." *Nursery Rhyme Time: Sing-a-long with Our Babies—and Yours!* Singing Babies, 2000. Compact disc.

"Paw-Paw Patch." *Playtime Favorites.* Kid Rhino, 1999. Compact disc.

"Peter Cottontail." Greg Scelsa and Steve Millang. *Holidays and Special Times.* Youngheart Music, 1989. Compact disc.

"Pop Goes the Weasel." Wonder Kids Choir. *Ultimate Kids Song Collection: Favorite Sing-a-Longs.* Madacy Entertainment, 2000. Compact disc.

"Rig-a-jig-jig (As I Was Walking)." Bob McGrath. *Songs and Games for Toddlers.* Bob's Kids Records, 2000. Compact disc.

"Rock-a-bye Baby." *Nursery Rhyme Time: Sing-a-long with Our Babies—and Yours!* Singing Babies, 2000. Compact disc.

"Row, Row, Row Your Boat." *Twenty-Five Fun Songs for Kids.* Madacy Entertainment, 2001. Compact disc.

"Sailing Sailing." *Best 101 Children's Songs.* Nancy Music, 1988. Compact disc.

"Six Little Ducks." Linda Arnold. *Sing Along Stew.* A&M Records, 1995. Compact disc.

"Skinnamarink." Dennis Buck. *Car Songs.* Kimbo, 1990. Audiocassette.

"Skip to My Lou." Pete Seeger. *Birds, Beasts, Bugs, and Fishes, Little and Big.* Smithsonian Folkways, 1998. Compact disc.

"Ten in the Bed." *Playtime Favorites.* Kid Rhino, 1999. Compact disc.

"Ten Little Indians." *Nursery Rhyme Time: Sing-a-long with Our Babies—and Yours!* Singing Babies, 2000. Compact disc.

"Three Blind Mice." Wonder Kids Choir. *Ultimate Kids Song Collection: Favorite Sing-a-Longs.* Madacy Entertainment, 2000. Compact disc.

"Twinkle Twinkle Little Star." Dennis Buck. *Car Songs.* Kimbo, 1990. Audiocassette.

"We Wish You a Merry Christmas." Lois Sharon and Bram. *Candles, Snow, and Mistletoe.* Elephant Records, 1993. Compact disc.

"Wheels on the Bus." *Playtime Favorites.* Kid Rhino, 1999. Compact disc.

"Where Has My Little Dog Gone (Oh Where, Oh)?" *Toddlers Sing Storytime.* Music for Little People, 2000. Compact disc.

"Who's That Knocking at My Door (Barnacle Bill, the Sailor)?" Louis Jordan. *Let the Good Times Roll: The Anthology, 1938–1953.* Decca, 1999. Compact disc.

Index

Judy Nichols resides in Wichita, Kansas, where she is a freelance storyteller, puppeteer, and library consultant. She was previously the youth services coordinator for the Wichita (Kansas) Public Library and a children's librarian at the Decatur (Illinois) Public Library and the Elkhart (Indiana) Public Library. Nichols has also worked in school and academic libraries in Georgia and Texas. She is a member of the National Storytelling Association and the Puppeteers of America.